Creating Faulkner's Reputation

Creating Faulkner's Reputation

THE POLITICS OF MODERN LITERARY CRITICISM

Lawrence H. Schwartz

THE UNIVERSITY OF TENNESSEE PRESS/KNOXVILLE

The paper in this book meets the minimum requirements of the
American National Standard for Permanence of Paper for Printed
Library Materials. ∞ The binding materials have been chosen
for strength and durability.

Library of Congress Cataloging in Publication Data

Schwartz, Lawrence H., 1947–
    Creating Faulkner's reputation.

    Bibliography: p.
    Includes index.
    1. Faulkner, William, 1897–1962—Criticism and
interpretation—History.   2. Criticism—United States—
History—20th century.   3. Canon (Literature)   I. Title.
PS3511.A86Z9663   1988   813'.52   87-27203
ISBN 0-87049-565-8 (cloth: alk. paper)
ISBN 0-87049-645-X (pbk.: alk. paper)

For my Parents and PT

Acknowledgments

Now, at the end of this very long project, I can reflect on the substantial social network of individuals and institutions that made possible the successful completion of this work. Over the years, many colleagues and friends have read various sections of the manuscript and have offered disparate but useful commentaries which helped to sharpen the argument. Their efforts were very much appreciated. In particular, and in several very different contexts, Bob Rosen, Bruce Franklin, James Gilbert, and Alvin Kernan offered important professional critiques. The book has been strengthened by their observations.

Of course, this type of research could not be conducted without the dedicated help of many librarians, archivists and curators. Their patience and professionalism made much of the investigation far easier. I want to thank the staffs in the manuscript sections at the Newberry Library, the University of Virginia, Princeton University, the Rockefeller Archives, New York University (Fales Library and the Tamiment Collection), Columbia University, and Yale University. In particular I want to thank Carolyn Sheehy, Diana Haskell, Nancy Ralston Strife, and Anne Freudenberg. At Montclair State College, the Interlibrary Loan Department was extraordinary (thank you, Larry Kirschenbaum and Ed Gil). I also appreciate the permission granted to review personal and corporate correspondence. My thanks go especially to Dorothy Commins, Helen Weybright, Random House, and the New American Library.

I have also been the recipient of much institutional support. The Montclair State College Research Committee has provided generous grants of released time from classroom teaching to be devoted to my research and writing. The Rockefeller Archive Center of the Rockefeller University awarded a timely research and travel grant. At an early stage, the National Endowment for the Humanities made possible a summer of research at Princeton University in Al Kernan's seminar on literature as a social institution. And over the years there were several helpful awards from the Montclair State College Alumni Association for travel and preparation of the manuscript for publication. At the University of Tennessee Press, I was most fortunate to have the encouragement of Carol Orr and the editorial skills of Lee Campbell Sioles.

Sections of the book were first published in two essays: 1) "Malcolm Cowley's Path to William Faulkner," in the *Journal of American Studies* and "Publishing William Faulkner: The 1940s" in the *Southern Quarterly*. For the respective journals, Arnold Goldman and Noel Polk provided many good editorial suggestions. For their careful attention, I am grateful.

By far, my largest personal debt is owed to Grover Furr. He supported this research from the very beginning. He was always willing to take time from a heavily committed schedule to discuss my ideas, comment on early drafts, and write extensive responses to what I often thought were finished passages. Because his criticisms were always couched in the most constructive and supportive language, he managed to prompt me to refine my analysis without making me feel discouraged. That's the best reader and friend an author can find.

Finally, Pat Thomas contributed much good sense to several parts of this analysis, and too many coerced hours of editing and proofreading. I especially thank her for living in such good humor with a distracted person. Her endurance was singularly important in support of an endeavor that took far more perseverance, both personal and professional, than we ever imagined.

Contents

Introduction

The sudden inflation of William Faulkner's literary reputation after World War II is at once the most dramatic and most obvious aspect of his writing career. I wondered how was it possible for a writer, out of print and generally ignored in the early 1940s, to be proclaimed, in 1950, a literary genius, perhaps the best American novelist of the century? This book investigates the development of Faulkner's literary fame in order to understand why, in the special context of the postwar period, this novelist emerged as a celebrated writer. What were the circumstances in the publishing industry, academia, and the popular media in the years 1945-50 which helped to establish his reputation?

At the start of the project, I assumed that to answer my questions would require little more than a review of major books and articles to filter out this part of his story, with the results presented in a single compact essay. However, in the dozens of books and scores of articles on the novelist's career, no cultural historian or literary critic had tried to examine in a serious, thorough, or scholarly way the mechanisms that came into play to elevate Faulkner. The absence of thoughtful commentary on this issue was a surprising revelation which meant an exciting opportunity to study an unexplored area, but one that turned out to be far more complex and difficult than I originally imagined.

What I discovered was that, before the award for the Nobel Prize in 1950, the few critics who praised Faulkner asserted his literary genius, and after the Prize they claimed it had been validated. To explain the rapidity with which his literary fortunes were reversed, they suggested, in almost mythic rags-to-riches terms, that Faulkner struggled in obscurity in the early 1940s until a few writers and critics without the blinders of 1930s Marxism recognized his achievement, though at first these adherents had trouble enlisting support for the novelist. But eventually the "truth" won out and Faulkner gained the deserved recognition. In the early 1940s, he was presented as a dedicated writer and uncompromising stylist, whose great creative virtue was his single-minded determination to write fiction on his own terms.

Many serious Faulkner scholars, including Malcolm Cowley and Robert Penn Warren, advanced this view. They argued that after the war Faulkner's reputation rose because he was a great writer whose greatness had been ignored; and the literary situation after the war was right for a reconsideration. With the Nobel Prize and subsequent literary fame, he was, they said, justly rewarded after years of obscurity and neglect because his work was simply the best. I found this inspiring, but as explanation for the precipitous rise in reputation it was not particularly satisfying.

The following study attempts to show how the confluence of literary, cultural, and commercial forces created and shaped Faulkner's literary reputation. It investigates the individuals and institutions responsible for raising him to world-wide fame and for drawing his work into the canon. It is a book that focuses on the "cultural mechanisms" that, in less than five years, made for the sudden turnabout. This analysis does not debunk Faulkner's genius or talent, or question the intrinsic literary merit of his novels and stories. The key issue is *not* Faulkner's greatness. But why was he perceived as great? Who proclaimed it and under what circumstances? Faulkner's work was essentially a constant; in fact, he produced little new writing in the 1940s. But the critics did alter their assessment of it. What can be seen in the sudden rise in Faulkner's reputation is the instability of aesthetic criteria. This analysis looks at the way in which aesthetic criteria changed, how the critics interpreted literary consequence in the 1940s, and what that meant for Faulkner. Literary reputations rise and fall dramatically because the critics reflect not universal, but relative, literary values which are, in large measure, historically determined.

The central premise of my study is that the process of literary tastemaking can be isolated and identified, and that literary fame and reputation can be studied in the same way as any other historical phenomenon. In every era, there are many excellent writers who never achieve widespread recognition, while there are also writers who achieve some measure of literary success in one period but find themselves set aside in another. In the 1940s, such social novelists as Richard Wright, Theodore Dreiser, Erskine Caldwell, and John Steinbeck, who were held in high regard in the 1930s, fell almost as dramatically as Faulkner rose. The Faulkner myth tends to suggest that his revival was, in a certain sense, inevitable. What my study suggests is that he was not a "great" writer just because he wrote fiction of high quality. I believe that in the context of the postwar era, and the emergent cultural cold war, there was a need to find an important American nationalist writer. How Faulkner came to be selected is the subject of this book.

My argument involves four basic points. First, there was a decided shift in the critical perception of Faulkner after the war (chapter 1). Led by the work of Cowley and Warren, writers argued that Faulkner had been misunderstood. In almost all the American literary histories of the period up to World War II, Faulkner was judged a talented, but limited secondary writer—hard to read, often macabre, and too involved with style. Cowley and Warren wanted to project a new direction for Faulkner criticism and to revise a lengthy heritage of negative commentary by the sociologically inclined critics of the 1930s, such as Alfred Kazin, Bernard De Voto, Oscar Cargill, Maxwell Geismar, and Clifton Fadiman, and of sharply hostile attacks from Marxists such as Granville Hicks. But Cowley and Warren also knew that there were Faulkner enthusiasts as well. For example, in the South, there were important writers and critics such as John Crowe Ransom, Allen Tate, Donald Davidson, Cleanth Brooks,

Stark Young, Hamilton Basso, Caroline Gordon, Katherine Anne Porter, and Eudora Welty; and in the North, support could be found from Robert Sherwood, James T. Farrell, Robert Cantwell, Kay Boyle, and Horace Gregory. And there were important essays on Faulkner by Conrad Aiken, Jean Paul Sartre, André Malraux, George Marion O'Donnell, Warren Beck, and Delmore Schwartz. In fact, by the early 1940s there were substantial positive appraisals upon which an argument for rereading Faulkner could be constructed. After the war, Faulkner was presented by Cowley, Warren, and others as an important novelist, a literary genius, and a serious moralist.

This reinterpretation coincided with United States political and economic hegemony at the end of the war. With that rise in power and position came, given the devastation in Europe, preeminence in culture. Like Jackson Pollock and the abstract expressionists, Faulkner became universalized as an emblem of the freedom of the individual under capitalism, as a chronicler of the plight of man in the modern world. Faulkner was seen to exemplify the same values that Western intellectuals saw in capitalism which made it morally superior to communism. He came to represent American literary modernism.

Second, the book publishing industry also changed during the war, making cheap paperbacks possible and creating a mass market for *some* of Faulkner's books (chapter 2), those with popular, non-serious qualities: sex, violence, intrigue. These sales, however, created the income necessary to keep his novels in print. And, without his novels in print, no revival would have been possible. Thus, his popular market was a necessary condition for Faulkner's resuscitation, though not sufficient in itself to guarantee a serious literary reputation. This discussion of Faulkner publishing analyzes the actual demand for and sales of his books during a decade when he had little commercial (or perceived cultural) value and was essentially saved from extinction by a few critics and chary publishers. These ties to commercial publishing should not be ignored. They were the fundamental and material roots of his professional life, shaping his goals, career, and reputation in the bleak period of artistic self-doubt and critical neglect, and the base, from 1946 to 1948, upon which an audience was built.

The third point, and the central focus of my study is presented in a series of related discussions (chapters 3, 4, and 5) that set the reinterpretation of Faulkner into the context of postwar cultural readjustment. The change reflected the Cold War confrontation between capitalism and communism (an ideological battle that still continues). It was explicitly anti-Communist and tied to the repudiation of the socially conscious literary traditions of naturalism/realism. This could not be done in the name of cultural "democracy" (because that concept had been a watchword of determinations of literary worth and relevance in the 1930s and, thus, symbolic of the politicization of literature), so it had to be done through an elitist aesthetic—an aesthetic that claimed important literature was remote, complex, iconoclastic, and inaccessible, and required interpretation. In the most direct terms, I try to demonstrate that a new literary consensus and dominant aesthetic were shaped by two principal literary elites, the New Critics and the New York intellectuals, and an important philanthropic organization, the Rockefeller Foundation. They came together in the 1940s to set a cultural agenda, and they used and promoted Faulkner for their own ends.

And fourth, with Faulkner serving the cultural, aesthetic, and intellectual needs of these groups, he became their exemplar in literature (chapters 6 and 7). There was no conspiracy to launch the novelist, but in the context of the postwar era, critics came to value his values. For example, the key work of several critics, Cowley, Mark Schorer, and Irving Howe, representing different communities within the literary elite, adopted common assumptions about the significance of literary formalism and modernism, and the limitations of naturalism. Had the aesthetic values of the 1930s persisted or had anti-Communism not become prevalent, Faulkner could not have achieved renown.

Two brief prefatory notes should be made on definitions of literary groups and sources. First, by New Critics I mean those poets, critics, and writers who developed formalist literary aesthetics based on the work of T.S. Eliot, I.A. Richards, and William Empson, dating from the 1920s. This movement had its early development in Nashville with the Agrarian/Fugitive group: Ransom, Tate, Warren, Brooks, and Davidson. Once the Agrarian ideology was dropped in the mid-1930s, the movement expanded rapidly. As commonly defined, the New Critics were those who were interested in explication of poetic texts and who published in and were involved with *Southern Review, Sewanee Review, Kenyon Review,* and the Kenyon School. Principal among them were: R.P. Blackmur, Yvor Winters, W.K. Wimsatt, René Wellek, Austin Warren, Robert Heilman, Robert Stallman, Mark Schorer, Arthur Mizener, William Van O'Connor. In the forties the New Critics had totally altered undergraduate teaching of literature and had become the pervasive movement in the academy. By New York intellectuals I mean critics and writers drawn to the *Partisan Review* in the late 1930s (after its clear break with the Communist Party) and throughout the 1940s. They included, for example, Philip Rahv, William Phillips, Lionel Trilling, Clement Greenberg, William Barrett, Dwight Macdonald, Diana Trilling, Sidney Hook, Irving Howe, Delmore Schwartz, Leslie Fiedler, and Alfred Kazin.

Second, I realize that my conclusions are not sympathetic to the main tendencies in Faulkner scholarship, but they were reached after a careful review and circumspect reading of primary research materials—letters, reports, memoranda, and diaries. The research was conducted in the William Faulkner Archives at the University of Virginia, the Allen Tate and Richard P. Blackmur Papers at Princeton University, the Malcolm Cowley Collection at the Newberry Library, the New American Library Archive at New York University, and the Rockefeller Foundation Archive.

The tremendous political and economic upheaval of war that made the United States, for a few short years, the most powerful nation on earth, profoundly altered cultural values. Earlier efforts to launch Faulkner met with failure until the demands of the Cold War propagated a new aestheticism. Without that change in aesthetic sensibility it seems unlikely that such a difficult writer would have achieved the wide recognition he did. Faulkner's reputation requires explanation; no more than any other historical event was it "inevitable." Such an explanation is the goal of this book.

CHAPTER ONE

Faulkner's Image:
From Prewar Nihilist
to Postwar Moralist

In 1944, when Malcolm Cowley began his research for *The Portable Faulkner* (1946), a book that many literary historians and critics see as the turning point in Faulkner's literary reputation, he quickly discovered that this author of seventeen published books and a score of short stories in the major mass circulation magazines of the 1930s was virtually unread in his own country.

> Consider what might be called his quoted value on the literary stock exchange. . . . In eleven of the books he had created a mythical county in northern Mississippi and had told its story from Indian days to what he regarded as the morally disastrous present; it was a sustained work of the imagination such as no other American writer had attempted. Apparently no one knew that Faulkner had attempted it. His seventeen books were effectively out of print and seemed likely to remain in that condition, since there was no public demand for them. How could one speak of Faulkner's value on the literary stock exchange? In 1944 his name wasn't even listed there.[1]

In fact, the situation could not have been worse for a living novelist. Only *Sanctuary* (1931), his most scandalous novel and his only commercial success, was in print. It was only after *Sanctuary* became a best seller that Faulkner had success in the magazines, such as the *Saturday Evening Post,* and could attract the lucrative screenwriting assignments in Hollywood. The books that are today considered literary masterpieces were unavailable, even in secondhand bookshops: *The Sound and the Fury* (1929), *As I Lay Dying* (1930),

Light in August (1931), *Absalom, Absalom!* (1936), and *The Hamlet* (1940).[2]

Cowley was unhappy not only that Faulkner was out of print but that for more than fifteen years critics had misinterpreted and misrepresented the books. He thought that a *Portable* might begin to redress what he perceived as unjustified neglect and indifference. With a speed that Cowley could hardly have imagined, by 1950, after the appearance of the *Portable,* which included the "Appendix" to *The Sound and the Fury,* publication of a new novel, *Intruder in the Dust* (1948), and the awarding of a Nobel Prize, Faulkner was not only back in print but had moved from the category of unappreciated southern novelist to become the major American literary voice of the mid-twentieth century. And as one English professor reported, by the beginning of the next decade, one could already speak of a "Faulkner cult."[3]

> We have heard a good deal some years ago about the Melville boom, and the James boom, but the present Faulkner boom surpasses them both. If you will look at the annual bibliographies of the *Publications of the Modern Language Association of America* for the years 1954–57, you will find that they contain a larger number of titles of books and articles on Faulkner than on any living writer in English. Faulkner has a total of 160 items; Eliot, 96; Hemingway, 78. Faulkner even rivals (always excepting Shakespeare, whose score for the four years is 719) the great English worthies long dead: his total of 160 is all the more impressive when we discover that Milton's is only 225 and Chaucer's 185.[3]

However, in July 1944, when Cowley wrote to Faulkner asking for his cooperation on the *Portable,* he gave the novelist a bitter statement of his negligible market worth.

> It's about what I suggested in my other letter—very funny, and a great credit to you, but bad for your pocket book. First, in publishing circles your name is mud. They are all convinced that your books won't sell, and it's a pity, isn't it? they say, with a sort of pleased look on their faces. . . . The bright boys among the critics did a swell job of incomprehending and unselling you, Fadiman especially. Now, when you talk to writers instead of publishers or publishers' pet critics about the *oeuvre*

of William Faulkner it's quite a different story; there you hear almost nothing but admiration, and the better the writer the greater the admiration is likely to be. Conrad Aiken, for example, puts you at the top of the heap. The funny thing is the academic and near-academic critics and the way they misunderstand and misstate your work. You probably haven't read Maxwell Geismar's book, "Writers in Crisis," . . . but when he comes to Faulkner, you might as well have written your novels in Minoan or Hittite for all the sense he makes of them.[4]

Cowley summarized quite neatly the general patterns of Faulkner criticism. In the 1920s, there were early admirers such as publishers Horace Liveright, Alfred Harcourt, and Harrison Smith, and support from novelist Sherwood Anderson. Faulkner's fellow southern writers, such as Donald Davidson, John Crowe Ransom, and Robert Penn Warren, wrote scattered book reviews of the first novels (generally appearing in the newspapers). However, sales of the early novels were poor, and *The Sound and the Fury* stimulated the critics but stumped the audience, selling just five hundred copies. In the 1930s, Cowley knew that Faulkner had attracted a great deal of attention, though most of it was superficial and hostile.[5]

In order to gain some perspective on the postwar changes in aesthetics and the interpretation of Faulkner's value, it is worth considering Cowley's sketch of the literary situation looking backward from 1944. Cowley's reference to publishers was prompted by recent conversations with Max Perkins, the famous Scribner's editor of Hemingway, Wolfe, and Fitzgerald. In January 1944, Cowley, while working on a profile of Perkins for the *New Yorker,* had discussed Faulkner's reputation. Perkins told Cowley that Faulkner "has fallen into a certain position which is not as high as it should be, and once that happens to a writer, it is extremely difficult to change the public's opinion." For Perkins, despite Faulkner's extraordinary talent, the novelist had no publishing future.[6] Given Cowley's respect for Perkins, this seemed to him an authoritative pronouncement of the attitude of the publishing industry during the middle of the war, though Faulkner's publishing relationships were actually more complex and more favorable, as we shall see in subsequent chapters.

The reference to Clifton Fadiman, book reviewer for the *New Yorker,* concerned his savage indictment of *Absalom, Absalom!*— a scathing but not atypical attack on both the Faulkner style and message.

> One may sum up both the substance and style by saying that every person in "Absalom, Absalom!" comes to no good end, and they all take a hell of a time coming even that far. . . . This cheerful little fable is filtered through the medium of a style peculiar to Mr. Faulkner. It seems peculiar to me, too. First we have the Non-Stop or Life Sentence. . . . Then we have what may be called Anti-Narrative, a set of complex devices used to keep the story from being told. Mr. Faulkner is very clever at this. He gets quite an interesting effect, for example, by tearing the Sutpen chronicle into pieces, as if a mad child were to go to work on it with a pair of shears . . . confusing the reader and otherwise enabling Mr. Faulkner to demonstrate that as a technician he has Joyce and Proust punch-drunk. . . . On the other hand, it is only fair to say that there are a score of pages . . . full of remarkable prose poetry, beautiful in itself, if magnificently irrelevant.[7]

Fadiman's final judgment simply was that he could not understand Faulkner and that this novel "seems to point to the final blowup of what was once a remarkable, if minor, talent." But Fadiman was hardly alone. Even Cowley, in his politicized days at the *New Republic,* also dismissed the book. He saw it as a modern-day Gothic romance in the Poe tradition, which aside from the technical innovations was of little interest.[8]

Perhaps the most far-reaching critique came from Bernard De Voto, a generally fair-minded literary journalist, who went beyond a review of the novel to attack Faulkner's infatuation with the macabre. Writing in the *Saturday Review of Literature,* De Voto called the novelist a mystic who had chosen "witchcraft" as a substitute for the "ordinary concerns of fiction." De Voto saw no value in Faulkner's exploration of "the primitive violence of the unconscious mind" or his fondness for "rape, mutilation, castration, incest, patricide, lynching, and necrophilia. . . ." All his technical skill and experimentation was directed toward revealing no "deeper and fuller truth" about his characters.

Those people remain wraiths blown at random through fog by winds of myth. The revelation remains just a series of horror stories that are essentially false—false because they happen to grotesques who have no psychology, no necessary motivations as what they have become out of what they were. They are also the targets of a fiercely rhetorical bombast diffused through the brilliant technique that promises us everything and gives us nothing, leaving them just wraiths.[9]

On the other hand, Maxwell Geismar did not think that Faulkner was trivial or a minor talent, rather "perhaps in sheer craft" the best American writer of his generation. In fact, he thought that *The Sound and the Fury* was a "magnificent" novel, marking Faulkner as a "major voice in American literature." But Geismar, in a very long and elaborate review of the novelist's development from 1929 to 1940, saw a great virtuoso talent wasted, his compassion turned into inhumanity.

From the troubled but tender and intensely human world of "The Sound and the Fury" . . . the writer has moved steadily toward the perverse and the pathological: and the denial of humanity which he uses his inversions to convey. From the touching drama of innocence, he has advanced to that of corruption.[10]

Cowley focused on Geismar's long analysis of Faulkner in *Writers in Crisis* because it summarized and perpetuated much of what Cowley saw as misguided antagonism toward the novelist. Geismar was tied too much to 1930s socially conscious literature and criticism. He was a critic who believed in the Democratic progressivism of the New Deal and in the importance of literature of social substance. He appreciated the literary rebellion of the young writers in the 1920s but saw it as lacking responsibility. When Hemingway, Dos Passos, Thomas Wolfe, and John Steinbeck began to react to the crisis of the 1930s by affirming their connection to America, Geismar saw the value of their work increase. For Geismar, the flowering of American literature culminated in the naturalism/realism of the 1930s as represented by John Steinbeck.[11]

Geismar wanted writers to abandon their solipsistic rebellion to help advance the Democratic reforms required by the crisis of the

Great Depression. In Faulkner, he saw only the unreconstructed rebel, a defender of the old order against all that was new and possible. For Geismar, Faulkner'was a writer trapped by the Old South.

> . . . this family tradition, this home uninterrupted except by visions of incest, rape, and murder, these ancestral halls in which echo only the sobs and shrieks of demons; a possessed gallery of the decaying and the demented who live in memory; memory which leads only backward in thinning circles of disaster until the cycle is wasted and spent in time. . . . With Faulkner the descending spiral of isolation, rebellion, and denial, the heritage of American negation reaches its final emphasis. With him, we make our last study of the influence of the nineteen-twenties, forming, lasting over, and wholly conditioning the artist of the thirties.[12]

Geismar's chapter, "The Negro and the Female," argued that throughout Faulkner's books the unifying theme was a portrayal of "The Negro and the Female," not as victims, but as "the evil cause" of the degeneration of the South. How similar to the Fascist use of the Jews, Geismar noted.

> I have used the title of Maurice Samuel's penetrating study of the Fascist superstitions, "The Great Hatred," to best describe Faulkner's work as a whole. For it is in the larger tradition of reversionary, neo-pagan, and neurotic discontent (from which Fascism stems) that much of Faulkner's writing must be placed—the anti-civilizational revolt rising out of modern social evils, nourished by ignorance of their true nature, and which succumbs to malice as their solution.[13]

Geismar was not disturbed by Faulkner's rejection of modern society, because such a gesture was typical of much of 1920s fiction. But in *Light in August* there emerged "the twin furies of Faulkner's deep southern Waste land; but a waste land, quite unlike Eliot's, of demons and incubae rather than pallid clerks, one which is built on diseased fury. . . ." There was no catharsis, no redemption from evil, no Dostoyevskian "salvation," just "the incessant breeding of evil by evil." Ultimately, Geismar found in this novel that "great hatred," a disdain for life: "And with the emphasis on necrophilia and cannibalism, on misogynists and miscegenation, with these murders and their dangling corpses, we are touching on the center of Faulkner's mature work. . . ."[14] In the big novels of the 1930s, *Light in August* and *Absalom, Absalom!,* Geismar saw Faulkner's abhorrence of modern civilization reflected in the emancipated Black (Joe Christmas and Jim Bond), portrayed as "the inhuman criminal degenerate who will dominate the civilization which freed him," and reflected in the pure southern Lady turned "wanton, graceless, and degraded."

. . . as the last step in his sequence of discontent, Faulkner mates the Female with the Negro, the savage as Faulkner feels for whom the southern Lady was sacrificed, and spawns out of his modern union the colored degenerate who is to reign supreme, the moronic emperor of the future.[15]

On the left, the criticism was even harsher. Of the early Faulkner books Granville Hicks wrote that "the world of William Faulkner echoes with the hideous trampling march of lust and disease, brutality, and death."[16] And in his Marxist analysis of the development of American literature, *The Great Tradition,* Hicks argued for Faulkner's irrelevance because the novelist did not try to explain the source of "misery and vileness" which so permeated his view of the South.

The ordinary affairs of this life are not enough for Faulkner; even the misery and disease born of generations of poverty and ignorance are not adequate themes for the expression of his horror and disgust. Nothing but crime and insanity will satisfy him. If he tried to see why life is horrible, he might be willing to occupy himself with the kind of suffering that he can see on every hand, the kind of crime that is committed every day, and the kind of corruption that gnaws at every human being in this rotten society. As it is, he can only pile violence upon violence in order to convey a mood that he will not or cannot analyze.[17]

For Hicks, Faulkner's preoccupation with style and technique was a facade, a way to express an intense enmity without an understanding of the object of his rancor: "Faulkner's unwillingness to try to understand the world about him not only robs his novels of true importance but brings them dangerously close to triviality." The violence, suffering, meanness, and despair were meant to shock, but the heightening of effect, as Hicks called it, only created "in the reader the most violent loathing."[18]

As Cowley well knew, in a decade dominated by social realism in both fiction and criticism, Faulkner was rejected, not just by the leftists, but by all those who wanted fiction to address the humane tradition of naturalism. For example, in Harry Hartwick's 1934 analysis of contemporary American fiction, the chapter on Faulkner was entitled, "The Cult of Cruelty," reflecting the view that Faulkner exploited pessimism, horror, and inhumanity to no positive effect. He was a nihilist who missed "the best spirit of naturalism" and drifted into his own "blind alley":

> The vital tradition of naturalism, which is at heart broad in its sympathies and warm in its "passionate recognition" of life, cannot rest upon such a specialized, reptilian art as that of Faulkner's; it requires thought to justify its style and meaning to adorn its emotion. It should be a . . . source of inspiration for all those who draw their values from Nature rather than Man, not a haunted house, dark and cold, inhabited only by spiders and morons.[19]

From this perspective, representative of critics sympathetic to the realist tradition, and not just from that of the Marxists, Faulkner was blind to his own world.

However, Cowley also noted in his letter to Faulkner, that, as to his reputation as a writer's writer, there were appreciative voices. In 1939, Conrad Aiken's defense appeared in the *Atlantic Monthly*. Aiken was one of the first critics to argue that Faulkner's style, while disconcerting, distracting, and demanding was thoroughly appropriate to the conscious artistic intent. "[W]hat sets him above—shall we say it firmly—all his American contemporaries, is his continuous preoccupation with the novel *as form*. . . ."

> What Mr. Faulkner is after, in a sense, is a *continuum*. He wants a medium without stops or pauses, a medium which is always *of the moment,* and of which the passage from moment to moment is as fluid and undetectable as in the life itself which he is purporting to give. It is

all inside and underneath, or as seen from within and below; the reader must therefore be steadily *drawn in;* he must be powerfully and unremittingly hypnotized . . . and this suggests, perhaps, a reason not only for the length and elaborateness of the sentence structure, but for the repetitiveness as well.[20]

Aiken was one of the first critics to make a claim for Faulkner as a literary genius (near to both James and Balzac), a genius of form and of inventiveness. Aiken believed there had been too much emphasis on Faulkner's violence and depravity. He suggested that it should be viewed more positively, an "inventiveness of the richest possible sort—a headlong and tumultuous abundance, an exuberant generosity and vitality, which makes most other contemporary fiction look very pale and chaste indeed."[21]

Aiken's emphasis on form and imaginative power was a precursor to much of the postwar arguments for Faulkner's value. But as Cowley also suggested, Aiken was not alone. Faulkner possessed international reputation as well. Two major French literary figures were very early admirers. André Malraux wrote a preface of high praise for *Sanctuary* in which he stated that Faulkner had achieved "the intrusion of Greek tragedy into the detective story." Malraux believed that Faulkner's power came from setting characters "face to face" with the horror of their own obsessions, though, of course, *Sanctuary* had achieved public support for more mundane reasons.

> The tragic poet expresses what obsesses him, not to exorcise the obsession . . . but to change its nature. . . . He does not defend himself against anguish by expressing it, but by expressing something else with it, by bringing it back into the universe. The deepest form of fascination, that of the artist, derives its strength from being both horror and the possibility of conceiving horror.[22]

While in Jean Paul Sartre's famous essay on time and technique in *The Sound and the Fury,* the obsession was viewed differently, an author overwhelmed by the past, "a lost man" cut off from a future. Though Sartre was greatly impressed with Faulkner's style and viewed him as the equal of the very best contemporary writers

(Proust, Joyce, Dos Passos, Gide, and Woolf), he disagreed thoroughly with Faulkner's pessimism.

> You won't recognize in yourself the Faulknerian man, a creature deprived of potentiality and explained only by what he was. . . . Man is not the sum of what he has, but the totality of what he does not yet have, of what he could have. . . . Faulkner's despair seems to me to be anterior to his metaphysic; for him, as for all of us, the future is barred. . . . We live in a time of incredible revolutions, and Faulkner uses his extraordinary art to describe a world dying of old age, with us gasping and choking in it.[23]

As politically minded artists, Malraux and Sartre rejected Faulkner's world view as too despairing. Malraux, despite the plaudits for *Sanctuary,* saw "no particular presentation of man" and "no values." Sartre believed Faulkner had created his own absurd vision of the world, one very "far from the creative imagination and from truth," but, for Sartre, "A barred future is still a future." Yet both Malraux and Sartre, like Aiken and even some of Faulkner's severest critics, were captivated by his art and his technical skill.

Finally, note should be made of George Marion O'Donnell's influential essay, "Faulkner's Mythology" in *Kenyon Review.* Also published in 1939, it was an effort to view the novelist's work, as a whole, as a conflict between two worlds, the old aristocratic South, represented by the founding families like Sartoris, and the aggressive new South, represented by the formerly landless whites who come to power after the Civil War, the Snopeses.

> It is a universal conflict. The Sartorises act traditionally, that is to say they act always with an ethically responsible will. They represent vital morality, humanism. Being antitraditional, the Snopeses are immoral from the Sartoris point of view. But they do not recognize this point of view; acting only for self-interest, they acknowledge no ethical duty. Really, then, they are amoral; they represent naturalism or animalism. And the Sartoris-Snopes conflict is fundamentally a struggle between humanism and naturalism.[24]

O'Donnell recognized that this was not a historically accurate depiction of the evolution of the South, but part of Faulkner's artistic achievement in creating a universal myth out of a personal tradition. In these terms, O'Donnell claimed that Faulkner "is really a traditional moralist, in the best sense."[25] Thus, by the end of the 1930s, there were at least several correctives to the general conviction that Faulkner's work was "immoral" and "nihilistic" or worse. O'Donnell's pattern and view of Faulkner as a "traditional man in the modern South" would be an important basis for the reconsideration of Faulkner after the war, especially for Cowley.

In sum, as Frederick Hoffman has suggested, after 1946, Faulkner's work achieved "a *succès d'estime*" because of Cowley's *Portable* and the Nobel Prize. In Hoffman's view, it was not seen until after the war that "this man who had described so powerfully and so frequently the ugly, chaotic, miserable, obscene, irrational world of man should have meant all along that he was upholding the 'eternal verities' and therefore had been without qualification on the side of the angels."[26] This was a dramatic change in perception. Even in 1942, in a long article about the evolution of contemporary southern literature, Cleanth Brooks, who would come to dominate the New Critical interpretation of Faulkner, had not recognized the universality of the novelist's message or his literary genius, and most definitely did not call him the leader of a literary movement.[27]

II

It is certainly safe to say that Faulkner was little appreciated in the 1930s, even by Cowley, who reviewed the major novels in the *New Republic*. But he was not ignored. At the end of the decade, when *The Wild Palms* was published, Faulkner made the cover of *Time* (January 1939). Robert Cantwell's accompanying essay placed the novelist as the central figure in a southern literary renaissance, and, in France, as the modern equivalent to Poe. He reported that Faulkner lived quietly, but well in his hometown, Oxford, Mississippi.

Faulkner bought a big, 90-year-old cedar-shaded house at the edge of Oxford, a Waco cabin plane, financed an aviator brother in a barnstorming venture. He still flies occasionally, but sold his plane after his brother was killed in a crash in 1935. In Oxford he lives quietly, writes, rides, hunts. . . . A landlord, a conservative Democrat, he says he finds it too difficult to run his own place (he has five tenants) to theorize about tenant farming, politics, or economics.[28]

During the middle of the worst years of the Depression, Faulkner made a handsome living from Hollywood screenwriting and sales of stories. From 1936 to 1942, Faulkner published five novels with Random House. The most popular was *The Wild Palms,* which sold 12,000 copies, earning Faulkner $4,500 in royalties. This demand was stimulated by "The Wild Palms" section of the book with its provocative love story. Faulkner's most profitable book during this period was *The Unvanquished* (1938). MGM bought the movie rights for $25,000, netting Faulkner about $19,000; this sum he invested immediately in a 320-acre farm, establishing himself as a gentleman farmer, but one without cash reserves. Unfortunately, this movie sale was the only substantial reward that the novelist would receive during the next decade. The book itself was not a strong seller and earned Faulkner about $2,300 on sales of 6,000 copies.

Overall, as a fiction writer, Faulkner had to face gloomy sales and earnings records: *Absalom, Absalom!* sold 8,000 copies (earning $3,000); *The Hamlet* (1940), 7,000 copies ($2,600); and *Go Down, Moses, and Other Stories* (1942), 4,000 copies ($1,500). Together, the five books published in these years, perhaps his most prolific period, brought Faulkner less than $15,000. In contrast, his yearly income doing Hollywood screenwriting, for each of the three years between 1936 and 1938 was never less than $20,000.[29] At the end of the decade, when Faulkner gave up screenwriting for several years and tried to support himself by writing, he found not only that his books were not selling but that the magazine market was drying up as well. He was having great difficulty earning the $5,000–6,000 per year that he needed just to support his large, extended family. In a May 1940 letter to his publisher, he analyzed his own financial situation:

Beginning at the age of thirty I, an artist, a sincere one and of the first class, who should be free even of his own economic responsibilities and with no moral conscience at all, began to become the sole, principal and partial support—food, shelter, heat, clothes, medicine, kotex, school fees, toilet paper and picture shows—of my mother . . . [a] brother's widow and child, a wife of my own and two step children, my own child; I inherited my father's debts and his dependents, white and black without inheriting yet from anyone one inch of land or one stick of furniture or one cent of money; the only thing I ever got for nothing after the first pair of long pants I received (cost: $7.50) was the $300.00 O. Henry prize last year. . . .[30]

In the summer of 1944, when Cowley turned his attention to Faulkner, the novelist had essentially stopped trying to publish fiction and returned to Hollywood screenwriting to guarantee that his bills would get paid, though his value there had fallen as well to a mere $300 per week, down from $1,000 per week in the 1930s. At the time Cowley did not know the extent of Faulkner's money difficulties.

By October 1944, Cowley's research was advanced enough to publish a short essay on Faulkner in the *New York Times Book Review*. The essay, "William Faulkner's Human Comedy," argued for the novelist's importance, expanding the analysis and reappraisal begun several years earlier in Cowley's reviews of *The Hamlet* and *Go Down, Moses*. He suggested that there was a central unifying theme in Faulkner's Yoknapatawpha novels:

[I]t is the decline of the planting aristocracy to which the Faulkners belonged; it is the rise of new men descended . . . from bushwackers and carpetbaggers; it is the poverty of the white farmers . . . it is the growing hostility between two races; it is the slow bleeding of the land itself and the decomposition of a whole society. . . .[31]

Taking aim at critics such as Geismar and Hicks, Cowley asserted that Faulkner had been misrepresented by those who stressed the Gothic and violent themes. Truly to understand this writer, Cowley argued, it was necessary to see his genuine love of the land and to appreciate the mythology associated with that love of nature: "He dwells with affection on its memories of a great past, on its habits of speech, on its warmth of family feeling; . . . and he tells how it was blessed."[32]

Four years earlier Cowley had started to revise his views; he saw in Faulkner's fiction much more of a plan than critics had granted. In April 1940, he reviewed *The Hamlet* and argued that Faulkner was telling the story of the South in the form of "legend:"

> Until now, almost all his books have been war novels—Civil War novels, in a sense, although most of them have been laid in the twentieth century. They have been based on aspects of the same plantation legend that appears . . . in "Gone With the Wind" . . . [H]e accepts the tradition, but in altered form making it less material than moral. . . . What he does tell us is that there used to be men in the South who were capable of good and evil, who observed or failed to observe a traditional code of ethics. These men, he says, were defeated in the Civil War, but not by the Northern armies. Surviving into a new era, they were weakened by a sense of guilt resulting from their relations with Negroes; and they were finally destroyed by new men rising from among the Poor Whites. The point is made symbolically in "Absalom, Absalom!" . . .[33]

Two years later, in the summer of 1942, reviewing *Go Down, Moses, and Other Stories,* Cowley first recognized that Faulkner had been at work on that legend for fifteen years. Here for the first time, Cowley argued against the critical neglect and lack of appreciation for this achievement:

> And there is no American writer who has been so consistently misrepresented by his critics, including myself. William Faulkner is not a pure Romantic in the Poe tradition as I asserted some years ago; on the contrary his recent work seems close to Mark Twain, with overtones of Turgenev. . . . [H]e is after Hemingway and perhaps Dos Passos, the most considerable novelist of his generation.[34]

By 1944, his tentative reappraisal had become the firm judgment that Faulkner was a "neglected" genius. Despite the difficulties imposed by Faulkner's style, Cowley asked for a rereading on the grounds that this novelist had created a special imaginative world. Furthermore, Faulkner was tied directly to two important literary trends of the nineteenth century:

> . . . that of the psychological horror story as developed by Hawthorne, Poe and Stephen Crane, among others; and that of realistic frontier

humor, with Mark Twain as its best example. . . . It is time for that work to be more widely read. We haven't so many good novelists in this country that we can afford to neglect one of our most distinguished talents.[35]

Faulkner read the October essay in the *Book Review* and liked it, and in early November, wrote to Cowley commenting on the "story" he tried to tell and the symbolism embedded in it. And Cowley reflected:

> I felt that truly effective symbols, like those in Faulkner's novels, were produced almost unconsciously, when the author was so deeply absorbed in his story that he made it larger than life. Faulkner's letter helped to confirm me in this belief, and I went back to work on the essay with renewed enthusiasm.[36]

These six months of careful, intense work on Faulkner yielded two more published essays. First, he wrote a long essay for the *Saturday Review;* it appeared in April 1945. This piece, "William Faulkner Revisited," focused at length on Faulkner's literary qualities so long neglected by the critics. He noted once again the creative intensity of Faulkner's fictive world:

> There in Oxford Faulkner performed a labor of imagination that has not been equaled in our time, and a double labor: first, to invent a Mississippi county very much as children invent a mythical kingdom, but to work over it until it becomes lifelike and consistent in all its parts; second, to make the story . . . stand as a parable or legend of the Deep South as a whole.[37]

Cowley argued that Faulkner resembled both Hawthorne and James: like Hawthorne, that isolated genius of the nineteenth century, "Faulkner . . . has a power, richness of life, and intensity to be found in no other American novelist of our time. He has—once more I am quoting from Henry James's essay on Hawthorne—'the element of simple genius, the quality of imagination.' " And, Faulkner's power, like James's, was not merely as an observer but as an artist whose richness of story and detail mesmerizes the reader:

Essentially he is not a novelist, in the sense of not being a writer who sets out to observe actions and characters then fits them into the architectural framework of a story. For all the weakness of his own poems, he is an epic or bardic poet in prose, a creator of myth that weaves together a legend of the South.[38]

In early December 1944, his friend Allen Tate, then editor of *Sewanee Review,* invited Cowley to submit a long analysis of Faulkner and to enter the essay in a contest co-sponsored by *Sewanee Review* and Prentice-Hall, whose trade-book editor, Gorham Munson, was leading the firm into the publishing of southern literature. In February, Cowley sent Tate a draft of the essay, "William Faulkner's Legend of the South." This third piece on Faulkner was published in *Sewanee Review* (July 1945) and was the prize-winning essay in the competition. Cowley continued to attack the 1930s view, one he had shared, of Faulkner as a southern aristocrat, a narrow regionalist whose difficult prose style and preoccupation with violence placed him in the second rank of writers. Cowley's main thrust, in this third essay, was to explain the legend as it unraveled in Faulkner's many novels, but there was also an added argument, an elaboration of George Marion O'Donnell's thesis, that Faulkner must be seen as an idealist and moralist:

Always in his mind he has an ideal picture of how the land and the people should be—a picture painted, many-windowed houses, fenced fields, overflowing barns, eyes lighting up with recognition; and always, being honest, he measures that picture against the land and people he has seen. And both pictures are not only physical but moral; for always in the background of his novels is a sense of moral standards and a feeling of outrage at their being violated or simply brushed aside. Seeing little hope in the future, he returns to the past, where he hopes to discover a legendary and recurrent pattern that will illuminate and lend dignity to the world about him.[39]

Cowley examined *Absalom, Absalom!* as Faulkner's essential statement about the South's tragic lesson, relating his now clear understanding of the unity in Faulkner's writing:

With a little cleverness, the whole novel might be explained as a connected and logical allegory, but this, I think, would be going beyond the author's intention. First of all, he was writing a story and one that affected him deeply, but he was also brooding over a social situation. More or less unconsciously, the incidents in the story came to represent the forces and elements in the social situation, since the mind naturally works in terms of symbols and parallels. In Faulkner's case, this form of parallelism is not confined to *Absalom, Absalom!* It can be found in the whole fictional framework that he has been celebrating in novel after novel, until his work has become a myth or legend of the South.[40]

In the summer of 1945, Cowley's hard work, persistence, and publishing successes convinced the Viking management to support a *Portable Faulkner.* On 9 August, he wrote to Faulkner announcing the agreement to publish a *Portable,* saying in part:

[T]he reason the book pleases me is that it gives me a chance to present your work as a whole at a time when every one of your books except "Sanctuary"—and I'm not even sure about that—is out of print. The result should be a better sale for your own new books and a bayonet prick in the ass of Random House to reprint the others.[41]

Cowley's goals were clear. First he wanted to end the critical neglect and to offer a base from which to confront the entirety of Faulkner's work, stressing the coherent design that tied together the Yoknapatawpha novels and stories; and he hoped to force a serious reconsideration by other critics. Second, he wanted Random House, Faulkner's publisher, to reissue novels as part of an effort to "launch" Faulkner's career anew.

From August to November 1945, he worked closely with Faulkner on the selections for the *Portable,* and by mid-November the typesetter's copy was ready. At the end of December, Cowley's introduction and prefaces were complete; the introduction was a carefully refined, polished, and expanded version derived from the three published essays. Cowley was quite pleased with the collection and saw it as a unified anthology, almost a novel in itself, telling the Yoknapatawpha story from its wilderness origins to 1945. "Other writers are being rediscovered and revalued," Cowley wrote to Marshall Best, his editor at Viking. "I think it's Faulkner's turn this year, for he's the best of them."[42]

Despite Caroline Gordon's laudatory, front-page review of the *Portable* for the *New York Times Book Review* (May 1946), Cowley's hope for a Faulkner revival was premature. The *Portable* itself was far from a commercial success—selling only twenty thousand copies from 1946 until November 1950, when Faulkner won the Nobel Prize. Given Faulkner's small audience and the wartime paper shortage, Robert N. Linscott, a senior editor at Random House, told Cowley, after reading his *New York Times Book Review* essay, that there were no immediate plans to reissue Faulkner novels. In fact, except for a Modern Library dual-volume of *The Sound and the Fury* and *As I Lay Dying* (1946), there was no further Faulkner publishing through Random House until *Intruder in the Dust* (1948). It is safe to say that the commercial revival of Faulkner came in response to the success of that novel, not to the appearance of the *Portable*.[43]

However, the critical value of the *Portable* was established in the summer of 1946 when Robert Penn Warren's two-part review essay appeared in the *New Republic*. His analysis was important in two ways: First, he outlined, for scholars and critics, the basic issues in Faulkner's vast literary achievement that needed exegesis, asking them to study Faulkner and recognize his worth. Second, Warren argued that Faulkner was far more than a southern regionalist; his message was "universal," transcending his southern emphasis:

> It is important, I think, that Faulkner's work be regarded not in terms of the South against the North, but in terms of issues which are common to our modern world. The legend is not merely a legend of the South, but is also a legend of our general plight and problem. The modern world is in confusion. It does suffer from lack of discipline, of sanctions, of community values, of sense of mission. It is a world in which self-interest, workableness, success, provide the standards. It is a world which is the victim of abstraction and of mechanisms, or at least, at moments, feels itself to be.[44]

Thus in the confusion of the postwar era, Warren asserted that Faulkner offered a respite, a steadiness of vision. In fact, he moved beyond Cowley's praise to argue that the novelist's concern with the eternal verities in the context of a vast artistic achievement merited Faulkner's elevation to the level of the grand literary masters.

Cowley's book, for its intelligence, sensitivity, and sobriety in the introduction, and for the ingenuity and judgment exhibited in the selections would be valuable at any time. But it is especially valuable at this time. Perhaps it can mark a turning point in Faulkner's reputation. That will be of slight service to Faulkner, who, as much as any writer of our place and time, can rest in confidence. He can afford to wait. But can we?[45]

This aesthetic and ideological emphasis proved to be a very significant part of Faulkner's literary revival—an aspect of the general retreat from the overt political concerns and engaged social realism of the previous decade.

III

When Robert Penn Warren reviewed Faulkner's rise to literary prominence from 1946 to 1966, he devoted a substantial part of the retrospective to the author's new-found acceptance immediately after the war. "What . . . the fiction of Faulkner gave was a release into life, into the sense of a grand and disturbing meaningfulness beneath the crust of life, into a moral reality beneath the crust of history." Faulkner's reemergence, Warren suggested, went beyond his acceptance by a few critics. Returning GI's came into college classrooms with a new sensibility that rendered Faulkner's work meaningful. Warren made the case that a new readership had emerged from the unprecedented ravages of war, and, in the most general and universal way, Faulkner's fiction addressed that world:

In that case, we are all GI's, and any reader may come, in mufti, to Faulkner's work with the same built-in questions as the GI of 1946, seeking the same revelatory images of experience. Perhaps the images of violence . . . are, to adapt a famous remark by Poe, not of the South but of the soul; and perhaps their Southernness has such a deep appeal because this order of violence . . . is associated with the assertion of, or the quest for, selfhood, the discovery of a role, or the declaration of a value, in the context of anonymous violence of blankness. . . . [A]nd all the images of isolation, self-imposed by a wrong relation to nature or to history, or visited blindly on the individual, are to be taken as images of the doom that we all, increasingly in our time, must struggle against; and the images of Southern alienation are only images of Everyman facing one of the possibilities in his world.[46]

The revival was attributable, as Warren and others have suggested, to the previously unrecognized, inherent artistic merit and universal worth of Faulkner's writing; he was, they argued, not just the best American novelist of the era but equal to the classic Europeans as well. Warren summarized the argument for the novelist as the new postwar moralist—imbued with tradition, yet with an avantgarde, modernist core:

> It can, perhaps, be plausibly argued that Faulkner is one of the few contemporary fiction writers—perhaps the only American—whose work is to any considerable degree concerned with the central issues of our time, who really picks at the scab of our time, in the way that . . . Melville, Dostoyevsky, Kafka, Conrad, Proust, Eliot, Yeats, and Camus, also do.[47]

Given this view, and starting from Malcolm Cowley's *The Portable Faulkner* in 1946, it has been generally asserted, by Warren, Cowley, and others, that the remarkable rise in Faulkner's reputation was, in a certain sense, inevitable because he was, in fact, a great writer and a literary genius, one who unjustly had been denied acclaim.

However, I will argue that, as modernism—the postwar *Zeitgeist*—became the aesthetic expression of the restructured political environment, Faulkner's fiction was integrated into the culture of the new conservative liberalism of postwar America. The novelist's revival was, in part, an aspect of the cultural revolution that followed from the revised political position of the United States and the new hegemony of its corporate interests. American literature and art were accorded a status commensurate with the new power of the United States. Faulkner became one of the beneficiaries of an aesthetic that was in complete accord with the new order. It was an aesthetic created by an intellectual elite committed to the survival and preeminence of the United States. This was no accident. Very early in the war, as we shall see, the leading literary critics, including the formerly dissident New York intellectuals, were positioning themselves to emerge from the conflict with enough influence and power to set the cultural agenda. In short, the ideological shift prompted by the war converted Faulkner into the postwar moralist and symbol of solitary literary genius, a shift in ideology that achieved public consciousness by 1948, just as Faulkner returned to the literary mainstream with *Intruder in the Dust,* as we shall see in subsequent chapters.

In 1947, the British journal *Horizon* reviewed the American cultural scene, with the New York intellectuals making the report: William Philips for literature and Clement Greenberg for painting. Philips's outlook was pessimistic. What he saw was a "democratic free-for-all" in which the best talent was destroyed because literary survival required accommodating the "middlebrow" audience. What he wanted for the postwar era was a "stable" intellectual elite capable of creating an environment in which writers of promise could explore their artistic possibilities without succumbing to the temptations of a commercial society, an intellectual elite ready to offer guidance in "traditional ideas and values and to create new ones." Perhaps, then a new literary movement of the highest quality could emerge or, absent a whole movement, one writer who would offer up the American nativist experience with an avant-garde, not a "provincial," outlook. Faulkner was just beginning to be considered in these terms, and so Philips could maintain that there was, in this period, a rather disturbing absence of high literary quality in a country which has assumed the moral and economic leadership of the world.

> In the past, our own creative energy has been nourished by new literary movements in Europe. Today, however, an impoverished and politically tottering Europe is not only dependent on the economic resources of the United States but is also, apparently more receptive than ever before to its cultural advances. The historical irony in this dual role of the United States is merely an extension of the contradiction at the heart of our civilization. For, on the one hand, our economic power and democratic myths behind our institutions are all that stand in the path of

Stalinist enslavement in Europe. On the other hand, the United States might well become the greatest exporter of *kitsch* the world has ever seen.[48]

Clement Greenberg, while similarly concerned about the threats to "high culture," was optimistic that new and heroic talent would emerge to provide a distinctly American presence. In fact, Greenberg believed Jackson Pollock to be that artist. Here was a painter, Greenberg asserted, who, in his "violence, exasperation and stridency," was the "radically American," abstract expressionist Gothic equivalent to Faulkner. Greenberg argued for the creation of a *"milieu"* in which American art and literature could attain international significance.

> We stand in need of a much greater infusion of consciousness than heretofore into what we call the creative. We need men of the world not too much amazed by experience, not too much at loss in the face of current events, not at all overpowered by their own feelings, men to some extent aware of what has been felt elsewhere since the beginning of recorded history.[49]

Of course, there can be no easy, one-to-one correspondence between literature and art, but Jackson Pollock's ascent to become the cultural and artistic hero of the abstract expressionist movement is very similar to Faulkner's rise in postwar American literature. According to art historian Serge Guilbaut, "the unprecedented national and international success of an American avant-garde was due not solely to aesthetic and stylistic considerations . . . but also, even more, to the movement's ideological resonance." Indeed, abstract art did not achieve its preeminence "solely because of its formal superiority." It is worth quoting Guilbaut at length:

> American art was described as the logical culmination of a longstanding and inexorable tendency toward abstraction. Once American culture was raised to the status of an international model, the significance of what was specifically American had to change: what had been characteristically American now became representative of "Western culture" as a whole. In this way American art was transformed from regional to international art and then to universal art. French "taste" and "finish"

gave way to American "force" and "violence" as universal cultural values. . . . In this respect, postwar American culture was placed on the same footing as American economic and military strength: in other words it was made responsible for the survival of democratic liberties in the "free" world.[50]

The two stages Guilbaut suggests—from nationalism to internationalism and from internationalism to universalism—holds for the progress of Faulkner's reputation as well. Beginning in 1946, critical interpretations by both American and European critics stressed the larger significance of his work and attacked earlier criticisms that had emphasized his provincialism. Then after the Nobel Prize, the dominant themes were accorded a universal value. As Guilbaut notes, the politicized art of the thirties and the nationalist art of the forties had to be set aside: "This kind of art no longer corresponded to reality, much less the needs of the Cold War."

> It is not my intention to impute to artists of the avant-garde any precise political motive or to suggest . . . some sort of conspiracy. What I argue is this: that from compromise to compromise, refusal to refusal, adjustment to adjustment, the rebellion of the artists, born of frustrations within the left, gradually changed its significance until ultimately it came to represent the values of the majority, but in a way (continuing the modernist tradition) that only a minority was capable of understanding. The ideology of the avant-garde was ironically made to coincide with what was becoming the dominant ideology, that embodied in Arthur Schlesinger, Jr.'s, book *The Vital Center.* . . .[51]

In the politics of Cold War anti-Communism, with Jackson Pollock identified as one of the world's important artists, "America now held all the trumps: the atom bomb, a strong economy, a powerful army, and now artistic supremacy, cultural superiority." American culture would be enlisted to fight for the democratic freedom of the West. The ideology of the "new liberalism" articulated by Schlesinger "not only made room for the avant-garde dissidence but accorded to such dissidence a position of paramount importance." The freedom of artistic expression which allowed wide-open experimentation transformed Pollock "into a symbol of man, free but frail; his work came to stand for modern anxiety."[52]

For Guilbaut's discussion of abstract expressionism, Schlesinger's argument about freedom's relationship to alienation and anxiety is crucial. However, another aspect of Schlesinger's case for the "vital center" is, perhaps, even more appropriate to the shift in literary values that had such an impact on Faulkner's career. In the struggle against totalitarianism, Schlesinger believed that the "reassertion of the ultimate integrity of the individual" was a central part of the "fundamental faith" in contemporary liberalism. It was exactly in terms of the assertion of the individual human will that Faulkner was reread by Cowley and Warren, as we have seen, and by New York critics and French existentialists such as Irving Howe and Claude-Edmond Magny, as we shall see.

It is also safe to say Faulkner came to represent the power of the individual will in struggle against the corrosive effects of a modern world, a world said to be in moral confusion and social decay. The argument for the importance of Faulkner's individualism became almost indistinguishable from Schlesinger's image of "democratic" man: "[M]an is capable of reason and of purpose, of great loyalty and of great virtue, yet he is also vulnerable to material power and to spiritual pride."

> There is on our side, of course, the long-run impossibility of totalitarianism. A totalitarian order offers no legitimate solution to the problem of freedom and anxiety. It does not restore basic securities; it does not create a world where men may expect lives of self-fulfillment. . . . Totalitarianism thwarts and represses too much of man ever to become in any sense a "good society." Terror is the essence of totalitarianism; and normal man, in the long run, instinctively organizes himself against terror.[53]

Faulkner's absorption in terror was revised to emphasize its function as resistance to domination, and his individualism was intimately tied to a homogeneous community, an environment which in some measure could sustain traditional values and resist the forces of modern materialism. And in Schlesinger's terms the only individualism that mattered was one in which a social context existed.

The individual requires a social context, not one imposed by coercion, but one freely emerging in response to his own needs and initiatives. Industrialism has inflicted savage wounds on the human sensibility; the cuts and gashes are to be healed only by a conviction of trust and solidarity with other human beings. . . . We require individualism which does not wall man off from community; we require community which sustains but does not suffocate the individual.

The reconciliation between the individual and the community, in Schlesinger's view, strengthened democracy and the prospect of conditions "where moral decisions are more or less likely to be made." In culture, the responsibility of the artist was to create "a rich emotional life, reflecting actual relations between the individual and the community." It was time, he argued, to restore belief and eliminate the desperation created by unbridled capitalism. The modern world left us lonely, Schlesinger asserted, but the struggle against such loneliness defined "democratic" man.[54]

IV

By 1950, Faulkner's poignant plea for humanity in his Nobel speech struck a resonant cultural chord: "I believe that man will not merely endure: he will prevail. He is immortal . . . because he has a soul, a spirit capable of compassion and sacrifice and endurance."[55] Of course, the French existentialists saw the larger significance early on, when they argued that the primary mission of literature in the modern world was to show the individual consciousness in struggle. "To describe," as Simone De Beauvoir explained, "in dramatic form the relationship of the individual to the world in which he stakes his freedom."[56]

With French literary critics guiding the postwar taste of Western Europe, they separated Faulkner from the "hard-boiled" school of 1930s American fiction, treating him in more existential terms. Living in a shattered world, they saw in his work a fundamental compassion that offered a compelling alternative to the ideological tendentiousness and pessimistic despair of much contemporary writing.

For French critics, Faulkner offered a view of existence that relied on personal values as a way to confront an increasingly anarchic and horrifying world—that is, he was a writer concerned with the mysteries and intricacies of life. Faulkner came to be praised for an authentic style and for creating a special imaginative universe, a "fiction" that could be divorced from, and set above, the social realism of the 1930s. In France, he was seen, first, as the most important American writer, and later, as a great modern master on a level with Proust and Joyce.[57]

In assessing Faulkner's Nobel Prize in relation to French readers, novelist Marcel Ayme reported, in December 1950, that his attachment to and love for the South made him the most important American writer, one whose tragic vision, poetic sensitivity, and "savage religiousness" proved resonant to French readers. For Ayme, there was in Faulkner's nightmare vision a "glimmer" of divine presence.

> . . . [T]he more brutal, cruel, bloodthirsty, lusty and wrathful the characters are, the more tangible is the presence of God. His universe is peopled mostly with crude, sometimes monstrous beings, describing them, we hesitate between *degenerate* and *primitive;* and yet, although plunged in the human substance of fate . . . are possessed by a superhuman force which we would say is that of God.[58]

The high regard for Faulkner and the other American moderns, as Perry Miller reported from the Continent in his essay "Europe's Faith in American Fiction," was more than just an infatuation with America. The writers were infused with a "reckless amateurism" that symbolized a "fundamental freedom," the essence of a living literature. The cultural focus of the world had shifted to the United States, and through our literature we could "communicate with free men everywhere. Because this is a literature of criticism in the name of fundamental man, it is a literature of freedom."[59]

In the United States, by 1952, the fight for literary modernism and aesthetic formalism had been won.[60] With the cultural Cold War in full bloom, the editors of *Partisan Review* in their introduction to the massive symposium, "Our Country and Our Culture," simply declared their allegiance to democracy as the only alternative to Russian totalitarianism—"America has become the protector of Western civilization" and its "cultural democracy is an outgrowth of political democracy under conditions of modern industrial development"[61]— and then turned their full attention to justifying the international significance of the avant-garde.

For the intellectual elite, the real battle was for the preservation of high culture. William Phillips, coeditor of *Partisan Review,* recognized the paradox that in this era the best avant-garde writers, Proust, Kafka, Mann, Eliot, and Faulkner, were hardly rebels, but asserted, in his contribution to the symposium, that "an avant-garde is necessary to keep the spirit of the imagination alive. . . ." He also thought it was valid for internationally recognized art to have native roots.

> . . . [T]he artist keeps a balance of opposing forces, which gives him the appearance of a suspended man. He seems suspended between tradition and revolt, nationalism and internationalism, the aesthetic and the civic, and between belonging and alienation. . . . If the artist in this country is to become an American, it is to correct the earlier denial of his native roots; and it cannot be at the expense of his internationalism, or of those feelings of anguish, dissidence, or estrangement which are also essential to his life.[62]

Indeed, critics were already making the case for Faulkner's attachment to the communal, mythical past and reading him into the international avant-garde and the new liberalism. Clearly, Faulkner's place in this modernist tradition was assured by the Nobel Prize, but the intellectual arguments for it were rooted in the postwar acceptance of an ideology that interpreted "great" art in these terms, as demonstrated by many of the contributions to this symposium. For example, Philip Rahv's contribution was a call to support the avant-garde as the only way to resist *kitsch* and mass culture. The prosperity in America after the war made it much harder for the artists and intellectuals to resist the temptations of materialism, what Rahv saw as the "*embourgeoisement* of the American intelligentsia."

Rahv reminded readers that the avant-garde has a special restorative function:

> . . . to preserve the integrity of art and the intellect amidst the conditions of alienation brought on by the major social forces of the modern era . . . by resisting the bourgeois incentives to accommodation, and perforce making a virtue of its separateness from the mass. That this strategy has in the main been successful is demonstrated by the only test that really counts—the test of creative achievement.

For Rahv and the other New York intellectuals, high artistic and literary achievement, on the order of T.S. Eliot, Jackson Pollock, or William Faulkner, was attributable to preservation of freedom of expression under the democratic traditions of the West, "without which the survival of the intelligence is inconceivable in a modern society, which lacks any organic basis, social or religious, unity of belief, or uniformity of conduct."[63]

Before the war, Faulkner's immorality, his submersion into the terror, corruption, barbarism, and decadence of the South, was associated with an American realism that made violence the centerpiece of the artist's rejection of modern society. After the war, Faulkner's virtue, so the argument went, was to depict the individual struggle against an irrational world as morality, the dilemma of existential choice. This was Schlesinger's point, and it was neatly summarized by Robert Penn Warren when addressing Faulkner's apparent stylistic inconsistencies and lack of clear intellectual center:

> . . . to struggle with the painful incoherences and paradoxes of life, and with the contradictory and often unworthy impulses and feelings in the self, in order to achieve meaning; but to struggle, in the awareness that meaning, if achieved, will always rest in perilous balance, and that the great undergirding and overarching meaning of life is the act of trying to create meaning through struggle.[64]

And by the time of the Nobel Prize, Faulkner's own life became a metaphor for that same effort. He began his Nobel speech by saying: "I feel that this award was not made to me as a man but to my work— a life's work in the agony and sweat of the human spirit, not for glory and least of all for profit, but to create out of the materials of the human spirit something which did not exist before."[65] For here was an unattached artist, not a bohemian, isolated and ignored, who, while highly regarded by other novelists and literary critics, had persisted in his craft when commercial success seemed impossible. Who better to represent the complexities and paradoxes of Cold War existential *angst,* artistic freedom, and unrelenting struggle?

The Nobel Prize alone would have made any author's reputation, but a reading of the publishing record and the intellectual developments from 1946 to 1950 shows that postwar cultural changes set the basis for his revival. And, by the mid-1950s, the intellectual elite had the power and authority (through university, foundation, publishing, and government ties), given the political requirements of cultural Cold War, to make that reputation in the college classrooms and in the international cultural congresses.

CHAPTER TWO

The Commerce of Culture:
Publishing Faulkner in the 1940s

The business of publishing serious fiction, whether profitably or, as often is the case, unprofitably, is an intensely egotistical activity, generally rationalized as an obligation to literature in an honorific sense.[1] In Faulkner's case, the publishing relationship with Random House was, by the late 1930s, conducted precisely on these terms. The Random House partners, Bennett Cerf, Donald Klopfer, and Robert Haas, fully expected the novelist to remain a "small-public" writer whose work would probably never be profitable. But, because they believed that Faulkner was a serious and deserving artist, the partners were fully committed to publish each new work.

In the prewar era of "personal" publishing, Faulkner's failure as a commercial novelist was not a deterrent to his publishers. Their commitment was based on deep feelings of friendship, sympathy, and respect; in fact, it was a relationship that often transcended the formalities and covenants of contracts. Repeatedly, they helped Faulkner solve financial problems, providing extra money whenever possible. Although they cautioned him not to expect a mass audience, they made it clear that the firm was always ready to publish new books. Yet, as pragmatic and experienced publishers, the partners were compelled to limit their financial support to amounts dictated by prudent business practice.[2]

However, at the end of the war, Random House dramatically increased its level of financial support. By 1946, the boom in book publishing during the war had made it possible for the firm to offer the novelist a substantial stipend as an advance on a new novel. The Random House management decided that it was important to see that Faulkner end a long literary silence. The partners saw this increased assistance as a way to share new-found prosperity with a long-suffering literary genius and also a way to sustain their reputation as a literary house. It is useful to examine why the firm was willing to invest part of the wartime profits to help return Faulkner to the literary mainstream when, in reality, as the partners repeatedly told Faulkner, there was no audience, and no possibility of creating one by reissuing his out-of-print novels.

The nature of the prewar Random House commitment to Faulkner was reflected in the novelist's failed attempt, in 1940, to find a new publisher, one who could advance enough cash to cover his immediate, substantial debts. Faulkner's indebtedness had already far surpassed both his current regular income, and the advances that Random House could "prudently" offer during the slack of business of the Great Depression. From 1936 to 1940, Random House published four Faulkner novels, which earned the author less than $15,000. In fact, by April 1940, he was "broke." He needed the cash generated by his most recent novel, *The Hamlet* (published in March) to pay immediate bills, while the money he required for the next few months was to come from short stories which Harold Ober, Faulkner's literary agent, was trying to place in the popular, high-paying magazines such as the *Saturday Evening Post* and *Colliers*. Unfortunately, the stories were not selling.[3]

By the end of April 1940, Faulkner, frantic and depressed, wrote to Haas saying that he needed $1,000 immediately to pay current bills with a guarantee of $9,000 for the next two years in monthly installments of $400. His commentary on the predicament was most telling:

> I had planned, after finishing *The Hamlet,* to try to earn enough from short stories by July 1 to carry me through the year, allow me six months

to write another novel. I wrote six short stories by March 15, trying to write the sort of pot boilers which the Post pays me $1000.00 each for because the best I could hope for good stories is 3 or 4 hundred, and the only mag. to buy them is Harper's etc.

So I wrote the six stories, but only one of them has sold yet. Actually I would have been better off now if I had written the good ones. . . .

Now I have about run out of mules to mortgage. . . . I will still have to keep trying to write trash stories which so far are not selling even fifty percent, because now I am like the gambler who simply has to double and pyramid, the poker player who can neither call nor throw in his hand but has got to raise. . . .[4]

Faulkner had plans for three books, but there was no possibility of concentrating on these new projects until his finances were stable.

Haas responded for the firm with a contract covering three novels and $9,000 for three years, providing $1,000 immediately for an "un-named" novel, $2,000 during the next twelve months, and $250 per month for the following two years; the firm would support novels at a rate of about $3,000 each. Haas explained quite frankly that, with books in general not selling, Faulkner could not expect to earn even his average return of $3,400 per title.[5] However, Faulkner needed more cash, asking, in reply, for an immediate $2,000 and a contract for one book. Contained in this new request was a poignant summary, quoted in chapter 1, of both his impoverishment, and his deep-felt isolation as an artist. Haas, trying to be supportive, agreed to a $2,000 advance and an additional $1,000 if needed. But Faulkner had recalculated his needs. He now required either $9,000 in the next two years or $5,000 for one year. In addition to the $2,000 already advanced and the extra $1,000, he still had to find $6,000 more to get him through 1941.

Also, he began to worry that his constant pleas for money were becoming a nuisance, which forced the firm to provide support on the basis of friendship:

Obviously this is too high a rate of spending for my value as a writer, unless I hit moving pictures or can write at least six commercial stories a year. I am still convinced that I can do it . . . when I become convinced that I cannot, I will liquidate what I am trying to hold on to. . . .

So besides the $3,000.00 advance on the new unwritten novel, I need $4,000.00 more by January 1. If your judgment forbids you to get more deeply involved, let me take the collected story idea and try to sell it somewhere else for that much advance. As I said before, I don't want the personal friendship between us, and Random House's unfailing past kindnesses . . . to become a burden to us both. I don't want the proposition to be on the basis of an importunity through friendship, to be accepted with a bitter taste in the mouth. . . .[6]

With regret, Haas reluctantly told Faulkner to try to get better terms because the firm could not offer more than the extra $1,000 (for a total of $3,000), though Haas asked for the opportunity to present a counter-offer to any proposal that went beyond one book.[7]

In mid-June 1940, Faulkner approached Harold Guinzburg of Viking Press and reached a tentative agreement covering two books with a $6,000 advance (of which $2,000 would be repaid to Random House).[8] As promised, Faulkner informed the firm, but with Haas involved with a special project for the War Department, Cerf entered the negotiations searching for a way to retain Faulkner without appearing to set unreasonable and punitive demands. Cerf had no desire to hold, or appear to hold, the novelist for ransom. He was proud to publish Faulkner but, if necessary, would release him, though not without some struggle.

Cerf's plan was a mixture of friendly support toward the novelist and shrewd business pragmatism. First, he asked Faulkner and Guinzburg to agree to ground rules under which the novelist would move only if Viking could offer more than Random House. Second, Cerf proposed to buy the book of stories with an advance of $2,000; thus Random House was ready to provide $5,000 for two books, though paid out in monthly installments. Third, he required Viking to purchase the plates and remaining inventory of *The Hamlet,* the first volume of a planned Snopes trilogy; if Random House would not publish the other volumes, Cerf was unwilling to hold the stock. And fourth, he asked for repayment of the advance on the new novel which, by the end of June, had reached $3,000.[9]

By insisting on compensation for *The Hamlet*, a reasonable demand and part of accepted publishing practice, Cerf found a way to keep Faulkner. He set the price for the plates and stock at a figure below cost. This was a generous gesture, exemplary of Cerf's desire to be fair. At the same time, it was an important trump card that raised the ante just enough to convince Guinzburg to withdraw, and to withdraw without rancor.[10]

To acquire Faulkner, Guinzburg now needed $7,500, not $6,000. At the beginning of July, he formally withdrew his offer, telling Faulkner that the original figure was already higher than careful business judgment should have allowed. The extra amount for the plates and stock of *The Hamlet*, though a fair price, made the deal prohibitively expensive. According to Guinzburg, had this been raised immediately, he would not have pursued Faulkner—not wanting to add the cost of a slow-moving book to a very generous, and perhaps unjustifiably high, advance.[11] Clearly in the era of personal publishing, there was tremendous prestige associated with control over "quality properties," even if unprofitable.

In stoic, indeed fatalistic terms, Faulkner accepted the settlement without protest. He realized that, after repaying Random House, the $3,000 in cash from Viking would just cover his immediate debts, thus making Guinzburg's large investment, in books not yet written and without much chance of commercial success, merely the old debt in a new form.[12] Faulkner had no further plans to try another publisher; instead, he would rely on Ober to sell stories quickly enough to support him during the next few months. Immediate disaster was averted when, between August and September 1940, Ober sold four stories. The novelist planned to keep writing short pieces for quick sale, delaying, until 1941, completion of the final long episode, "The Bear," for what he called the "race-relations" book. Thus, in 1940, he had earned $4,100 from stories and about $400 in royalties from Random House. By January, with advances having gone to cover accumulated debts, Faulkner was in trouble again.

Cerf sensed Faulkner's despair but claimed that the present financial arrangement was the best that the firm could do given the depressed market for books. And as a way to help Faulkner, during this difficult period, Harold Ober refused to collect his usual 10 percent fee.[13] For the publisher, Faulkner represented the pride and prestige of publishing serious fiction, and, along with Eugene O'Neill, he formed the centerpiece of the firm's list in contemporary literature. Cerf encouraged Faulkner to remain with Random House, but in 1940, given Faulkner's limited audience and the strictures of his style, the publishers' pride and prestige came to be offset by the balance sheet. Clearly, the partners were willing to retain Faulkner and publish his books on a break-even basis. However, in 1940, extended and deep support for the author was not a possibility; it was not even given serious consideration. They would provide advances based on what his books could reasonably expect to earn, but no more.[14]

In sum the Viking episode had a disastrous effect on Faulkner, marking the beginning of an eight-year period of distraction and diminished artistic productivity, dominated by doubts about the quality and worth of his writing. The incident demonstrated to Faulkner, irrefutably and finally (as he thought then), that he had "mortgaged" his full value as a serious artist. He no longer could afford to write novels that would not sell, and, as a pragmatic man, he consciously set that work aside in the conviction that his economic survival now depended completely on magazine fiction and a return to Hollywood screenwriting. In retrospect, Donald Klopfer thought that the motivation to retain Faulkner was based on the personal ties formed in the 1930s and on the sincere belief that he was a "special" writer. However, Klopfer also acknowledged, given the Nobel Prize, how lucky they had been to keep him from moving to Viking.[15]

II

Faulkner held out in Mississippi from January 1941 until July 1942 when, desperate and with no real prospects for publishing enough fiction to sustain him, he returned to Hollywood as a screenwriter. In May 1941, he had arranged a $1,500 advance for *Go Down, Moses, and Other Stories* which, when published a year later in the first foreboding spring of World War II, sold just enough to cover the advance. For the year Random House reported $300 in royalties for all his work remaining in print. Ober could report more success. In March 1941, he sold "The Tall Men" to the *Saturday Evening Post* for $1,000, and in November, "The Bear," for another $1,000 to the *Post;* in February 1942, he sold "Two Soldiers" to the *Post,* also for $1,000. But then the magazines stopped buying. There would be no major sale of a Faulkner story to a popular magazine until after 1950. During the eighteen-month period ending in July 1942, Faulkner earned about $4,800 ($1,800 from books and $3,000 from magazines).[16]

In the summer of 1942, Faulkner reported to Cerf that his economic survival required a Hollywood assignment. While Cerf's response, as usual, was sympathetic, it held no new solutions or offers, though Cerf did make one suggestion. With the recent increases in the book business, why not, he asked, try to write a simple and direct novel in the style of the short story "Turnabout" to disarm those critics who said that Faulkner was a fine writer, but too difficult and obscure?[17] Faulkner made no reply. In fact, he had been trying for two years to produce enough of that "simple" writing to pay his bills, but could not find a successful formula to guarantee consistent sales in the magazines.

For Faulkner it was now impossible to consider taking time to try to produce a popular novel on speculation. Furthermore, he was now convinced that all of his fiction, the long string of out-of-print books and the succession of popularized but unplaced short stories, would never again support him. In his view, Hollywood screenwriting was his only reliable source of steady income. With no audience, Faulkner was forced to retire as novelist, a silence imposed by economic necessity. During the next three years (1942–45), therefore, Faulkner organized his life in two spheres, alternating the long months in Hollywood with regular returns to Oxford, trying not to be overcome totally by anger, frustration, and depression. The period became the least productive and most worrisome in the novelist's professional life, as he struggled to earn enough money to maintain his family, home, and holdings in Mississippi.[18]

Faulkner's relationship with Random House remained essentially unchanged until 1946 when Haas, Ober, and Cerf extricated the novelist from his Warner Brothers contract, freeing him to write a new novel, supported by advances from the firm. Haas and Ober were enthusiastic about the new novel, a World War I fable, believing it to be the best way to end the writer's "schizophrenic" existence, which had perpetuated and deepened his emotional despair and stifled his creativity.[19] They were convinced that the novel could only be written in Oxford with Faulkner free from the nagging worries about money and his Hollywood contract. Their new strategy was to keep Faulkner at home and at work on his novel, hoping that, protected and isolated, he would quickly produce a new and important book. In this way Ober and Haas felt that Faulkner could contribute to the modest but tangible revival of interest in his work, prompted by Cowley, as we have seen, while also rebuilding his seriously diminished self-confidence.[20]

Starting in January 1946, Haas, Ober, and Cerf began the concerted efforts to secure Faulkner's literary and film rights to his fable, and to arrange an indefinite leave of absence from Warner Brothers. They quickly found that their major problem was not to secure a release from the studio but to convince Faulkner to accept money from Random House on an extended basis, to stay in Mississippi, and to write. With only $500 in the bank, Faulkner was planning to return to Hollywood in March, as part of his now familiar migration, having been in Oxford since the previous September.[21]

Given the uncertainties, Faulkner believed the easiest and safest decision was to return to Hollywood, but there were tensions and contradictions.[22] To maintain his family and farm in Oxford, he needed the weekly Hollywood paycheck (now at $500), knowing that six months in California brought him six months' leave in Oxford. While he had never been happy with his work as a screenwriter, Faulkner was reluctant to sever the Warner Brothers contract with its guaranteed income to risk *all* on a novel that was proving exceedingly difficult to write, and one whose literary rights were clouded.[23]

Even though he was now deeply involved with the story as the basis for a long novel, and a major work, he refused to proceed until the studio released both screen and literary rights. Perhaps most importantly, Faulkner still did not want to accept an advance from Random House for a short extension of his present stay in Oxford, since he was convinced that the novel could not be finished quickly even if all the other issues were settled. His reluctance to stay at home and complete the novel was the heritage of six years of despair about the value of his writing and his position as an artist. Furthermore, Faulkner believed that Random House offered financial support out of a sense of loyalty. He was too proud to accept money in this way, regarding advances as debts that could be paid in only one currency—books.

In March 1946, Haas, Ober, and Cerf convinced Jack Warner and his studio managers to release the rights to the fable and to grant Faulkner an extended leave to complete the novel. At the end of March, Ober wrote to Faulkner outlining the settlement, and telling him that he was now free to finish the novel; Ober's advice was to stop worrying and to stay in Oxford with the blessings and financial support of Random House. Initially, the firm provided $1,000 and agreed to sent two $500 payments in May and June.[24]

By June, with 150 pages of the book in hand, Haas felt confident that Faulkner could be finished in a year, and converted the firm's commitment to a guaranteed advance of $6,000, to be paid in monthly installments of $500. Haas acknowledged that this was a big advance, the largest of the novelist's career—and technically $8,000, since $2,000 had already been paid in 1940 for his next novel. However, he told Faulkner that everyone at Random House was in favor of the project and that he should stay in Oxford for as long as necessary to finish the book.[25]

Although Faulkner worked steadily for the next eighteen months, with 300 pages written by March 1947 and 500 pages by the end of December, it was still not finished. Throughout this period, Ober and Haas continued to provide encouragement. For them the primary goal was to see that Faulkner had a *new* book, and they worked to guarantee that he was not distracted.[26] Throughout the late spring of 1947 Faulkner worked on revisions, and then, at the beginning of the summer, he started to compose a whole new section of the novel. By the end of August Haas had 100 pages of the new section, "Notes on a Horse Thief."[27] But in September it was clear to Faulkner that the novel could not be finished by January 1, 1948.

> My inclination is to stay here and work on the mss. too. But I am going to need more money. . . . I don't intend to ask Random House for extra money because you will let me have it and I will be getting that much deeper not only into an unfinished book but into about all I have which might be called capital.[28]

This was disconcerting news for Haas, and in mid-October he again wrote to Faulkner to stop considering a return to Hollywood and offered to send $2,400 to defray immediate expenses in addition to the monthly stipend.[29] Faulkner reluctantly accepted, and within a month he had completed the "horse thief" episode. He sent it to Ober for placement in the *Partisan Review,* whose editors had offered a $1,000 fee. But at the end of November, the piece was rejected, and Faulkner became despondent. The piece, in his view, was finished, polished, and ready for publication, and he had counted on the money to pay taxes.[30] Faulkner now believed that they had all misjudged the entire project. In January 1948, he abandoned work on the fable and started to write *Intruder in the Dust* in an effort to prove to himself that he could still write a good story. Also he wanted a complete work to give to Random House for two years of active support, and to pay off the accumulated $12,000 "debt." He wrote quickly, completing the manuscript by April, with publication set for September.

Once Faulkner produced a new book, the power of Random House was applied to insure its commercial success, to stimulate the Faulkner revival, and to provide the novelist with personal financial security. The publicity campaign for the novel and the sale of the movie rights were "the catalyst for Faulkner's commercial revival." A cultural base already had been created during the previous two years by Cowley and the *Portable,* the linkage between the New Critics and the New York intellectuals, and the praise of European existential critics. Now, in the autumn of 1948, Faulkner had a new visibility, and the firm moved ahead quickly and confidently to establish a Faulkner revival. With *Intruder,* Random House pushed Faulkner into the literary mainstream and into the postwar book boom. Bennett Cerf felt the book was flawed as a mystery, and still ponderous in Faulkner's usual style, but that it could and should be made into a publishing event.[31]

After the war Faulkner's stubborn refusal to alter his style and his old-fashioned individualism became virtues, emblems of his value and greatness. Still Cerf's advice of June 1942 to write a "popular" book had been exceptionally well timed and prescient, but Faulkner's retreat from literature after 1942 was the rational response to his failure to find a place in the literary mainstream and to accommodate a mass audience. Ironically, the novelist's decision to retreat and return to Hollywood coincided with the unprecedented boom in the book business.

> And that the man crouching in a Mississippi hole trying to shape into some form of art his summation and conception of the human heart and spirit in terms of the cerebral, the simple imagination, is as out of place and in the way as a man trying to make an Egyptian water wheel in the middle of the Bessemer foundry would be.
>
> What is your opinion of this stuff? Will anybody read it in the next 25 years? Are Random House by taking me on absolute faith as they have, wasting their money on it?[32]

His withdrawal seemed to conform to a basic pattern in the professional lives of the so-called "classic" writers. Faulkner, like his nineteenth-century counterparts (Melville, Hawthorne, and James, for example), was a writer in "collision" with his culture, a writer whose works were generally rejected as too difficult, obscure, and idiosyncratic.[33]

III

Before continuing with the analysis of Faulkner publishing, it is worth looking at the influence of the war on the publishing industry. Domestically, the war created, in a triple sense, a permanent revolution in the book industry, profoundly affecting both the image-making trade publishing (general fiction and nonfiction), and the less publicly visible, but highly profitable, textbook, reference, and religious publishing. First, in the war economy, with most consumer goods severely restricted or rationed, books were readily available. Under circumstances in which wage earners found few items on which to spend increased salaries, the demand for books went up sharply. Second, the obvious widespread concern about the conflict itself generated an almost insatiable demand for information, news, and analysis. Third, this general increase in demand generated new income and high profits, prompting publishers to revise their marketing formulas and to restructure their distribution networks.

Despite paper restrictions, by the end of the war, the United States book industry had expanded to its productive limits; there was no idle book manufacturing machinery to accommodate further increased production. In fact, it was the only "healthy" book industry in the capitalist world. The war also stimulated a new international perspective. One of the earliest ventures was the Overseas Editions, organized by the Council of Books in Wartime, a series of books in English or translation that would be distributed in the liberated areas of Western Europe.[34]

This marked the transition of the book trade into a mass-market industry. Many commentators, including Malcolm Cowley, realized the great potential of the mass market but were also concerned about the effects of the "best seller" phenomenon. It was feared that literary quality would suffer and that serious writers, such as Faulkner, would be discouraged. They feared that avant-garde culture might be displaced by kitsch.[35]

There is much historical evidence that suggests the economic expression of post–World War II American foreign policy was imperialist, the attempt to dominate and control the world economy for the benefit of the United States' ruling elite and its corporate interests. While the major political struggle was directed at the Soviet Union, the secondary matter of securing ascendency over other industrial states and emerging Third World nations was also of crucial importance. In the arena of book publishing the attempt was to shift the balance of authority, prestige, and profits to American firms. Furthermore, the notion that "Books Are Weapons in the War of Ideas" (the slogan of the Council of Books in Wartime) did not end with the surrender of Germany and Japan but carried over into the Cold War era as an important part of the ideological confrontation with the Soviet Union. Beyond the political, military, and economic designs, the policy planners also delineated ideological battle lines as well. Thus the cultural Cold War was very much a part of an expansive American foreign policy in the postwar period. On the ideological front, American art and literature would have to serve important and new symbolic functions.[36]

While the demographic and technical bases for the postwar evolution of the book industry, such as paperbacks and the juvenile and education markets created by the "baby boom," have often been discussed and analyzed, the significance of the publishing revolution in terms of the politics of World War II is generally ignored.[37] The American book publishing industry was swept into new prosperity and international significance in the general global expansion of United States business at war's end, filling the vacuum left by both allies and former enemies. With the absence of British, French, German, and Japanese competition, American publishers move aggressively, under a series of postwar government support and propaganda programs, to create, for the first time, an export market. United States publishers consolidated their virtual monopoly of the Latin American region, and staked out areas previously controlled by former colonial powers. American texts and authors had access to a world-wide market, achieving, given the revised position of the United States, a leading role in intellectual, scientific, and cultural affairs.[38]

This was recognized early on as an immediate postwar objective. For example *Publisher's Weekly* reported on the United States International Book Association meeting at Princeton University in January 1946: "It is important, all speakers agreed, to bring U.S. book exports more into line with the present cultural, economic, and political position of the country in world affairs. . . ." The journal noted that Spruille Braden, assistant secretary of state, "declared that increased foreign circulation of American literature is essential to the success of American foreign policy, for it will do much to make the U.S. better understood abroad."[39]

Peter Jennison, one of the participants in the USIA program, believed that the cooperative efforts between government and publishers were necessary to make American books easily available abroad. He believed that books ". . . serve as instruments of foreign policy in ways that many products of major American industries cannot; and that therefore they are deserving of public support in special ways."

> Books are, of course, industrial commodities in commerce; but beyond that, they are unique conveyors in permanent form of a nation's thought, expression, achievements, and aspirations. And as such, they serve national policy as instruments of persuasion in the ideological context of the mid-twentieth century.[40]

Jennison also argued for distribution of distinguished works of literature as part of the cultural activism in the Cold War:

> Americans need not endeavor to reach a mass audience with a large quantity of American books generally, but to insure that works of significant non-fiction and serious fiction are made easily available, in inexpensive editions, to European intellectuals, scholars, government officials, editors and writers, in an effort to counteract deliberate misrepresentation and misinterpretation of the United States, but to provide an antidote for the kind of anti-Americanism which flourishes subjectively. All too often Western European publishers and critics dramatize the charge that American culture, if it exists at all, is immature, derivative, sensational, materialistic, or mechanical. This view is largely based on the American works they select for translation or for information.[41]

The Random House partners were in an exceptionally advantageous position to exploit the opportunities of the war and the new prosperity. Although only a moderate-sized firm in 1940, issuing about thirty to forty new titles (mainly fiction) each year, the firm had survived the Depression as a financially stable company, built on the depression-proof base of the Modern Library. By the end of the war, Random House had become one of the most successful and respected trade publishers in the country, acquiring important war books, developing popular trade titles, cultivating its juvenile department, and continuing its commitment to "high brow" authors as well. Because its prewar business had almost doubled by 1946, it now had the resources to move into new markets. In a rather remarkable and unique way, Random House, through its partners, especially Cerf, the ubiquitous businessman, humorist, radio and TV personality, columnist, and author, became "wired in" to the literati, cultural elite, and mass entertainment industry.[42]

The firm's prestige had its origins in the 1930s, when Robert Haas, one of the founders of the Book-of-the-Month Club, joined the firm, bringing to it Faulkner, Robinson Jeffers, Isak Dinesen, Andre Malraux, Robert Graves, and Edgar Snow. Random House already had Eugene O'Neill safely secured on its list, had helped to establish new civil liberties for publishing with the famous *Ulysses* obscenity case in 1933, and had published such classics as Proust's *Remembrance of Things Past*. Its list of distinguished and popular authors continued to expand gradually, eventually including Gertrude Stein, W.H. Auden, William Saroyan, Sinclair Lewis, John O'Hara, James Michener, Theodor Geisel (Dr. Seuss), and others. During the war, the firm moved aggressively to publish best-selling nonfiction (its first 100,000 seller was *Guadalcanal Diary*), and Cerf guaranteed a place for Random House in the paperback revolution through part ownership of Grosset and Dunlap and Bantam Books.[43]

Immediately after the war, the firm began to expand its juvenile and education departments, investing more than a half a million dollars in the *American College Dictionary* and creating the very successful Landmark and Allabout children's books, while the trade list continued to be successful throughout the 1950s. By the end of the 1950s Random House was ready to accelerate its expansion, merging with Alfred Knopf, buying L.W. Singer Co. (a Syracuse-based publisher of school texts), acquiring Pantheon books, and selling stock to the public. After the issuance of the first public shares of Random House stock in 1960, Cerf could confidently state to a meeting of Wall Street executives that 80 percent of Random House business came from safe, depression-proof, and lifetime ventures, with only the remaining fraction subject to the far more uncertain vicissitudes of trade publishing. The dramatic conclusion to the story occurred in 1965 when RCA paid $40 million for Random House. In addition to the personal motivations of the partners and their beliefs about the cultural responsibilities of serious publishing, Random House's increased support for Faulkner was made possible by the first surges of this remarkable change in the publishing industry.[44]

The force of the Random House efforts as a leading and influential publisher after 1948, like the political requirements of Cold War, is not usually considered as part of the Faulkner revival. But the circumstances in book publishing at the end of the war were important contributory factors in making the case for the novelist's elevation. By every measure—sales, production, and audience—the once clubbish and reserved book business was converted during the war into a bonanza mass-market industry. By 1945, book sales had reached the one-half billion mark, twice the 1939 level. The book reprinters were flourishing in the new era of the 25-cent paperback. Paperback production in 1945 reached 83 million copies of 112 titles, compared to 1939 when Pocket Books issued 1.5 million copies of 34 titles to open the contemporary era of paperback publishing in the United States. The book clubs were reaching a vast new audience in the mid-1940s, accounting for about 10 percent of book sales. For example, Book-of-the-Month Club attained a membership of 918,000 in 1946, distributing about 10 million books a year, and guaranteeing minimum sales of more than 300,000 copies (six times its average sale of ten years before) or about $100,000 for each main selection. And of course, the army audience alone was immense, with the Council of Books in Wartime publishing 1,180 titles and 123,500,000 copies in

Armed Services Editions. As the leading historian of the book industry explained, "With the end of the war, a publishing era also came to
an end, one that had begun with the close of the First World War.
It could fairly be said that the modern era in publishing began
in 1946."[45]

In the present period of the "blockbuster" novel, when advances
in excess of one million dollars are routinely paid to established
authors, it requires some effort of imagination to believe that William
Faulkner could not make a living as a novelist. From 1936, when
Random House became Faulkner's publisher, until the advent of the
mass-distributed paperback in 1947, he virtually had no audience—a
classic example of a so-called important writer who remained unread
and unappreciated in his own country. He understood this paradox
quite clearly:

> Thank you for the Ellery Queen check. What a commentary. In
> France I am the father of a literary movement. In Europe I am considered
> the best modern American and among the first of all writers. In America,
> I eke out a hack's motion picture wages by winning second prize in a
> manuscript mystery story contest.[46]

However, from 1946 to 1948, just as some critics were arguing for
a new interpretation of Faulkner, the author's ties to the literary
marketplace were also undergoing a change, one that formed the
base upon which an audience was built.

IV

As we have seen, Faulkner's failure as a "commercial" novelist
created desperate money problems which forced him in 1942, as the
only way to guarantee a steady income, to resume his screenwriting
career. Once back in Hollywood, Faulkner virtually abandoned "serious" fiction writing—except for the "Compson Appendix" to *The
Sound and the Fury* for *The Portable Faulkner* and desultory work on
a novel that would take ten years to complete, *A Fable* (1954). After
1946, with the beginning of the postwar publishing boom, Random

House was joined by other publishers to begin producing Faulkner books.[47]

Of course the Cowley *Portable* published by Viking was extremely significant, but the publishing history of the volume is itself a metaphor for Faulkner's position in American letters in the mid-1940s. As we have seen, by the summer of 1945, Cowley's success in placing his three Faulkner essays convinced Viking management to support a *Portable*.[48] However, the immediate stumbling block for Viking was to acquire the rights to the Faulkner material from Random House. During the first two weeks of July 1945, Marshall Best, Cowley's editor at Viking, worked out an agreement with Bennett Cerf, cofounder of Random House, for a six-hundred-page (200,000-word) volume. Cerf's only restriction was to exclude excerpts from *Sanctuary*.[49]

Viking agreed to pay a royalty of 10 percent of the $2.00 selling price, and guaranteed $2,500 for the project; Cowley's editing fee was to be deducted from the guarantee. The Viking management did not have high sales expectations, but they saw Faulkner as a quality writer who might begin to attract some readership in the postwar period. Viking was prepared to take a modest risk, believing that the book would stay in print over a long period of time as part of the Portable series. Although Harold Guinzburg, Viking's founder, failed in 1940 to get Faulkner to leave Random house, he would at least have something by the author on the Viking list.

As expected, the *Portable Faulkner* was far from a commercial bonanza, selling a total of 20,000 copies in four years. The *Portable Hemingway,* in contrast, had enjoyed immediate success, and sold exceptionally well—30,000 copies in the first year, 45,000 total during the five-year licensing agreement with Scribners.[50] Nevertheless, in response to the *Portable,* Random House planned to reissue *The Sound and the Fury* (including the new "Compson Appendix" written in October 1945 for Cowley's *Portable*) and *As I Lay Dying.* These novels were to be released in the fall of 1946 as a dual-volume in the Modern Library series—a reissue arranged by two Faulkner devotees within the firm, editors Saxe Commins and Robert Linscott. Although Cowley wanted to see Faulkner returned to print, he was unenthusiastic about the proposed volume, believing it to be counter-productive to his efforts to resuscitate the novelist. In February 1945 he wrote to Linscott expressing his reservations about the literary merits of *As I Lay Dying* and, more importantly, stating his concerns about possibly flooding a very limited "Faulkner market":

> I think it's a great pity that you are planning to issue this book next fall. Viking is putting a good deal of money into the Faulkner Portable . . . and if the book gets reviews (as I hope it will) and shows any signs of selling . . . they might make a good advertising appropriation too . . . and *then* the way would really be prepared for a reissue of Faulkner's other books. This business of relaunching him requires cooperation rather than rivalry.[51]

In fact, the Random House management had no immediate plans to "relaunch" Faulkner, and, because of limited sales, there were no further reissues. Instead, beginning in 1946, the firm provided Faulkner with a $500 per month stipend as an advance on his new novel, the fable about World War I, which management hoped he could complete within a year. For Random House, Faulkner's commercial revival would not begin until three years later, after the surprising popular success of *Intruder in the Dust* (1948).

However, despite the lull at Random House in the two years from 1946 to 1948, Faulkner publishing was not at a standstill, owing to an entirely new development: the postwar "paperback revolution." Inexpensive paperback reprints became the most active publishing arena for Faulkner fiction, and one that has not received careful study for its role either in the development of Faulkner's reputation or in the emergence of postwar American literature in general. Kurt Enoch and Victor Weybright, the New York managers of United States publishing for Penguin Books (London), arranged with Random House to license *Sanctuary* (published in April 1947). After separating from Penguin to form the New American Library of World Literature, Enoch and Weybright also licensed *The Wild Palms* (February 1948). The novels were produced in 25-cent editions, with mass distribution through magazine and newspaper wholesalers to news dealers and drug stores—representing about 100,000 outlets around the country, compared to the 900 major bookstores that traditionally handled hardbound volumes. Enoch and Weybright believed that a vast new reading audience could be reached through mass distribution. As Weybright explained, titles were selected based on two factors:

> [F]irst, literary quality and importance; second, acceptance of a book by the mass audience. It is true that many of our best selling books have dealt with human relations in which sex has been the motivating force. However, we have never published, and never will publish, a book which panders to the public by erotic vulgarity. . . .
>
> It all depends on what one knows of literature and literary standards. *Strange Fruit* is a good book, universally acclaimed by the critics; some other books that we could mention, published by our competitors, are trash. No one can deny that sex is one of the most interesting subjects in the world. . . .
>
> Let me repeat, I can understand how any one handling a great volume of current publications can have his attention called to specific instances in our books which at first glance may seem low. It is the frame of reference which gives the clue to the subject. There are dubious pages in the Bible, if read out of context.[52]

It is true that Weybright and Enoch wanted to offer quality books at a low price for a mass audience. However, the early formula in fiction still required easy readability and titillating content—sex, violence, or scandal—with appropriately provocative cover designs; thus, Penguin opted first for *Sanctuary,* Faulkner's best-known and most shocking book, followed by *The Wild Palms* (printed without the intertwining "Old Man" sections). Weybright explained:

> Our decision and determination to make Faulkner available to the common reader was not a stunt, but based on careful planning to add Faulkner's work to a list of distinguished writers, in the mass market, and to promote interest in his work by those who had discovered the pleasures of literature in the Armed Services Editions. . . .

And, according to Enoch, the phrase "good reading for the millions" was not just the firm's slogan but represented their philosophy to make "good" books universally available.[53] Their plan was to legitimize paperbacks by establishing a list of quality nonfiction and fiction titles, which could not be easily dismissed or attacked as tawdry pulp publishing.

In November 1946, Weybright approached Bennett Cerf to discuss the possibility of reprinting Faulkner titles. By the end of the month they had an agreement for one book, *Sanctuary*—exclusive of Faulkner's introduction. Weybright offered a $2,250 guarantee (one-half payable upon signing the contract, and the other half upon publication) with royalty payments scheduled at 1 cent per copy on the first 150,000 copies, and 1.5 cents in excess of 150,000. Cerf was amazed that Weybright thought 25-cent books could be profitable, and was skeptical that Faulkner would sell.[54]

However, Weybright and Enoch understood the mass market, and by May 1948, 470,000 copies of *Sanctuary* had been sold. Faulkner earned some $6,000 in three years from this book, but, according to Weybright, "he was totally unimpressed by the high volume of our reprint sales even though he liked the revenue."[55] Probably, Faulkner disliked the notoriety surrounding this novel, often complaining that he would be remembered forever as the "corn-cob man."

The success of *Sanctuary* and Erskine Caldwell's *God's Little Acre* (which sold some 3.5 million copies from March 1946 to January 1948) prompted the Penguin editorial department to study other Faulkner titles very carefully. In mid-July 1947, Arabel J. Porter, an editorial assistant, recommended that either *The Wild Palms* or *As I Lay Dying* should be published as the successor to *Sanctuary*. *The Wild Palms* was selected because it was the easier to read, though Porter also suggested deleting the bland counterpoint story, "The Old Man."[56] Weybright wrote to Cerf in mid-August, and Robert Haas responded for the firm asking for a clear decision about "The Old Man" sections. Five days later Weybright made an offer to Haas:

> We have taken your advice and made up our minds. We should very much like to reprint *The Wild Palms*, omitting *The Old Man* . . . if William Faulkner would agree. . . . It would be our hope, of course, that

the book would sell far in excess of the 100,000 copies, since it should appeal to the readers who have discovered or rediscovered Faulkner through our edition of *Sanctuary.* It is quite possible that if *The Wild Palms* proves fairly successful we would like to come to you again with a proposal to reprint *The Old Man* as a special book, even though it would make a rather short book, and in our experience books that are too thin don't sell well in 25¢ editions.

If Faulkner agrees, we should like to reprint *The Wild Palms* not later than the first half of 1949, so that we can take advantage of the Faulkner audience now being stimulated by *Sanctuary.*[57]

Within a week, Haas had secured Faulkner's permission to reprint the novel (omitting "The Old Man" sections) with a $1,000 guarantee. The book was scheduled for release February 1, 1948, as the first Signet novel of the newly created firm, the New American Library of World Literature, Inc. (NAL), with Enoch, president and general manager, and Weybright, chairman-of-the-board and editor-in-chief. But there was one last roadblock: Weybright could not find a copy of the book to sent to the typesetter! Not only was Faulkner out-of-print, his work was not even readily available in the second-hand bookshops. Weybright had to borrow the author's autographed copy from Random House.

This novel sold exceptionally well. By April, NAL had printed 639,000 copies of the novel and distributed 551,000 copies—total Random House sales of the trade edition were only 12,393 copies.[58] While Weybright had been very confident about the success of *Sanctuary,* the strong sales of the second Faulkner title was a welcome and reassuring surprise.

As *The Wild Palms* was being distributed, Weybright decided to ask Haas for permission to license "The Old Man" as a separate book. But Haas explained that the exclusive rights were given to Viking Press for inclusion in their *Portable;* therefore, permission to publish had to be arranged with Harold Guinzburg. In Weybright's response of February 5, he alerted Haas to forthcoming NAL publicity concerning Faulkner:

Thanks alot for your note about Faulkner's *The Old Man.* I am hopeful that, in due course, Viking will let us handle it. We would be happy to give their Portable a handsome boost in our blurbs; already as you will note in Harvey Breit's note in next Sunday's *Times,* we have helped to revive literary as well as popular appreciation of Faulkner's works, which we hope will be to the advantage of the Portable as well as your own Faulkner books which are in print.[59]

Weybright did secure the rights to *The Old Man,* publishing it in November 1948 as a third Faulkner title under the Signet imprint. It was a weak seller, not breaking the 200,000 mark.

Harvey Breit's article, "Repeat Performances, Reappraised," to which Weybright had referred, was a summary of newly released reprints. Breit, a staunch Faulkner partisan at the *New York Times,* took this opportunity to attack the critics for failing to see Faulkner's worth. For example, pointing to Milton Hindus's introduction to the recent reprint of *Death on the Installment Plan* (New Directions) by Louis Ferdinand Celine, Breit argued passionately for a reconsideration of Faulkner:

> Yet for Milton Hindus to write in his introduction to this New Directions reissue . . . that, in comparison with Celine, the Faulkners "seem to me mere puffs of wind" (leaning heavily on Clifton Fadiman's estimate) seems to me an indulgently unintelligent statement. Why in the name of what critical order, does Faulkner have to be the whipping boy of Celine? . . . And if the Dilsey section of "The Sound and the Fury" is part of the "waxwork horrors" that Mr. Fadiman says they are and Mr. Hindus subscribes to them it is *their* . . . responsibility to cite warmer blood . . . something I feel they cannot do without going to Tolstoy or Dostoyevsky or Balzac or Flaubert; in short, to nothing less than the unquestionable great masters of fiction.
> A FAULKNER novel, "The Wild Palms," published first in 1939, is a Penguin (25¢) reprint; it is Faulkner on the simpler level of "Sanctuary" where the lush and very beautiful prose with its accompanying poetic compressions give way to the intricate, though easily grasped, realistic style. As can be "guessed" from the above paragraph, I believe Faulkner to be the finest author writing in America today; as such, I believe too, that everything he has written is worth at least one reading.[60]

Three days after this piece appeared Weybright wrote to Haas reaffirming NAL's commitment to Faulkner, and noting again that both *Sanctuary* and *The Wild Palms* were selling strongly. Weybright planned to reprint more Faulkner in the near future.[61]

V

In the winter of 1947–48, while Enoch and Weybright were growing more confident about their new publishing program, Faulkner was depressed. Since the spring of 1946, he had been relying on advances from Random House to write his new novel and avoid a return to Hollywood. But, according to his biographer, Faulkner was struggling with this book as he never had before:

> Alone in his workroom, or lying wakeful in the early hours of the morning when the insomnia descended upon him, he must have wondered whether this gestation had not been disastrous from the beginning. He had felt that he had been trading his remaining time as an artist for Hollywood's money. Now perhaps he had done almost the same thing again, this time to himself. . . . Perhaps he was wasting his precious time on a work that would continue to resist his efforts. . . .
>
> As he surveyed his situation that snowy, icy mid-January of 1948, it must have had a disagreeable sameness about it. He had been sending material to (Harold) Ober for a long time now, and he seemed little closer to publication. . . . Ober had nearly 500 pages of the fable, including the horse race story, and it was now the most complicated manuscript he had ever worked with.[62]

In January 1948, Faulkner dropped work on the fable and began writing a short detective novel that he was sure he could complete. It was *Intruder in the Dust*. Faulkner finished the manuscript in April but wanted to delay in order to sell segments of the novel to magazines for additional income. His editors and publishers at Random House unanimously urged him to proceed with immediate book publication, wanting no delays in the first new Faulkner novel in *six years*.

Meanwhile, there had been another important development at Random House which was to have a long-term, positive influence on Faulkner publishing. Albert Erskine joined the firm's editorial staff in 1947 and, beginning with *Intruder in the Dust,* worked with Saxe Commins as one of Faulkner's primary editors. A southerner, educated at Louisiana State University, Erskine was a Faulkner enthusiast whose literary judgments were shaped by his close association with Cleanth Brooks and Robert Penn Warren at the *Southern Review,* and by his marriage to Katherine Anne Porter. He quickly became Faulkner's chief lobbyist, pressing hard to have the firm reissue at least a few of the out-of-print books. Erskine provided an important link to the academic New Critics who were beginning to proclaim Faulkner as literary genius.[63]

Submitting to the praise and entreaties of his editors and publishers, Faulkner agreed to early publication of the novel. On April 27, 1948, Cerf wrote a one-page "reader's report," noting that despite minor trouble spots *Intruder in the Dust* should be printed without substantial revision and publicized as a major release.[64] After reading the manuscript, Cerf began to explore the possibility of a film version of the novel, and he successfully negotiated a $50,000 contract with MGM in July. This netted Faulkner $40,000 (Random House received its standard 20 percent fee), providing him with his first financial cushion in more than a decade, and guaranteed him at least four years of economic independence and security.[65] More importantly, perhaps, the book sold well—12,000 copies by the end of September. As Cerf had expected, the advance publicity generated by the movie contract contributed to the novel's early success.

Interest in the book and the novelist was sustained for another full year. The movie was filmed on location in Oxford, Mississippi, during the spring of 1949, and in October it was released, with the world premiere in Faulkner's hometown movie theater.[66] However, in addition to the publicity surrounding the making of the movie, the book was also controversial. Far more political than earlier Faulkner novels, it confronted the issues of southern racism and justice at a moment when the problems and tensions of the civil rights movement in the postwar era began to simmer; thus, its contemporary focus attracted an audience and many reviews. These elements made *Intruder in the Dust* a publishing anomaly in the novelist's pre–Nobel

Prize career, because it was his best-selling book: 23,000 copies in the trade edition. In two years, Faulkner earned more than $10,000 in royalties—for him an unprecedented income from a single book.

With this success, there was a new exuberance and confidence at Random House. The editors and management wanted to move ahead on an often-discussed and often-postponed volume of collected stories, though Faulkner was more interested in writing another mystery novel. In late October 1948, Faulkner treated himself to a two-week New York City vacation as a reward for hard work and as a celebration of his new good fortune—his first New York visit in eight years. But in addition to rest and relaxation, there were also serious discussions with Commins, Erskine, Haas, Cerf, and Klopfer to plan more publishing. Haas was strongly in favor of publishing the short story collection and had made a specific proposal to Faulkner the previous March, based on a list of stories compiled by Erskine.[67] They also discussed the possibilities of reissuing several out-of-print titles, notably *Light in August* and *Absalom, Absalom!* Also, Faulkner reported that the fable remained unfinished.

In late November, Faulkner wrote to Commins reflecting on their New York discussions. He wanted to publish a collection of pieces about Gavin Stevens, the lawyer in *Intruder* (released in 1949, as *Knight's Gambit*), before the short story volume appeared. He also told Commins that he preferred to see *Absalom, Absalom!* reissued, since he thought it was superior to *Light in August*. Commins responded for the firm with unmistakable optimism, a clear signal that commercial success was now possible. In addition to NAL, the firm had also given reprint rights to James Laughlin's avant-garde press, New Directions, for *Light in August*.

> There can't be too much of a good thing! That is why I am all for doing both the "Gavin Stevens" volume and the Collected Stories too. We can easily decide on the order of their appearance. I for one would be inclined to give the Stevens volume precedence, but that can be worked out when we receive the manuscript. . . .
>
> I talked it over with Bob Haas and Donald Klopfer (Bennett is away on a lecture tour) and they both enthusiastically agree with what I have set

forth here. So whenever you are ready merely send me the Stevens manuscript and we'll go to it.

As to reprints, New Directions, having just issued *Light in August,* has exclusive rights in this field for a year after we notify them of our intention to reprint elsewhere. So I guess that's out for awhile. We certainly will consider *Absalom, Absalom!* and when Bennett gets back, we'll discuss it in a full meeting.[68]

The full meeting and further discussion led to a suggested reversal of publishing order. In late January 1949, Commins wrote to Faulkner arguing that the collected stories should precede the Gavin Stevens book for two reasons: First, he said, there was the obvious demand for the collection, since most of the stories were no longer available in a convenient form; and second, they would be criticized for not including something from the Stevens book in a supposed comprehensive collection. The counsel from Random House was to publish *Knight's Gambit* subsequent to the collected stories.[69] However, Faulkner was still uncertain about the merit of the short story volume and concentrated his efforts, instead, on the Stevens material for *Knight's Gambit.* Faulkner thought a collection of stories might be a bit presumptuous—i.e., it was being published, in his view, not because the stories were "good," but to fill a void and to take advantage of the recent success of *Intruder in the Dust.* Commins knew from experience how intractable Faulkner could be and did not force him to adopt their plan. In June 1949, Faulkner submitted the manuscript for *Knight's Gambit,* with publication scheduled for November. For the next year, Commins and others at the firm subtly cajoled and pressured Faulkner, trying to convince him that the stories were of value and could stand alone as a fine collection.

In short, the lobbying efforts of Commins, Erskine, and Linscott on behalf of the novelist were successful, and, by the end of 1949, plans to publish more Faulkner were moving apace. When it was discovered that the plates for *The Wild Palms, The Hamlet,* and *Go Down, Moses, and Other Stories* had not been destroyed as part of the wartime metal conservation program of the War Production Board, Erskine convinced management to reissue these books. Also

Erskine had "engineered" the Modern Library reissue of *Light in August,* scheduled for release in Fall 1950.[70] Finally, the volume of short stories was set for publication in August 1950.

Thus, it was not a spectacular rebirth, but rather a judicious response to Faulkner's expanding reputation at home and abroad. he had been elected to the American Academy of Arts and Letters in November 1948, and there were "loud rumors" of the possibility of a Nobel Prize in November 1949. In his campaign, Erskine capitalized on the rise of Faulkner's status within the literary establishment (initiated, in large measure, by Cowley's *Portable*) and, in concert with Commins and other devotees on the editorial staff, argued for the firm's responsibility to have more in print than *Sanctuary* alone.

While NAL's success in the mass market was not overlooked as a measure of the novelist's appeal, the reality for Random House management was that, in trade editions, Faulkner novels still had limited audience. For example, despite the continuing publicity surrounding the movie premiere of *Intruder in the Dust* and the strong sales of that novel, *Knight's Gambit* sold fewer than eight thousand copies. Nor were the recently reissued trade editions of the three novels in demand.[71] However, everyone in the firm was convinced that a short story volume would sell; the major goal was to have it published as quickly as possible. Given the general boom in the book business and the firm's wartime profits, Random House could comfortably afford to relaunch Faulkner.

Faulkner made a brief trip to new York in early February 1950 and finally agreed to the short story book, planned for August publication. After the visit, Commins sent a confirmation letter telling Faulkner not to worry, that Random House would make no literary claims about these stories or the collection, except to announce the fact that the magazines and books in which they had originally appeared were no longer available.[72] In May, when Faulkner saw the galleys, he was quite pleased and wrote to Commins:

> You and Don (Klopfer) were both right about the collection and I was wrong; I mean about the time and place for it. I was worse than wrong;

stupid; I didn't seem to understand what "cc!lection" meant. It's all right; the stuff stands up amazingly well after a few years, 10 and 20. I had forgotten a lot of it; I spent a whole evening laughing to myself about the mules and the shingles.[73]

Prior to publication, the volume received an important endorsement when, in July, Klopfer negotiated an agreement with Book-of-the-Month Club to offer the stories as an alternate selection for September. As Klopfer explained to Faulkner, the guarantee was small, only $2,500 (with half going to Faulkner), but the publicity and exposure were excellent.[74]

The management had correctly predicted the appeal. Reviews upon publication were generally positive, leading to a strong nationwide sale (even with a $4.75 retail price). Faulkner was on the rise! This brisk activity prompted a letter from Cerf in mid-October (Cerf usually left Faulkner in the good care of Haas, and rarely wrote to the author). He alerted Faulkner to the forthcoming royalty statement, reflecting his new success, and presented him with two new pipes as gifts from the firm, telling him how truly pleased they were to be his publisher. Within a month, the era of obscurity would end, and with it, all doubts about lagging sales.[75]

At the same time, there was further activity at NAL. During the busy summer of 1948, while Cerf sought to sell a movie version of *Intruder in the Dust,* he also sent galleys of the novel to Weybright for possible reprinting. In late July, Weybright wrote to Cerf saying that he liked the new book very much.

> We certainly want to reprint *Intruder in the Dust* in our Faulkner series. We shall soon have completed our staff survey of Faulkner's previous works—which involves rereading by all hands here—so that we should have a title or two to nominate before long. Meanwhile, *The Old Man* is scheduled for November.[76]

Despite the success of *Intruder in the Dust,* Weybright delayed making Cerf an offer on that novel for almost an entire year. While it was important for NAL to have quality writers such as Faulkner on their list, the young firm needed to do well with each title. *The Old Man,* hardly sensationalist, was not selling, and, given the weak response to that novel, in the winter of 1948–49 Weybright decided not to proceed quickly with another Faulkner title. Instead, he had asked his editorial staff to make a thorough review for novels compatible with their basic fiction format: books that were easy to read, containing at least some sex and/or violence. Weybright really wanted another novel equivalent to *The Wild Palms*, but no book emerged as a clear choice. Weybright decided to purchase *Intruder in the Dust* to maintain friendly business relations with Random House and to guarantee access to the older Faulkner novels, when and if they decided to reprint those works. In June 1949, NAL bought the rights to *Intruder in the Dust* for the then substantial fee of three thousand dollars and agreed to publish the paperback edition simultaneously with the movie premiere in the fall. Weybright, however, did not believe that this novel would sell; it was too "highbrow" for the mass market.[77]

The staff review was not completed until October 1949. Donald Demarest, an editorial assistant and perhaps the most informed reader of Faulkner at NAL, presented the novels in order of literary excellence: *The Sound and the Fury* (which he noted as very difficult), *Light in August, Intruder in the Dust, the Wild Palms, As I Lay Dying* (also noted as difficult), *Sanctuary, Pylon,* and *The Unvanquished.* However, the suggested order of publication was inverted: *The Unvanquished, Pylon,* and *Light in August. The Unvanquished* was chosen, according to Arabel Porter, because it was the easiest to read, and *Pylon* because the characters in the novel had a "soldier of fortune" quality that the editorial staff felt was popular among their readers.[78] Also in mid-November, Porter reported to Weybright that she had met with Albert Erskine who told her of the Random House plans to reissue *Light in August* and *Absalom, Absalom!* in the Modern Library series and to produce the short story collection. Erskine recommended that NAL reprint *Go Down, Moses and Other Stories, Sartoris,* and *The Unvanquished,* a suggestion clearly compatible with his campaign to make Faulkner more generally available.[79]

In January 1950, before a decision was made on these titles, NAL also bought *Knight's Gambit,* though not planning to release it before December.[80] Weybright told Cerf that they were not sure which

Faulkner title should precede *Knight's Gambit;* Weybright's uncertainty continued into the spring. In March, Demarest suggested *Sartoris* as the next title, since both *Light in August* and a short story volume were to be published by Random House. He told Weybright that *Sartoris,* like *Pylon,* was a simple enough story, including enough "action" to attract their readers, and that it would stimulate sales after the lethargic response to both *The Old Man* and *Intruder in the Dust.* [81]

Finally, in the fall of 1950, a plan for reprinting other Faulkner titles was formulated. Weybright would secure rights to *Soldier's Pay* from Liveright, *Sartoris* from Harcourt (Faulkner's early publishers in the 1920s), and *Pylon* from Random House, selecting *Pylon* as the book to follow *Knight's Gambit.* In September, Weybright offered Cerf a $2,000 guarantee for *Pylon,* which Cerf must have found to be both amusing and generous, because he wagered $50 that it would not sell enough to cover the guarantee. Weybright accepted the wager, but with a reverse twist: "I am really glad that *Pylon* finally emerged as a matter of urgent decision—and I take pleasure in enclosing our contract herewith. It's a bet: you owe me $50 if it doesn't earn its guarantee, and I owe you $50 if it does. I have every hope of losing my bet."[82] Of course, on the coattails of the Nobel Prize the book easily covered its guarantee.

The NAL published *Pylon* in April 1951, followed by *Soldier's Pay* in August. But *Sartoris* was postponed until 1953 because Weybright was convinced it would not sell. Instead, in May 1951, he decided to reprint *The Unvanquished.* Weybright's cover letter to the contract neatly summarized, for Cerf, NAL's contribution to the Faulkner revival during the previous four years.

> Herewith the contract on Faulkner's *The Unvanquished*—for 1952—and with it my appreciation of your swift understanding of the next phase in our Faulkner reprint program. . . . The advanced and accrued revenue, substantial as it has been, only partially reflects the effect of our bold introduction and promotion of Faulkner as a universal writer for a universal audience. I like to feel—and I hope you agree—that we have had more than a modest effect upon the direct Random House and Mod-

ern Library sale of Faulkner's books to a number of people who have enjoyed a taste of an author they once considered esoteric, have come back for more in your editions as well as our reprint series. Ultimately, we hope to trail your entire Faulkner list with Signet editions of all his major work.[83]

In short, Enoch and Weybright successfully exploited Faulkner's seamier side in *Sanctuary* and *The Wild Palms* because they were perspicacious enough to see the commercial value of the novelist's concern with love, sex, and violence in the South—those disturbing stories of passion and death, often tied to a curious sense of country humor which attracted a new audience. However, they were also shaping NAL into an eclectic publishing house, where a variety of "highbrow" authors found a place on their list along with Mickey Spillane and Ian Fleming.[84] Their commercial instincts led them to the sensationalist *Sanctuary* and *The Wild Palms,* but they were to benefit from an inexorable demand for other Faulkner titles after the Nobel Prize, especially as the professors made him required reading in colleges and universities. Of course, the Nobel Prize changed the entire complexion and value of all Faulkner publishing. As a Nobel laureate, Faulkner was now famous, *publicly* recognized and lauded as a great author.

VI

When it was announced in November 1950 that Faulkner had received the 1949 Nobel Prize for literature, Charles Poore featured the novelist in his *New York Times* column, "Books of the Times." Poore was trying to explain the contradiction between Faulkner's new literary prestige and his lack of a reading audience. This article provides a convenient bench mark of the novelist's publishing record.

Poore declared that, "The most famous thing about William Faulkner, a great American storyteller who last week won last year's Nobel Prize in literature, is his obscurity. An enormously popular notion holds that he is not popular at all." Poore claimed that, rumors notwithstanding, Faulkner was not quite an unknown and little-read author, and tried to substantiate this assertion with recent sales figures reported by Faulkner's publishers: Random House had sold 70,000 copies of *Sanctuary* (1931), 13,000 of *The Wild Palms* (1939), 23,000 of *Intruder in the Dust* (1948), and 34,000 of *The Sound and the Fury* and *As I Lay Dying* (1946). Viking had sold 20,000 copies of the *Portable* (1946). And NAL had sold 1,103,424 copies of *Sanctuary* (1947), 989,362 of *The Wild Palms* (1948), 37,040 of *Intruder in the Dust* (1949), and had scheduled *Knight's Gambit* for release on December 1, 1950, with a first printing of 300,000 copies.[85]

These dramatic figures tend to overstate Faulkner's recovery from the moribund conditions of the early 1940s and to ignore the books that sold poorly. Poore's statistics are not just sales figures, they include, for the recently released (post-1946) titles, total copies *printed*, i.e., all of the New American Library books and probably Random House's *Intruder in the Dust* and *The Sound and the Fury/ As I Lay Dying* (a dual-volume Modern Library release). However, Poore was recording a changed position for Faulkner.[86]

The success of Signet and Mentor titles proved Enoch's and Wey-bright's hunch that such writers could be sold widely. They changed the nature of publishing mass-marketed books and helped to create the basis for a paperback revolution. Their decision to include Faulkner in the early NAL program made him a beneficiary of the rewards of the mass market and helped to keep him in print. Of course, after the Nobel Prize, the G.I. Bill, and the advent of the university bookstore, the prosperity of Faulkner paperback publishing was insured. The unpublished correspondence and internal memos show that the most uninhibited and optimistic Faulkner publisher in the 1940s was NAL, gambling that certain "highbrow" quality writers could be popularized and marketed to a mass audience.

At Random House, high wartime profits made it possible for the firm to reissue several titles and, most importantly, to offer Faulkner increased financial support to write a new novel, his first in six years. The firm was prepared to advance fairly generous sums for the completion of the book, his World War I fable. In this instance, based on the long-standing commitment to Faulkner and on management's desire to sustain a reputation, in part, as a literary publisher, Random House was now ready to break even on Faulkner, or even to publish at a slight loss.

In 1948, *Intruder in the Dust* was successful enough to end the deficit financing of the novelist, and the sale of movie rights to MGM for fifty thousand dollars proved to be his economic salvation. In fact, the novel was the catalyst for Faulkner's commercial revival, thanks, in large measure, to the efforts of Saxe Commins and Albert Erskine. By November 1950, Random House had available the recently reissued Modern Library edition of *Light in August,* with an introduction by Richard Rovere, the *Collected Stories of William Faulkner, Knight's Gambit, Intruder in the Dust, The Wild Palms, The Hamlet, Go Down, Moses, and Other Stories,* and, of course, *Sanctuary.* For 1951, the firm planned the Modern Library reissue of *Absalom, Absalom!* with an introduction by Harvey Breit; Faulkner believed that he would be finished with *Requiem for a Nun* as well. Thus, Random House avoided the embarrassment of not having in print several works of a living Nobel laureate, and was ready to accommodate the immediate demand created by the Nobel Prize.

As presented above, Faulkner's publishing history in the United States in the 1940s clearly demonstrates two facts: First, that, except for the titillating *Sanctuary* and *The Wild Palms* (in both trade and paperback editions) and the movie-induced interest in *Intruder in the Dust,* there were virtually no substantial or quick profits to be made from Faulkner books. Second, that, for this author of almost a score of novels and dozens of stories (often sold to the most popular and widely read magazines), there was *no* reliable and sustaining audience. In the mass market, as we have seen, several works were scandalous enough to achieve some notoriety and wide distribution—thus helping to keep a few more Faulkner titles in print. Yet, between 1942 and 1948 he earned less than ten thousand dollars from the publication of original work and reprints. Long-term financial stability from book sales did not occur until after the Nobel Prize when there was a demand for his out-of-print works, as well as for all his subsequent books.

Efforts to re-launch Faulkner did not substantially alter his second-rank status. There was a perceptible commercial revival based on popular and sensational qualities which gave Faulkner more visibility, rather than literary prominence. In the late 1940s, that exposure seemed a necessary precondition to creating an image of the novelist as a symbol for the new era. The critics would have to make the case for a serious literary reputation.

CHAPTER THREE

The Origins of a
New Literary Consensus:
The New Critics and
the New York Intellectuals

To understand the arguments that were advanced in favor of William Faulkner's literary superiority we must examine the underlying ideological assumptions shared by the New Critics and New York intellectuals. By the mid-1940s, these prominent and powerful literary critics had come to agree that, since the "historical" responsibility to preserve freedom now belonged to the United States, those with "taste" and "appreciation" (the true men of letters) were to be in charge of culture. As the cultural elite, they represented, in their own self-defined terms, the antithesis of "totalitarianism" in the arts. They were the self-proclaimed defenders against "barbarism." In the dialectic of the Cold War, as they joined together in their journals, universities, grants programs, and cultural congresses, they claimed to be serving the advance of culture, not the State. However, they saw no contradiction between their cultural values and the requirements of the State.

By the early 1950s there already existed a fully realized and government-subsidized machinery for waging a cultural Cold War. The American Committee for Cultural Freedom and the Congress for Cultural Freedom organized hundreds of artists, writers, intellectuals, and journalists to battle for the supremacy of Western culture. Both Allen Tate and William Faulkner accepted Sidney Hook's invitation to speak at the International Exposition of the Arts in Paris (May 15–30, 1952) sponsored by the Congress for Cultural Freedom. Tate, writing to his close friend Donald Davidson, explained his participation in terms of a thoroughly changed ideological setting:

> I am one of six Americans. We travel round-trip 11,000 miles to speak twelve minutes; hence the precis of the longer speech. I might add that the American branch of the Congress was founded to oppose and discredit the infamous Waldorf Conference in 1949. It is the only "organization" I've ever joined, because it is the only international group opposed to Communism that means business. It will amuse you to know that Red [Robert Penn Warren] was invited to go, but Yale wouldn't give him leave! The others . . . are Faulkner, Farrell (reformed Marxist), Glenway Wescott, Katherine Ann Porter, and Auden. The curious thing about this list is my old friend Archie MacLeish is not on it. . . . A change has come over the spirit of these "Conferences." Think of an old reactionary like me being there.[1]

The reconciliation of conservative New Critics and radical New York intellectuals was one of the paradoxes of the Cold War. How they came together will be analyzed in detail, but one precondition was that their prewar involvement with political movements had to be set aside. For the exponents of New Criticism this meant pulling back from the overt political program of radical Agrarianism as outlined in the symposium *I'll Take My Stand: The South and the Agrarian Tradition* (1930). Ransom, Tate, and Warren all were contributors and, to varying degrees, involved with creating a political movement based on the premises found in *I'll Take My Stand.*

The essence of this Agrarian manifesto was a rejection of a new South built around industrial capitalism, because they saw in such modernization an emphasis on urban life and the possibility of an integrated society—the wrong kind of progress. They argued for the old values of the South, for its antebellum provincialism and unreconstructed traditionalism, both of which offered little room for compromise on race issues. They believed in a social hierarchy and a cultural aristocracy, and dismissed social reforms that stressed equality or egalitarianism. They were self-professed "unreconstructed" reactionaries in politics, and in literature, as completely elitist as their mentor, T.S. Eliot.[2]

Yet even as they began to play at politics in the late 1920s, they knew that their *métier* was poetry and literature. As Ransom explained to Tate in 1926, "'For you and me and the elite whom I know art is the true religion and no other is needed.'"[3] By the mid-1930s they turned their full energy and attention to literary concerns. With the deepening economic crisis of the Great Depression and frightening world-wide political upheaval, they came to believe that for literature to survive it had to be separated from extremist politics of the right and the left. They also well understood that their radical Agrarianism was a conservative doctrine perilously close to Fascism, an untenable politics in America by the end of the 1930s.

Their proselytizing for the New Criticism and literary elitism was their way of protecting art from the disorder of the modern industrial world. As Tate wrote in 1935, "The 'message' of modern art at present is that social man is living, without religion, morality, or art (without the high form that concentrates all three in an organic whole) in a mere system of money references. . . ."[4] And in 1936, Ransom proposed to Tate that they work together to create an "American Academy of Letters" dedicated to setting clear literary standards in praise of writing that honored the traditionalism which they agreed was the basis of "great" art. Ransom believed that creating a national group would be a way to elevate the truly worthy without giving the appearance of having formed a southern clique. Ransom proposed a group of twenty-five members to start, with two to be added each year, and with yearly book awards. He proposed this group: James Branch Cabell, Cather, Ralph Cram, William Dodd, Dreiser, John Gould Fletcher, Douglas Freeman, Frost, Glasgow, Joseph Wood Krutch, Marianne Moore, Paul Elmer More, Pound, Ransom, Santayana, Gilbert Seldes, Tate, Mark Van Doren, John Wade, Wharton, Yvor Winters, and Stark Young.[5]

At the time, Tate was unenthusiastic, worrying that it might fail and prove to be an embarrassment and, thus, harmful. Instead, he wanted to concentrate on making the case for modernist literature and the New Criticism. Once established, their literary authority, Tate believed, could be asserted with confidence. In the next decade, the movement achieved academic legitimacy: Ransom at Kenyon College; Warren at the University of Minnesota (1942) and Yale (1950); Brooks at Yale (1947); Tate at Minnesota (1951); Winters at Stanford University (1949); Blackmur at Princeton (1948); Robert Heilman at the University of Washington (1948); Austin Warren at the University of Michigan (1948); Arthur Mizener at Cornell (1951); and Mark Schorer at the University of California at Berkeley (1945). With such a national network and broad acceptance of the New Critics, their political roots could be ignored, or conveniently disregarded, as Tate hinted.

> You evidently believe that agrarianism was a failure; I think it was and *is* a very great success; but then I never expected it to have any political influence. It is a reaffirmation of the human tradition, and to reaffirm that is an end in itself. . . .[6]

In a series of essays beginning in 1936, Tate argued for the formalist aesthetics and inherent traditionalism of New Criticism. Following the lead of Eliot, Tate defended high art and those who understand art's separate function.

> The point of view here, then, is that historicism, scientism, psychologism, biologism, in general the confident use of the scientific vocabularies in the spiritual realm, has created or at any rate is the expression of a spiritual disorder. . . . It is my contention here that the high forms of literature offer us the only complete, and thus the most responsible, version of our experience. . . .
>
> The function of criticism should have been, in our time, as in all times, to maintain and to demonstrate the special, unique, and complete knowledge which great forms of literature afford us."[7]

When Tate became editor of *Sewanee Review* in 1944, he surveyed the state of American letters. "American literature and criticism," Tate wrote, "have sunk since the war to predictable depths of confusion and vulgarity the menace of which could be matched by the inertia and smugness of the first decade of this century."[8] He was particularly outraged by the popular critics, such as Van Wyck Brooks and Bernard De Voto, because their attachment to literary nationalism was helping to erode literary standards. In addition, Tate took aim at the Marxists:

> "Having done much to disorganize an entire generation, which might otherwise have been prepared to carry American literature through the apathetic crisis of the war, the Stalinist wing of this school is now talking very much like Mr. De Voto about democracy and nationalism, the wonderful union of which will probably become the religion of the next age. . . . I am not a democrat if Mr. Bernard De Voto is a democrat. . . ."[9]

Tate believed that serious writing was sacrificed to the war, with too much emphasis on "social-minded" writing which gave a wider audience to Dos Passos and created the illusion that Stephen Vincent Benét was a "great poet."

> For when we deliberately undertake to export America we have got to feel a cause in it, and we succeed in sending out "representative" writers, good and bad (the good to the bad in a ratio of about one to five), who after the social changes of ten years will cease to represent anything more than an historical document, unless, being also good writers, they merely represent literature.[10]

To protect "imaginative literature" in the current crisis of war Tate demanded that art be held to the highest standards by artists and critics. Scholars who were caught up in politics, or even history, were repudiating literature. In short, Tate reflected the underlying antidemocratic sentiments of the New Criticism. However, in the conservative liberalism of the postwar years, the New Critics lived quite comfortably with state-sponsored culture and foundation grants.

For the New York intellectuals, the path to anti-Communist liberalism was also direct—they had become vehement anti-Communists by the end of the 1930s—but far more paradoxical, as related by Alexander Bloom, in *Prodigal Sons: The New York Intellectuals and Their World*. Starting out as radical intellectuals (some Marxists, Communists, or Trotskyists) who tied themselves to the international avant-garde (European modernism), the New York intellectuals perceived themselves in the 1930s as alienated and bohemian, but by the war realized that they commanded influence, not as a progressive intelligentsia but as a literary elite. Bloom writes:

> The New York intellectuals began as radicals, moved to liberalism, and sometimes ended up as conservatives. But they were always intellectuals. *Partisan Review* started as a magazine dedicated to radical literature and then rededicated itself to radical culture, only outside the world of proletarian literature and Communist party politics. The New Yorkers held out for the preeminence of art, not devoid of social context but reflective of it. . . . They brought the modernist heroes of the 1920s into the world of radical politics, without sacrificing cultural standards or radicalism, they believed.[11]

They believed in the special function of the radical literary community, a "coterie" of both artists and intellectuals, who would sustain avant-garde culture and "revolutionary modernism." As Bloom explains, "In revolutionary modernism the New York intellectuals argued a theory of literature and of culture which satisfied their intellectual demands while allowing them to believe they had not sacrificed their radicalism."[12]

However, this cultural adjustment was also a political one, which Arthur Schlesinger defined as the shift to the "Vital Center" of American liberalism (chapter 1). For Philip Rahv and William Phillips at *Partisan Review,* the major effort at the end of the war seemed to be to find a way to accommodate larger social issues to cultural elitism. For example, in a 1946 summary of the magazine's publishing history they explained that it was their purpose to cultivate a wide-ranging literary expression while retaining a serious interest in political ideas. They saw the journal as part of the "little magazine" tradition, but outside of it too. For them, *Partisan Review* combined literary experimentation and political analysis:

> But our principal interest, editorially, was in bringing about a rapprochement between the radical tradition on the one hand and the tradition of modern literature on the other—a rapprochement that virtually all left-wing magazines had in the past done their utmost to prevent.[13]

In the postwar world, they chose the United States, and their socialism had become indistinguishable from democratic "liberalism." For example, in 1945, Rahv's review of Arthur Koestler's *The Yogi and the Commissar* stated that there was no reason to support Russia against Western democracies, since the Soviet Union was now so very far removed from its socialist origins:

> Hence the conclusion is inescapable that the democratic institutions of the West are just as much worth defending, despite their subservience to bourgeois aims. . . . The test of socialism is not unilateral: it cannot be confined to economic arrangements; the social, political, and ethical conditions must be tested with equal seriousness. . . . Socialism is above all libertarian. Socialism is incompatible with an hierarchical organization of society. Socialism is freedom, democracy, and equality.[14]

Their politics were unequivocally anti-Soviet, a position most clearly delineated in their strident editorial "The Liberal Fifth Column," written by William Barrett and published (unsigned) in the summer of 1946. They repudiated liberals who still apologized for Stalin and Russia, and who still defended the Communist Party. For the editors of *Partisan Review,* the liberals in the *New Republic,* the *Nation,* and *PM* who still advocated cooperation were "fifth columnists." The editors explained that their own interest in socialism could not now be separated from "the struggle to preserve the liberties still existing in the Western world."

> . . . [W]e propose to support the American policy of resistance to Stalinism so long as this policy meets the test of genuinely liberal and democratic standards to promote a democratic cause. . . .
>
> This approach rests on the belief that the Western democratic powers are today the only major force capable of curbing the aggressions of Stalinism. . . . The truth is that the countries of democratic capitalism are now the only places in the world where we can speak of civil liberties, intellectual freedom, and the possibilities of human advance. . . .

The *Review* was to remain a journal of culture and politics, but not the politics of dissidence: "Every politically conscious person recognizes that Stalinism is the central political question today and the principal threat to all socialist and democratic activity. . . ."[15] In

short, the battle against Soviet totalitarianism required choosing cap-
italistic democracy. In the Cold War era, there was to be no opposition to United States adventurism or imperialism. According to the
editors, the prospect for revolutionary change was now greatly restricted, and their energy was better directed to advancing the cultural avant-garde. They turned away from 1930s radical politics and
the associated literature of social realism and protest.

Where is one to look for the source of this fusion of New Critics
with New York intellectuals, a reconciliation in culture which made
modernism, formalism, and anti-Communism into the postwar cultural *Zeitgeist,* and which had such a profound effect on literature
and the arts? The roots of the literary part of this Cold War consensus
are located in the wartime activities of the editors of the three leading
literary journals, *Kenyon Review, Partisan Review,* and *Sewanee Review,* as they tried to guarantee the survival of their magazines.
Ransom and Tate, along with Lionel Trilling, Philip Rahv, and Richard Blackmur, joined together to work with the Humanities Division
of the Rockefeller Foundation, when, in 1943, the officers of the
Division began to consider ways to support contemporary American
literary culture.

The confidential and uncensored dialogues of these journal editors
and the Foundation officers show very clearly the nature of their
shared values and assumptions about the evolution of aesthetic formalism and the direction of American literary culture. They also
provide an important counterpoint to published essays, editorials,
and memoirs which too often have stressed antagonism between the
New Critics and New York intellectuals. For fifteen years, with
the help of the Foundation (and almost $500,000 in aid), these men
and their close literary compatriots worked together to find money
and institutional support for themselves and their literary projects. In
the mid-1940s, they quite consciously and actively took on the job of
developing, shaping, and justifying specific cultural values. The
common defense of culture by the coalition of New Critics and New
York intellectuals occurred almost a full decade before a formal
state-sponsored Cold War apparatus was in place.

II

As early as March 1942, the Humanities Division of the Rockefeller Foundation began to consider plans to strengthen the study of humanities in the United States. A complete analysis of the giving programs would be a study in itself. The records of the Division reflect an extraordinary expanse of interests, activities, and interpersonal relationships. Clearly, the officers of the Division perceived their primary role as planners, more concerned with ideas and strategy than with distribution of money. When a project or individual received a grant the officers preferred to award it "quietly" and anonymously to avoid being viewed in public as being both "rich and smart." In the 1940s, the amounts appropriated for literary purposes were small relative to the total budget, itself only about $1.5 million per year.[16]

The immediate concern of the Division was to help the government during wartime through expanded support to colleges and universities and individual scholars to prepare younger specialists in foreign languages and cultures—Japanese and Russian, in particular, but also Slavic, Near Eastern, and Chinese. The more long-term goal was to build up an international perspective in the humanities which would avoid parochial approaches to intercultural activities in peacetime.[17] During the war, much of the activities of the officers were focused on the Americas (the United States and Latin America). But when open hostilities ended, the main task was international "cultural rehabilitation"—restoration of facilities, protection of documents and artifacts, and help for displaced scholars and experts. The officers conducted tours of Europe, Eastern Asia, and the Orient. For example, John Marshall, associate director, went to England in 1945 to discuss wartime literary trends with such leading figures as Eliot, Herbert Read, F.R. Leavis, and Edwin Muir. They agreed that it would be beneficial to provide support through a fellowship program to selected younger writers "dislocated" by the war. When the Foundation's board of trustees approved the Atlantic Awards in Literature for younger British writers, it also authorized a study of ways to support literature in the United States.[18]

In a 1948 summary report on the Humanities programs for the previous five years, David H. Stevens, director for the Humanities Division, explained the philosophical basis for a world-wide perspective:

> Of importance is not only what life will be in the future or how it will be lived, but why. Many of the traditional sanctions and motivations of civilization have become obscured or have disappeared entirely in the last two decades. But the qualitative is not simply the unknown function of the quantitative. The size and well-being of the world's population will be controlled to a large extent by physical and economic factors, by the available food and industry. . . . Ultimately, however, the determining factor for both quantitative and qualitative existence is the will to live. Belief in the future is an essential if our world is to survive, and to create and strengthen this belief is one of the functions of the humanities. [19]

The report briefly summarized the fifteen-year history of the Humanities Division. It had provided grants and fellowships through traditional academic channels for American humanists to study the life and languages of areas of the world that had received too little attention—mainly non-Western cultures. The war demonstrated the significance of this work by establishing the value of an international perspective and the correctness of the struggle against parochial nativism.

Part of the planning for the postwar era was to consider new directions for the Humanities Division, and one obvious concern was the situation in literature. The officers began a study of writing and writers in the United States to see if there were ways to help support American literary culture. According to Stevens, it was clear that while large sums of money were available to supply mass entertainment "the contemporary arts are not finding material support sufficient to enable them to reach the small audience they undoubtedly command, and through which they gain the limited hearing that is essential for their vitality and growth." In the postwar era, clear evidence of artistic freedom was an important part of the agenda:

> The error of Hitler and of the Soviet Union in telling artists to turn from work that has engaged the interest of artists and critics everywhere

to production more readily appreciable to the mass of citizens is plain for all to see. Equally grave may be the error of other societies which, allowing their artists freedom to create according to their own choice, fail to give them the material support their art requires to survive and grow.[20]

During a period of four years from 1943 to 1947, the officers of the Humanities Division slowly worked out a strategy. They understood that the international aspects of the arts were equivalent in their importance to science and academic scholarship, but they also recognized that money alone could not buy a work of art. Stevens discussed some of these concerns in the 1948 report:

> In the sciences and in humanistic studies, the Foundation has depended largely on scientific or academic personnel and institutions, both as a source of judgment on the merit of requests, and for the administration of its grants. . . . But in the arts, the term *academic* is hardly used to characterize work at the forefront of their development; if the Foundation is to limit its concern with the arts to what can be done through personnel in institutions, it will be neglecting much that might be of most benefit to the arts in general.[21]

Of course, the experts would be consulted to provide guidance to the Foundation, but identifying worthy projects and superior individuals in the arts seemed far more difficult than in the sciences and traditional academic areas, as Stevens noted.

> The truly contemporary in the arts is appreciated by a rather small proportion of the entire population. In fact, work in the laboratory of the imagination—work which will eventually prove its permanence and find its audience—appears to be of questional significance when it obtains immediate hearing beyond that proportionately small group within the total population.[22]

The basic tension within the Division was between Stevens, who felt that money should be channeled through universities for fellowships in criticism and writing, and Marshall, who advocated support for selected literary journals that published writers outside the traditional university system. "Unhappily," Stevens wrote, "'responsible' institutions in the arts tend, perhaps more rapidly than in other fields, to become unresponsive to the truly contemporary; and responsive institutions when they exist may seem, and often are, irresponsible." The Foundation worked to support only "responsible" institutions. In short, the Foundation operated on the "trickle down" theory, giving encouragement, in Arnold Toynbee's terms, to the "creative minority." It was believed that the excellence of creations of the intellectual and artistic elite would, in time, be felt by the society at large.[23]

III

The Foundation's direct involvement with contemporary literary culture began in November 1943, when Stevens and Marshall agreed to negotiate a small emergency grant of $7,500 for John Crowe Ransom to guarantee the continuation of *Kenyon Review*. During the discussions with the officers in the summer of 1943, Ransom explained that *Kenyon Review* had a small but devoted audience—unreservedly "high brow"—who appreciated the uncompromisingly technical treatment of aesthetics offered by the magazine.

In January 1944, the grant for *Kenyon Review* went through.[24] It was to help defray publishing expenses for three years because wartime conditions had forced Kenyon College to withdraw its subsidy—at that time the annual operating budget for the Review was $5,500. The officers justified the grant on the basis of Ransom's exemplary academic reputation. They also believed that Ransom and *Kenyon Review* were providing important leadership in the humanities by publishing "quality" literary criticism and original poetry for a select readership.

The Foundation also agreed to provide editorial support for Ransom in the form of two one-year fellowships, for Eric Bentley in 1944 and Robert Penn Warren in 1946. Warren's tenure at Kenyon was an important turning point for Faulkner's academic reputation. He converted a review of Cowley's *Portable* into a lengthy and what proved to be a most influential essay on the need to reread and reconsider Faulkner. And with Tate, Ransom, and Cowley, he tried to launch an academic reconsideration of the novelist by publishing a special Faulkner issue of *Kenyon Review.*

At the same time, Ransom also began to lobby the Foundation for his planned school of English Studies. He told Stevens that he had been convinced for more than ten years that the universities should incorporate professional criticism into the curriculum by merging English, philosophy, and aesthetics into a theoretical program. Just before the war broke out he was trying to get Frank Aydelotte, director of the Institute for Advanced Study at Princeton, to organize such a program in critical method which would select and educate the finest students to become professional critics. Ransom was thoroughly convinced that, for literary culture to advance, elitist education and journals such as *Kenyon Review* were an absolute necessity. He believed that the best efforts in this direction were being made at Princeton and a very few other colleges in the country. However, he wanted to see critical studies made into a legitimate academic discipline, guided by the best critics, and systematically introduced into the college curriculum.[25] But it would be three years before the Foundation was ready to support the Kenyon School of English.

Once aid for *Kenyon Review* had been arranged, Ransom did try to interest the officers in one other project. Allen Tate was moving from the Library of Congress to the editorship of *Sewanee Review,* and Ransom suggested to Stevens that the Foundation should consider support for Tate's new effort as well. On the advice of Ransom and Archibald MacLeish, then Librarian, Tate wrote directly to Stevens and explained that his goal was to have *Sewanee Review* take on the work of the defunct *Southern Review.* He planned to make *Sewanee Review* into a journal devoted to both contemporary literature and formalist criticism, an approach to the literary journal advocated by his friend and mentor T.S. Eliot.

Tate and Eliot had written about the importance, in a utilitarian age, of maintaining quality literary journals to guard against the deterioration of language. They often discussed the threat to culture of wartime nationalism and misplaced democratic egalitarianism, which tended to inflate the value of a mediocre literature. Tate, taking Ransom's lead, also made a forceful argument to Stevens for the value of supporting those cultural journals which held to the highest standards and which conducted discussions at levels that precluded a wide audience. Tate believed that these critical journals stimulated the imaginative arts and helped to promote the best modern literature. He applauded *Kenyon Review* but told Stevens that the *Sewanee Review* would be dedicated to a criticism that more deliberately encouraged contemporary literature. Tate believed Ransom was doing important work on criticism from the philosophical and aesthetic perspective, but he had his own agenda. What was needed, he explained, was a way to renew study of past literature by joining it to the important living literature of the present.[26]

It was clear to Stevens and Marshall that in order to get the trustees to support a program for American literature it was necessary to have a clear plan. The modest award to *Kenyon Review* was justified as an emergency. But until they could present some "theory" for the support of writers or little magazines, there would be no other grants. Tate's request was turned down. However, in the winter of 1944, they commissioned critic Richard Blackmur to study the small literary journal. Blackmur had already received a series of modest grants from the Rockefeller Foundation which had first subsidized his Princeton staff positions at the Institute for Advanced Studies, then in the School of Economics and Politics, and next as a fellow in the Creative Arts Program. Blackmur's report was both a historical review of the little magazines and a commentary on their current financial problems. Essentially, he explained that little magazines were by their nature limited in appeal and short lived, but extremely influential.[27]

Blackmur published a revised version of his report in Tate's *Sewanee Review*. The essay, "The Economy of the American Writer: Preliminary Notes," asserted that the lucrative market system of the mass circulation magazines was a real threat to cultural values. It was a system that "dissolves all but the lowest values and preserves only the cheapest values: those which can be satisfactorily translated into money. . . ." He argued for increasing the rates of pay to contributors in the literary journals so that writers could produce their best work. There were ten thousand or so professional writers, he said, who couldn't make a decent living from writing, and a few hundred very good ones who "must under present conditions compete in the open market for a limited possibility of paid publication. It follows that most of them must, like the society which they express, lower their standards; or as an alternative earn their livings otherwise and devote only their spare time to their arts."

According to Blackmur, the important literary journals needed to be subsidized in order to maintain the highest cultural values.

> [W]ith the possible exception of Soviet Russia, and I am very doubtful there, there is no country in the world in which there is at this time, or likely to be in the future, either a dominant class or dominant institutions which assert a high aesthetic value against either the market system or its evident successor, the monopoly system. This is contrary to the most part of history—at least in those times when the arts greatly flourished.[28]

In short, Blackmur advocated here, and in the Foundation report, that levels of pay to contributors had to be increased in these literary journals to both encourage and hold the important writers. Such small, quality journals simply could not compete in the marketplace and had to have subsidies.

Blackmur, of course, was closely associated with *Kenyon Review, Partisan Review,* and *Sewanee Review* (as a former editor of *Kenyon Review* and a contributor to all three). Even though Blackmur was to have prepared the report as a confidential study, it was perfectly obvious to the editors, who were also personal friends, that he was working on behalf of the Foundation. In fact, he had solicited specific statements from Tate, Ransom, and Rahv to permit them a clear opportunity to outline both their current serious financial problems and their postwar plans. For example, Tate told Blackmur, off the record, that he thought *Kenyon Review* was becoming too academic and stale and that he could convert *Sewanee Review* into a stronger "critical" journal.

Rahv was also candid. He thought *Partisan Review*'s prospects were never better now that American writing was taking a new turn after a prolonged wartime drought, but the magazine was desperately short of cash. Blackmur knew this already from Delmore Schwartz, a *Partisan Review* editor and one of his regular correspondents. In November 1943 Schwartz had written to inquire if Blackmur had any "money" connections to direct toward the magazine. Schwartz reported that often people were reluctant to contribute because of the magazine's political reputation, which he thought was an irrational reaction, since *Partisan Review* was, in the views of all the editors, a "cultural" journal. By 1944, as Blackmur knew, the magazine was being shaped into the quintessential cosmopolitan literary journal of the intellectual avant-garde. Rahv and Phillips defined themselves as "literary" men who, in cultural matters, were in step with their counterparts at *Kenyon Review* and *Sewanee Review*. They planned to continue *Partisan Review*'s internationalist and modernist orientation and its advocacy of the leading European novelists (Kafka, Mann, and Joyce) while waiting out the wartime lull. They saw no clear American literary movement, but at least a few writers were trying for a new voice—mainly the New York family: Saul Bellow, Mary McCarthy, Randall Jarrell, and Isaac Rosenfeld, for example.[29]

At the April 1945 board of trustees meeting, Stevens and Marshall used the Blackmur report and his essay to suggest a comprehensive review of support for contemporary writing. But they were still uncertain about how to proceed. After the board meeting, John Marshall discussed the Blackmur essay and the general problem with Ransom, Tate, Blackmur, Schwartz, and John Berryman. Blackmur tried again to press for quick Foundation support. He told Marshall that raising rates for contributors was not the only problem, but that it was an important issue, one that could serve the immediate needs of the journals and the profession of writing. Blackmur urged the granting of endowments to selected journals on a strictly experimental basis.[30] Ransom, Tate, and Schwartz supported Blackmur's request. They told Marshall that their three journals represented the highest standards and were led by "literary men" of established reputation. The editors made it clear that they were not really in competition with one another—each had a small but identifiably distinct audience. Raising rates to contributors, they agreed, would have an immediate positive effect.

However, Marshall and Stevens were still not prepared to act. They wanted to be convinced that the journals had tried all other methods toward self-sufficiency. Marshall believed that a quick decision on money was not nearly as important as understanding the dilemma of these journals with respect to the larger questions about literature and culture. He saw three interrelated issues: how these journals served and nourished literary and cultural life, how large their potential audience was, and how well they were managed. Marshall arranged for a serious and rational study to determine the needs and the form of support, something never before undertaken. If it turned out that Blackmur was correct and the journals could never truly be self-supporting, then Marshall was prepared to offer reasonable aid.[31] However, it would be more than a year before the Foundation was ready to accept specific proposals. In addition to the review of audience and business practices, the delay was also partly necessitated by the demands on the officers at war's end and by a desire to see if peacetime would improve publishing conditions. Probably neither Tate's brief, one-year tenure as *Sewanee* editor nor *Partisan Review*'s mixing of political analysis with literary criticism helped to convince the Foundation of the stability of these journals. The officers also knew that if the journals could not survive without the grants, the trustees would not approve aid.

IV

During the 1944-to-1946 period of early negotiations with the Foundation, Ransom offered little public commentary on the general questions of cultural developments. But Tate, Rahv, and Phillips made several strong statements. For example, Tate's first *Sewanee Review* editorial, in autumn 1944 (discussed in the first section of this chapter), claimed that the modern literary movement which had generated a group of great poets and writers was at an end. He hoped that "imagination" would not be a casualty of the war; one of his goals as *Sewanee Review* editor was to keep "the imagination alive." He was dismayed at the low level of literature in the United States at present, and he despaired over the literary nationalism at center stage which simply praised literature when it offered up democratic themes.

> The Sewanee Review will oppose, when it is necessary for a literary review to consider politics, the democratic or any other state, if like the fascist state it shall make an all-engrossing demand for our loyalty and shall thus become the national religion. Then regardless of what the state may call itself, it will be totalitarian. [32]

Tate was worried that the war had created, for export, a kind of official literature which was elevated at the expense of the "best" writing.

Phillips, like Tate, was also decrying the sorry state of letters. He believed writers were too conformist, in fact, little more than pietistic, anti-Fascist nationalists.

> The rediscovery of America has become practically an occupational disease not only of the popular writers and reviewers but also of people who once had at least one foot in the movements of literary revolt. . . . And this impulse to boost our national stock has been accompanied by a wave of anti-intellectualism that threatens to destroy the still remaining traces of the radical and modernist spirit that developed in the last war.

Phillips viewed the 1930s as the era of the "political fling," with too many writers misled by politics, but now felt too many intellectuals had succumbed to the patriotism of the times: "Only in such a debased atmosphere can cash-and-carry writers like Saroyan and Steinbeck, for example, be treated with the respect and attention ordinarily reserved for figures of genuine distinction." [33]

Tate's strong advocacy of cultural traditionalism and contemporary literature was best viewed, perhaps, in the summer 1945 *Sewanee Review* in which he published, along with his editorial on writers and cultural institutions, Eliot's influential essay "The Man of Letters and the Future of Europe" and Cowley's "William Faulkner's Legend of the South." Eliot's essay was very much concerned with the direction and preservation of traditional cultural values in the postwar era. He argued for the cultivation of the true man of letters, a writer for "whom his writing is primarily an *art,* who is as much concerned with style as with content; the understanding of whose writings, therefore, depends as much upon the appreciation of style as upon comprehensions of content."

Eliot was worried that the heritage of the war would be the subordination of the man of letters to the government. Official encouragement and patronage could too easily lead men of letters to become "servants of the State." He claimed that "modern governments are very much aware of the new invention, 'cultural propaganda' . . . and we must be alert to the fact that all propaganda can be perverted." In his view, industrialism was the real problem, totalitarianism simply its political expression.

> I have suggested that the cultural health of Europe including the cultural health of its component parts, is incompatible with extreme forms of both nationalism and internationalism. . . . Not the least of the effects of industrialism is that we become mechanized in mind, and consequently attempt to provide solutions in terms of *engineering,* for problems which are essentially problems of life.[34]

Of course, Tate's position was not very far removed from this. His widely read essay "The New Provincialism" was another strong plea for the need to connect the humane literature of the present to the humane literature of the past, and for a literary regionalism tied to a civilized Christian culture.

> . . . that mere regionalism as we have heard it talked about in recent years is not enough. For this picturesque regionalism of local color is a by-product of nationalism. And it is not informed enough to support mature literature. . . .
> . . . Regionalism without civilization—which means with us, regionalism without classical Christian culture—becomes provincialism. . . . For provincialism is that state of mind in which regional men lose their

origins in the past and its continuity into the present, and begin every day as if there had been no yesterday.[35]

Tate acknowledged that this was quite impossible in a totalitarian country, but the prevailing literary nationalism in the United States was also not a solution. Even the kind of democratic nationalism represented by Dos Passos was merely a "provincial literature with world horizons" and, as such, too limiting because it shut out the value of the past and of tradition. In these terms, Faulkner's regionalism also made him a provincial, though of somewhat more power than Dos Passos because Faulkner was so thoroughly enmeshed in the mythic "past." In the early 1940s, Faulkner was only a regional writer and was only just beginning to be interpreted as a traditional moralist (by O'Donnell and Cowley) with the kind of larger significance that Tate and others claimed for great literature.

Tate was disturbed by the fact that the special and distinctive southern literature failed to get the appropriate critical consideration. Northern critics, he claimed, rejected the traditionalists in favor of the sociological novelists; these critics merely focused on themes of race prejudice and class oppression congruent with their own "liberal" notions of social justice:

> If the Southern subject is the destruction by war and the later degradation of the South by carpetbaggers and scalawags and a consequent lack of moral force and imagination in the cynical materialism of the New South, then the sociologists of fiction and so-called traditionalists are trying to talk about the same thing. But with this difference—and it is the difference between two worlds: the provincial world of the present, which sees in material welfare and legal justice the whole solution to the human problem; and the classical-Christian world, based upon the regional consciousness, which held that honor, truth, imagination, human dignity, and limited acquisitiveness, could alone justify a social order however rich and efficient it may be. . . .[36]

Here he reaffirmed the value of modern southern literary consciousness made a decade earlier in "The Profession of Letters in the South" (*Virginia Quarterly Review,* 1935), where he drew the analogy between the rise of great English literature at the end of the feudal period and that of the South at the end of its rural era. In "The New Provincialism," he wrote: "With the war of 1914–1918, the South re-entered the world—but gave a backward glance as it stepped over the border: that backward glance gave us the Southern renascence, a literature conscious of the past in the present." But Tate always took the position that Faulkner was not alone in creating the Southern Legend, that it would be a powerful literary myth even without Faulkner. If Faulkner was to rise, then Tate wanted to make sure that the considerable southern literary movement also would be elevated. In the mid-1940s he argued for a group of southern traditionalists who wrote about the same myth: Stark Young, Elizabeth Madox Roberts (Young and Roberts were his personal favorites), Katherine Anne Porter, Robert Penn Warren, Caroline Gordon, Ellen Glasgow (especially in *The Sheltered Life*), and William Faulkner "who is the most powerful and original novelist in the United States and one of the best in the modern world."

Tate was not convinced that the southern renaissance represented a movement of "first importance," but he felt that it was "distinctive enough to call for a special criticism which it failed to get."[37] In the 1930s, the Marxist influence, with its emphasis on social justice, tended to attack the southern traditionalists for their insensitivity to race prejudice and class oppression in the South. It was time for a reconsideration.

Tate's literary essays were, in large part, an elaboration of the ideas articulated by Eliot in his famous essay, "Tradition and the Individual Talent" (1920), which discussed the relationship of important new art to past literary tradition and argued for art as a separate form of knowledge. Tate called for the preservation of high culture, the autonomy of the arts, and the encouragement of only the very best talents. This he undertook as a battle to preserve his own vision of the Platonic ideal, but it also conveniently merged with the Rockefeller conception of elitist cultural activity. For example in the 1936 "preface to Reactionary Essays on Poetry and Ideas," Tate stated: "For by experiencing the past along with the present he [the Poet] makes present the past, and masters it; and he is at the center of the experience out of which the future must come." And in the conclusion to his essay "Miss Emily and the Bibliographers," he claimed that "the literature of the past lives in the literature of the present and nowhere else; that it is all present literature."[38]

What must be discovered, in other words, was a great literature rooted in the regional consciousness, but one that also transcended provincial nationalism to achieve universality. In the 1950s, this would be the southern literary renaissance, with Faulkner as its central figure. After the war, Faulkner would be read in terms of both the traditionalism of Eliot, Tate, and the New Critics and the revolutionary modernism of the New York intellectuals. However, before the war, Tate and the other New Critics did not make the specific connection to Faulkner. For example, Faulkner was not included in Ransom's list of first candidates for the proposed American Academy, and Tate offered no suggestion to include him.

Thus, in 1942, when Tate and John Peale Bishop edited the prose and poetry anthology *American Harvest,* they claimed to have selected work from the 1920 to 1940 period which to them demonstrated "the presence in America for the first time of a literature in the sense which the French understand that word." It was a representative, catholic collection, though obviously skewed to the South in prose and to the editor's close colleagues in poetry, with Fitzgerald the major glaring omission. It included nothing from the proletarian or "sociological" movement. To Tate and Bishop, the anthology represented the emergence of a powerful new literary culture: "It is safe to say that from no other land than ours, within the limits of time we set ourselves, could there have been gathered together a body of writing so various and so vigorous, so serious in intent and so accomplished in craft."[39]

What was missing was a writer of genius. There was no writer in the collection, they said, who was comparable to either the great nineteenth-century Americans or the important contemporary Europeans. No modern American was equal to Hawthorne, Melville, or James, or to Proust, Mann, or Yeats. Also in 1942, Mark Schorer, one of the youngest and more vigorous New Critics, discussed the general sense of doom and victimization that pervaded modern fiction writers. His essay "The Chronicle of Doubt" primarily focused on British fiction between the wars, but he did provide a brief overview of American literature as well. American writers, he said, also suffered from a pervasive nihilism and an absorption with the horrors of the modern world that contemporary intellectual movements had placed at the center of their conceptions of the individual.

Schorer saw a group of highly talented writers (Hemingway, Fitzgerald, Wescott, Aiken, Faulkner, O'Hara, Boyle, Porter, and Dos Passos) but claimed that "never before has the novel had so little to say." Ironically, in 1942, these writers were limited and handicapped because all they possessed was technique!

> History had hamstrung these men. It took away their valid subject matter and gave them nothing in return. The technical elaborations which they pursued took away from them, one after another, the main ingredients of the novel as it had developed before them: the author's own privilege of wisdom, the heroic element, the plot, with the representation of purposive action, and those objective values which alone give meaning to character. What did this leave? It left a glittering technical accomplishment and a picture of man as the victim of flux, of his own animalism; of many as disenabled for meaningful action and like the writers themselves, the pawn of history. [40]

Before the war, the most fully elaborated critique of contemporary American literature by one of the New York intellectuals was Alfred Kazin's in *On Native Grounds*. Somewhat in the same vein as Schorer, Kazin also expressed disdain for novelists who were more preoccupied with technique than with content. He argued that the writers outside of the general pattern of social realism in the 1930s— Faulkner, Wolfe, and Henry Miller—used their extraordinary technical skill to explore the "demoralization and collapse of society." These "specialists in doom" were addressing their own isolation and individualism, in novels of epic proportion, but were not concerned at all with social themes.

Kazin believed that Faulkner should be seen, along with Henry Miller and Thomas Wolfe, as part of a movement away from 1930s naturalism; their work was "a reaction against a literature of surface realism" and unfortunately fixated on "the loneliness of the individual sensibility."

> Few writers, certainly, have ever exploited so many of the devices of naturalism; and it is curious but significant that Faulkner, one of the patron saints of the cult of violence, a writer who has presented younger novelists with a veritable patrimony of brutality and calculated terrorism and the technique of shock, should actually represent a rejection of naturalism. . . .[41]

Faulkner, in Kazin's terms, was part romantic and part "tormented" individualist and, with Miller and Wolfe, a writer whose distinctive American voice was obsessed with "the evil that lurks under the surface of contemporary society and thought."

> Different as Wolfe and Faulkner are, the common note one hears in them is one of terror. They represent, like the surrealists, like the anxious and moving search for spiritual integrity in so much contemporary poetry, the loneliness of the individual sensibility in a period of unparalleled dissolution and insecurity; and they represent even more vividly a reaction against a literature of surface realism that merely records the facts of that dissolution.[42]

Specifically, Kazin tied Faulkner to the 1930s cult of violence, with "an overstylized Gothic, which had to be seen through a maze of confused lyricism and technical legerdemain." There did not seem to be a central design: ". . . [D]espite his extraordinary talents no writer has ever seemed so ambitious and so purposeless, so overwhelming in imaginative energy and so thwarted in his application of it." Here was a writer who indulged in "Poe-like terror" where everyone seems "unutterably lost and doomed."

> It is not strange, then, that his scene should always be some swamp of the spirit, or that his subject should always be murder, rape, prostitution, incest, arson, idiocy. . . . Faulkner's corn-fed, tobacco-drooling phantoms are not the constituents of a representative American epic, protagonists in a great modern tragedy; they are the tonal expression of Faulkner's own torment. . . . No writer ever made so much of his fail-

ure; in no writer of his stature is the suggestion of some cardinal failure so ambiguous and yet so penetrating.[43]

In Kazin's view, Faulkner was a writer out of control, whose stories were epic in conception, but whose meaning was parochial, local, and pessimistic. He was a novelist so consumed with technique that the mesmerizing language "seems to spring from an obscure and profligate confusion, a manifest absence of purpose, rather than from an elaborate but coherent aim."[44] It is all "a discursive fog," too violent, too obscure, and too solipsistic. His technical virtuosity was achieved at the expense of meaning; his style was so complex that "it has been possible to read every point of view into his work and to prove them all; and his mania for the South gave him no perspective on it, except to see all as "lost and doomed."

> Technically he soon proved himself almost inordinately subtle and ambitious, the one modern American novelist whose devotion to form has earned him a place among even the great experimentalists in modern poetry. Yet this remarkable imaginative energy, so lividly and almost painfully impressed upon all his work, did not spring from a conscious and procreative criticism of society or conduct or tradition, from some absolute knowledge. . . . No writer, least of all a novelist so remarkable inventive and robust of imagination, works in problems of pure technique alone. . . .[45]

Isolation, despair, and individualism seemed to have little meaning beyond the reflection of malaise in modern American life. Kazin believed in the rhetorical virtuosity but saw little to value in a fiction so devoid of meaning.

Even the New York intellectual most sympathetic to the New Critics, Delmore Schwartz, saw Faulkner in similar terms. For both critics, Faulkner's violence was taken literally as the center of his art. Writing in 1941, Delmore Schwartz tried to interpret the novelist's highly idiomatic style and to explain his obsession with evil and violence.

> Again and again, violence ensues, horror triumphs, injustice is the victor, irrationality overcomes all, all human purpose and effort is in vain,

mistaken, and defeated. . . . In Faulkner, signifying nothing signifies all, it is the ultimate revelation. . . .[46]

Schwartz suggested that Faulkner was demonstrating how the values of the Old South were at odds with the materialism of the New South. The old values of pride, gallantry, and racial paternalism had no place in the modern environment, and the irrational behavior in Faulkner's fiction both exposed and betrayed those values:

> . . . [T]he alien environment is irrational because those values are foreign to it; and Life is irrational because those values fail to be embodied, are always frustrated and destroyed. . . .
>
> But in the main, the body of his writing, both in its successes and its failures, seems to be engendered by an obsession with values which cannot be realized with sufficient intensity except through violation and perversion.[47]

After 1946, this general line of criticism was offset by another interpretation. Far from being a writer without values, Faulkner was reinterpreted as a writer with a moral frame of reference who had created a whole imaginative world where the old-fashioned verities still had meaning, a writer obsessed, not with literal evil and violence, but with the power of the individual human spirit to survive. After the war, technical virtuosity was the mark of modernism, where content was secondary to form, and terror was interpreted as existential *angst*. But in order for this interpretation to gain acceptance, the immediate cultural problem, at the close of the war, was to restore a clear purpose to literature. The literary intelligentsia, the New Critics and New York intellectuals, began to move briskly along the same path toward that restoration.

The Retreat from Radicalism and Literary Naturalism: Malcolm Cowley's Discovery of Faulkner

Starting from Cowley's *Portable,* Faulkner came to be interpreted as the great American avant-garde novelist who represented the dominance of Western humanist values. Clearly, the *Portable* was, as Warren noted, "the great watershed for Faulkner's reputation." It was the catalyst that began the novelist's literary rehabilitation. Cowley's long introductory essay and careful ordering of selections made Faulkner's fiction more accessible to both the critics (in Europe and the United States) and the public. In literary terms Warren identified two features that made Cowley's work important:

> First, Cowley's Introduction, developing but substantially modifying a line of interpretation originally suggested, in 1939, by George Marion O'Donnell, persuasively insisted on the significant coherence of Faulkner's work taken as a whole. Second, the selection itself was made with taste and cunning to support the thesis.

In a general sense Warren believed that after the war cultural circumstances had changed. The fact that a former left-wing radical had shifted sides to become an enthusiastic advocate ". . . gave a certain piquancy, and in some circles, an air of authority and respectability to his estimate of Faulkner. Fourth, the time was ripe."[1]

Warren's simple declaration that "the time was ripe" is obviously not an adequate explanation, but it is suggestive of an altered aesthetic environment in the 1940s. Certainly, Faulkner had not changed. The "important" novels had been completed almost a decade earlier, and from 1942 to 1948 there was no new book and, except for the Compson Appendix to *The Sound and the Fury,* no published new fiction. Cowley's involvement with Faulkner represented a personal renunciation of Marxist culture and radical politics, but also was reflective of the broader intellectual realignment hinted at by Warren. Cowley never adopted the precepts of New Criticism, but he did turn away from literary naturalism to focus on matters of style, symbol, and myth in contemporary American fiction. Looking back at his shifting literary emphasis, he noted:

> It was not at all a crowded field at the time. In the academic world Melville, Hawthorne, and Whitman showed signs of becoming growth industries, but contemporary writing was still a disputed area in which discoveries could be made. It was a time when the New Critics were coming forward with their "close readings" of masterpieces. . . . I too believed that the work itself should be the focus of the critic's attention, but I was also deeply interested in authors . . . and the myths that they embodied in their work. . . . I liked to speculate on the relation between an author and his audience. Perhaps from the 1930s, I had retained the stubborn belief that literature, while having its own laws, is also a part of history.[2]

Cowley's evolution from literary radical to "non-ideological" literary historian was obviously important for Faulkner. Though in *The Faulkner-Cowley File,* Cowley suggested that he was just "hastening" an inevitable revival. In taking up Faulkner, Cowley consciously thrust himself into the literary mainstream of aesthetic formalism and avant-garde modernism, and participated in creating a new dominant aesthetic. With this personal adjustment came new literary values for Cowley. His efforts on Faulkner's behalf were on one level a single-handed crusade for one novelist, but they also illustrate the extent to which this new formalist aesthetic was a central factor in Faulkner's rise.

Cowley's intellectual and political evolution was not atypical. He was never in the Communist Party, although he enthusiastically supported its anti-Fascist activities throughout the 1930s. He was especially active in the cultural programs of the Popular Front period.

For writers and critics the most visible forum was the League of American Writers, which he helped to create in 1935. He had once served as one of its officers, along with Hemingway, Archibald MacLeish, Langston Hughes, Meridel Le Sueur, Van Wyck Brooks, and many other well-known writers.

The League was a coalition of Communists, radical intellectuals, and political sympathizers. It was held together by a commitment to fight Fascism and to advance the literature of social responsibility. The twenty-fifth anniversary issue of the *New Masses* (December 15, 1936), the major cultural magazine of the literary left and the Communist Party, reflected the cultural Popular Front at its unified and tranquil best. Appearing in that issue were the leading Party spokesmen on culture—Joseph Freeman, Mike Gold, Granville Hicks, and Isidor Schneider—and with them a variety of contributors in and out of the Communist Party: Earl Browder, John Strachy, Rex Stout, Agnes Smedley, John Dos Passos, George Seldes, Scott Nearing, Upton Sinclair, Sherwood Anderson, Theodore Dreiser, Vincent Sheean, Albert Halper, Howard Lawson, Richard Wright, Langston Hughes, William Gropper, and others.[3]

In the conclusion to his analysis of the expatriate literary movement of the twenties, *Exile's Return* (1934), Cowley outlined his beliefs about the social role of writers and literature. Should artists take part in the class struggle? Cowley believed they should and wanted them to choose the side of the oppressed.

> Artists used to think that the world outside had become colorless and dull in comparison with the bright inner world they so tenderly nourished; now it is the inner world that has been enfeebled as a result of isolation; it is the outer world that is strong and colorful and demands to be imaginatively portrayed. The subjects are everywhere. There are great days ahead for artists if they can survive in the struggle and keep their honest vision and learn to measure themselves by the stature of their times.[4]

By the end of the 1930s, Cowley became disillusioned with Marxism. He felt the Communist Party was devoting too much energy to blind support of the Soviet Union and that literary matters had become too subservient to the politics. In October 1938, Edmund Wilson advised Malcolm Cowley to get out of politics, both "revolutionary and literary alike . . . because what you're really practicing is not politics but literature. . . ." Within two years, in the wake of the Hitler-Stalin pact and the war, Cowley had withdrawn from radical politics. In early 1940, politically confused and dispirited, he wrote to Wilson:

> I am left standing pretty much alone, in the air, unsupported, a situation that is much more uncomfortable for me than it would be for you. Since my normal instinct is toward cooperation. For the moment I want to get out of every God damned thing.[5]

Cowley publicly announced his resignation from the League of American Writers in August 1940. Cowley was not alone. Granville Hicks, Archibald MacLeish, Lewis Mumford, and Matthew Josephson, for example, resigned from active involvement. Cowley reported resignations from one hundred of the League's eight hundred members and from one third of its officers. Deciding to avoid all further public political debates, he retreated to his Connecticut farmhouse. "Anyone who was as close to the radical movement as I was is going to be deeply shaken by breaking connection with it," he explained to his close friend Kenneth Burke. "At that point the religious metaphor is absolutely accurate. You leave a church, and like a defrocked priest you can't think about anything else for a while."[6]

Although still writing for the *New Republic* Cowley no longer had editorial responsibilities in the New York office and so had more time to devote to literary history—though, in December 1941, he accepted an invitation from Archibald MacLeish to work in the Office of Facts and Figures in Washington, D.C. Almost immediately, however, he was attacked by the Dies Committee for his previous political ties to "subversive" organizations. In consequence he resigned and returned to Connecticut in April 1942, resolved "not to join anything in the future. Not to sign statements written by others. Not to let my name appear on letterheads."[7] He planned to dedicate himself to a free-lance writing career far removed from politics and controversy.

Cowley's shift in aesthetic emphasis began in the winter of 1940 in a moment of acute moral, political, and intellectual crisis. It was at this same time (see chapter 1) that Cowley slowly started to revise his judgments about Faulkner's fiction—in the reviews of *The Hamlet* and *Go Down, Moses.*

II

Thus, in 1942, Cowley decided to become a literary historian of his own generation, extending the analysis begun in *Exile's Return* (1934). Although he believed that his generation had produced many splendid works and several novels of real genius, no recent American writer, except for Henry James, was comparable to the truly great writers such as Tolstoy, Dickens, Dostoyevsky, Hardy, Shaw, Mann, and Gide—writers who sustained the production of quality fiction beyond middle-age. Cowley's judgment of Henry James offers an insight into his aesthetics after his break from leftist literary politics and his reconsideration of Faulkner's value. In the winter of 1945, in a two-part review essay in the *New Republic,* Cowley discussed the reemergence of James's literary reputation.

> Henry James is the great example in our time of an author whose reputation fluctuated during his life, declined before his death and has now reached a higher point than ever before. . . . [H]is work is more widely discussed and has more admirers than during his lifetime. It has become a commonplace remark to call him the greatest or even the only American novelist.[8]

Cowley argued that beyond the quality of the writing and the "rough justice" of posthumous recognition, there were two cultural elements working for the revival of James. First, there was the development of a kind of literary nationalism in the late 1930s, evoking a concern about America's past literary heritage—creating at the same time a new academic interest in Melville, Hawthorne, Poe, and Twain. James's sustained and prodigious writing career, despite his expatriation, offered the academic critics a vast opportunity to establish the significance of America's "usable past." The second development was a pervasive reaction against political and social standards in art:

> It began simply as a reaction against proletarian novels and Marxian criticism, but by now it has developed much further, into a reaction against historical or genetic criticism of any type. Nothing satisfies its leaders except absolute, permanent, unchanging moral and esthetic values. Works of art are being judged in and for themselves, as if independent of a social background; and the works most likely to be praised are those most widely removed from any social movement and least contaminated with ideas . . . He [James] never mentions social forces, although they figure in his work indirectly and almost secretly. He is the great example in this country of the "pure" novelist.[9]

For Cowley, James represented a heroic writer who dedicated his lifetime to his art and worked, like the European masters, on a grand scale. In a second part of the essay, Cowley focused on F.O. Matthiessen's *Henry James: The Major Phase* and the issues of unity and coherence in James's literary career. Most of this analysis was devoted to the debate over the quality of the later novels and the effect of James's expatriation on those novels. Cowley suggested that an important part of James's genius derived directly from his expatriate existence, which separated the novelist from social life:

> James was not merely . . . expatriated in the sense of making his home in England. He was self-exiled from England too, until the First World War; he spent most of his life in the world of creation. . . . In order to become a great novelist, he made himself purely a spectator of life . . . and thereby he lost his sense of participation in life. . . . At the same time, however, the liberty gained through being unpopular helped him to create independent and self-sustaining works of art.[10]

What is to be remembered from the later novels, according to Cowley, is "their rare quality of self-dependent life." James's writing retains its value because it is totally self-contained even though it is often narrow, snobbish, and unfashionable. Cowley explained:

> James said in his preface to *Roderick Hudson* that the novelist's subject was like the painter's: it consisted in "the related state, to each other, of

certain figures and things." . . . [W]e note everything in his later novels exists, develops, declines, is extinguished or transformed, *in* relation to something outside, to the reader's supposed knowledge of historical incidents or social forces. . . . [T]he best of those novels have an inner life that illuminates the life about us. . . .[11]

This marked a clear aesthetic separation from the social realism of the 1930s and Marxism. By the early 1940s, Cowley was convinced that the period of social fiction had come to an end and a new feeling in the arts could be discerned. He described it as "a rebirth of faith in the old values, in love, in friendship, in heroism, in man himself, and a hatred of every social institution that perverts them." Faulkner fit into this aesthetic quite well, since so much of the critical analysis of his work had stressed, incorrectly, its despair and pessimism. Cowley also saw that contemporary writing was not being carefully analyzed: academic critics were absorbed in the past with little sense of modern writing; and book reviewers, while aware of modern trends, were unable to place modern literature in a historical perspective or to judge it in terms of the European classics. Cowley felt particularly suited to this task, i.e., to writing American literary history that included modern authors and to making aesthetic judgments.[12] In short, this new emphasis was a step toward defining a new literary mainstream.

Cowley focused his literary research on contemporary American writers, individually and in groups, and tentatively looked for interconnections and literary antecedents. For Cowley, writers such as Hemingway, Faulkner, Dos Passos, Wolfe, and Fitzgerald were the "second flowering" of American literature.

In the 1940s . . . I began writing longer studies of their work. By then the work was being widely praised, except in the universities, but I was trying to show that it had more depth and broader implications. . . . Also there was Faulkner, whose books were scandalously neglected, and there was still the task of presenting the generation as a whole. I was delighted to find that the studies, as they continued, were helping to set in motion whole battalions of scholars. . . .[13]

He saw in these disparate individuals a cohesive literary generation sharing common artistic values that transcended politics, geography, and class. And he now believed that these modern American writers were following an artistic path illuminated and sanctified by their avant-garde precursors, Joyce, Eliot, and Proust.[14]

When he decided to concentrate his critical efforts on what he called *his* literary generation, Cowley sidestepped the proletarian and oppositionist writing that emerged and flourished during the Depression decade. Instead, he searched out, for praise, writers of his era who created fiction in the manner of James, choosing a group of writers who, except for Dos Passos, were artistically unmoved by social concerns. He recognized the enduring value of such works as *For Whom the Bell Tolls, U.S.A., The Great Gatsby, The Sound and the Fury, A Farewell to Arms, Tender Is the Night,* and *The Hamlet*—perhaps they were masterpieces. In a way, Cowley needed Faulkner to fill out the pattern for contemporary writers. Faulkner had to be resuscitated because he was connected to the nineteenth-century heritage of Hawthorne, Melville, Poe, and James, and he was also intimately tied to the European moderns. In Faulkner, Cowley found *his* Henry James—if not James's literary coequal, then at least a genius who had been wrongfully ignored. He came to see Faulkner as the "greatest" of the American moderns.

In February 1944, Cowley wrote to the novelist suggesting a long essay "to see whether it mightn't help to redress the balance between his worth and reputation."[15] While waiting for Faulkner's reply, Cowley was immersed in five other projects (in addition to desultory book reviewing for the *New Republic)* in an attempt to earn a living as an independent, free-lance editor/writer: (1) researching material for a single-volume history of American literature on an advance from Doubleday Doran (a book never completed); (2) writing a profile of Scribners' editor Max Perkins for April publication in the *New Yorker;* (3) translating Gide's *Imaginary Conversations;* (4) planning a chapter for the massive collaborative, *Literary History of the United States* (1947), sponsored by the Rockefeller Foundation; and (5) beginning to compile *The Portable Hemingway* for Viking Press.

However, for Cowley, the most fortuitous event of that spring occurred in April when Stanley Preston Young, then managing editor of the Bollingen Press, told Cowley that the Mellon family was establishing a foundation to help writers and suggested that Cowley formulate and formally submit a grant proposal. On April 11 he sent a long letter to Young outlining a five-year program for research and writing, with the book on American literary history (Doubleday Doran) as its centerpiece. Young forwarded the letter to Mary Mellon and arranged for her to meet Cowley. She agreed to support the project and, on May 1, 1944, entered into a contract with Cowley, guaranteeing him $5,500 per year for five years. Sheltered and financially independent, Cowley was free to write and research. His careful work on Hemingway and then his revised reading of Faulkner were the first returns from the Mellon subvention.[16]

In late July 1944, once the Hemingway *Portable* was finished, Cowley turned his full attention to Faulkner. First, he tried to convince Viking Press in cooperation with Random House to issue a Faulkner *Portable* as a companion volume to *The Portable Hemingway* (scheduled for September publication). But the Viking management did not feel that there would be enough of an audience. Not at all disheartened he shifted direction, asking for and receiving a commitment from Harrison Smith, then publisher of the *Saturday Review of Literature,* to print a long analysis of Faulkner by Cowley. This work would lead to the series of essays that gained approval for a *Portable* (see chapter 1).

Support for Cowley's advocacy of Faulkner's value came quickly from his southern literary friends Tate, Warren, and Caroline Gordon. Prior to publication of "William Faulkner's Legend of the South" in *Sewanee Review,* Cowley submitted a draft to Tate and Gordon (who were married to each other at the time). Both were enthusiastic about the piece (see chapter 1). Gordon felt that most other critics had misrepresented Faulkner. Cowley, however, was correct to see Faulkner's "tragic vision" of the South as a commentary on the general human condition, she wrote. Tate offered one suggestion to give the essay a broader implication. Because Cowley seemed to suggest that Faulkner was the creator of the "Southern myth," Tate argued for a more inclusive view, noting that Faulkner was a very powerful spokesman but not the myth's creator. He was, instead, one of several southern writers who relied on a common cultural heritage—Warren, Gordon, Tate, Thomas Stribling, and others.[17]

Cowley's deep sympathies for southern life and culture had begun in 1933 when he had spent two early-summer months with Tate and Gordon on their farm in northern Tennessee finishing the manuscript for *Exile's Return.* Despite very sharp differences about politics at that time, Cowley found that he had few disagreements about art and literature with the Tates, Robert Penn Warren, and their literary-Agrarian friends. In fact, they shared an idealism, agreeing that good writing finally transcended region and politics.

Being embraced by Gordon, Warren, and Tate eased Cowley's transition from left-wing book reviewer to "non-ideological" literary historian. Moreover, the involvement and encouragement of Warren and Tate (representing the ascendant New Criticism) helped to validate and elevate not just Faulkner but Cowley. Warren and Cowley very consciously attacked the arguments found in such critiques as Kazin's *On Native Grounds* and Geismar's *Writers in Crisis* that Faulkner's writing was obscure, violent, and lacked coherence.

In 1945, Cowley was commissioned to do two additional chapters in Spiller's symposium *Literary History of the United States* (making a total of three chapters), and, in 1949, he was elected to the National Institute of Arts and Letters. Also, by the end of the decade, he was receiving invitations to teach and lecture at major American universities, was hired by Harold Guinzburg, president of Viking Press, as an advisory editor at a salary of three hundred dollars per month, and was receiving lucrative assignments from the *New Yorker* and *Life.* By the end of the 1940s, Cowley had palpable proof of his new stature within the literary establishment.

III

As a socially and historically minded critic, Cowley deprecated the narrow textual concerns of the New Critics; yet at the same time, in the mid-1940s, he immersed himself in writers whose new styles and myths needed explication. Of course, these writers were primarily concerned with the world "within"—the Jamesian world transposed to the twentieth-century. Cowley repudiated the heritage of social realism, with its emphasis on the outer world, in favor of modernism, with its focus on the "psychological."[18] In 1947, he published an essay in *Kenyon Review* on American naturalism. He praised the rebelliousness of the American naturalists and their struggle to tell the truth about America despite the restraints of the prevailing genteel values in literature:

> And what shall we say in judgment? . . . Its results have been good, I think, in so far as it has forced its adherents to stand in opposition to American orthodoxy. Honest writing in this country has always been the work of opposition. . . .[19]

However, this was now qualified approval; too often, he felt that this opposition (both that of the nineteenth-century naturalists and of the Depression-era neo-naturalists) had in fact cheapened the writers' subjects because, while dramatizing issues, they were guilty of over-simplification:

> With few exceptions they [the naturalists] have no faith in reform, whether it be the reform of the individual by his own decision or the reform of society by reasoned courses of action. The changes they depict are the result of laws and forces and tendencies beyond human control. That is the great difference between the naturalists and the proletarian or Marxian novelists of the 1930s. The proletarian writers . . . believed that men acting together could make a new world. But they borrowed the objective and exterior technique of the naturalists which was unsuited to their essentially religious purpose.[20]

Cowley was also repelled by their lack of style; with the exception of Dos Passos and Steinbeck, "they have all used language as a blunt instrument." Their real contribution despite their "defective hearing" was, he claimed, to search out new material and to write about the difficult, unpleasant, and ugly side of American life which truly "broadened the scope of American fiction." Crane, Norris, Dreiser,

Sinclair, London, Dos Passos, Farrell, and Wright helped to create a clearer understanding of the urban industrial age in its "unseemly" variety. Yet for Cowley, in the mid-1940s, their work stood as a literature of surfaces with little subtlety and limited value:

> It is concerned with observed behavior and with explanations for that behavior in terms of heredity or environment. It presents the exterior world, often in striking visual images; but unlike the work of Henry James or Sherwood Anderson, or William Faulkner . . . it does not try to explore the world within.[21]

By chiding the naturalists for their superficiality and crude use of language, Cowley made it appear that his separation from the naturalist tradition was primarily an aesthetic matter—i.e., naturalism cannot be the basis of great art because it is inherently narrow and didactic. But, more importantly, he was repudiating the tradition of rebellion in naturalism which produced the valuable social and political novels of protest that characterized American literary realism. This fiction emerged from the social struggles of the industrial era, giving voice to the masses in a literature that was anti-elitist in substance and style. However, in the 1940s, Cowley came to believe that the inheritors of the dominant nineteenth-century tradition were those talents of his generation who were both stylists and mythmakers, not naturalists.

In 1951, when *Exile's Return* was reissued, Cowley changed the epilogue from the predictive "Yesterday and Tomorrow" to an adventurist but backward-looking chapter, "New Year's Eve." In the revised version, Cowley saw the Lost Generation as a group of rebellious individuals who ran away from convention, the sham of World War I rhetoric, the materialism of the 1920s, and the horror of the Depression. Except for the unanimity over the Spanish Civil War, they rejected the politics of the left in the 1930s. Cowley claimed, "They didn't look forward, really, to a new collective society based on economic planning and the intelligent use of machines . . . in their hearts they looked toward the past." Aesthetically, he said they turned to Europe and studied the modernists, Flaubert, Proust, Gide, Rimbaud, Mallarmé, Joyce, and Eliot.[22]

Cowley's further separation from the naturalistic movement was clearly drawn in an essay, published in 1954, which assessed the postwar literary scene and tried to establish its value after an evolution of some sixty years: "Naturalism: No Teacup Tragedies." He still believed that naturalism was an important literary tradition but claimed emphatically, "It isn't my tradition, for I disagree with its doctrines and even more with the slipshod manner in which they usually applied."[23] He rejected as false the notion that writers should be objective and dispassionate observers more concerned with data than with style.

While Cowley also reaffirmed the significance of naturalism for its truth-telling and its rebelliousness, he asserted that naturalism could not be the basis of great art because it was inherently narrow and didactic. To illustrate these strengths and weaknesses, he cited the Soviet experience with "socialist realism," making this invidious comparison:

> The Western ideal of novels based on personal experience is essentially right and the present Russian ideal of socially useful novels produced to order is wrong. The Western ideal is right because novels should be true at all levels and because such truth can't be achieved without a long accumulation of feelings and observations. The Russian ideal is wrong because social aims and political programs . . . are likely to be accepted only on the top level of the mind.[24]

In the postwar period, Cowley saw no continuation of the tradition of socially conscious art, but neither did he see another vital literary movement taking its place. Except for Faulkner, recent literature was anemic and uninteresting to Cowley; it was based on narrow life experiences.

> If the novelists looked deeply enough into their own hearts and minds, they would find a broader image of American life than most of them have been presenting. . . . I think of one example, that of William Faulkner . . . his books contained a picture of the Deep South and an

interpretation of Southern history—even a system of values and a myth of the sort that critics had been admiring in Hawthorne and Melville. [25]

In short, Cowley devoted his career, after 1940, to research on contemporary American writers, but he came to this work disillusioned with Marxism. He declared his allegiance to literature and elite literary values, and announced his disaffection with the literature of social conscience. After 1942, once Cowley had "come over" to Faulkner, he participated with the New Critics, the New York intellectuals, and the Rockefeller Foundation to shape the postwar cultural agenda, though for the hardcore anti-Stalinists at *Partisan Review* Cowley was never fully forgiven for his long-term Party ties. Ultimately, Cowley was an idealist who, like his formalist literary friends, placed art above politics, and who claimed that literature in its fully realized form was universal and apolitical.

CHAPTER FIVE

Forging a Postwar Aesthetic:
The Rockefeller Foundation
and the New Literary Consensus

In the summer of 1946, after several years of study and review, the officers of the Rockefeller Foundation Humanities Division were ready to make a modest but direct financial commitment toward American literary culture. The Division, based on the analysis provided by Blackmur and the connection to Ransom's *Kenyon Review,* was considering three ways of supporting American letters: subsidies to selected literary journals to raise the rates paid to contributors; grants in literary criticism to special institutes or schools, such as Ransom's Kenyon School of English or one suggested by Blackmur at Princeton; and fellowships awarded directly to writers selected by the editors of literary journals.

In mid-July 1946, John Marshall (associate director of the Humanities Division) suggested to David Stevens (director) that the Foundation take specific action to encourage "creative writing and criticism." Marshall wanted to get applications from several of the best little magazines, review them, and try a three-year experiment. He viewed the Foundation's involvement as temporary. The money was to be a catalyst, with the aid provided in such a way to avoid the appearance that the Foundation itself was making aesthetic and literary judgments.[1]

Stevens was not completely convinced. He was far more comfortable with awards granted through universities in the form of academic fellowships to alter the teaching of criticism and the training of younger critics, but he agreed to let Marshall and Blackmur prepare a specific proposal. Marshall concurred with Blackmur's 1944 report for the Foundation (published in *Sewanee Review* as "The Economy of the American Writer") that encouragement of these journals would help to promote real literary change, and seemed a far more promising arena than the universities.[2] On September 18, 1946, Marshall arranged to meet at Princeton with Blackmur and Walter W. Stewart, a Rockefeller trustee and member of the Institute for Advanced Study at Princeton, to organize a program.

In planning for the meeting Marshall wrote two analyses, one covering raising rates and the other dealing with literary fellowships and money for editorial expenses. In arguing for support, Marshall cited a recently published analysis of small magazines by Frederick Hoffman, Charles Allen, and Carolyn Ulrich, *The Little Magazine: A History and a Bibliography* (Princeton, 1946). It reflected Blackmur's thesis that little magazines, while short-lived, had demonstrable positive effects on the arts by providing outlets for the avant-garde (see chapter 3). According to this study, a large part of the modernist literary tradition was connected to these little magazines. Marshall believed that they "represent what might be called the cutting edge of literary advance."[3] Marshall wanted journals chosen on the basis of their "literary importance" by a panel of "independent" literary experts and critics; but he and Blackmur already believed that *Kenyon Review, Sewanee Review, Partisan Review, Accent,* and *Poetry* were clearly at the top of the list.

When considering the whole issue of such grants, one must keep in mind that the publishing scale was small. *Kenyon Review* had a circulation of about 2,500 at this time, Tate had raised *Sewanee Review*'s circulation from about 500 to 2,000, and *Partisan Review* had doubled to 6,000 an issue, switching from quarterly to bimonthly publication. It was thought that a circulation of 7,500 was legitimately possible for *Kenyon Review* and *Sewanee Review,* but 10,000 was the estimated threshold necessary for self-sufficiency. Only *Partisan Review* ever reached that level, and escalating costs always mandated a subsidy. Yearly budgets for all three were at the $10,000 level.

Marshall also prepared an analysis for a literary fellowship program. Direct awards were the traditional province of the Guggenheim Foundation, but those went to more recognized writers. Marshall, not wanting to interfere with this well-established program, proposed a program for *younger* writers. This would also be a way to offer Foundation support directly, but discreetly, to the journals for their general expenses. However, it would be five more years before the Foundation was ready to contribute to such a fellowship program.[4]

The plan that emerged from the September meeting required the creation of a small panel of three critics who would draft a letter to poll a larger panel. The large panel, in turn, would be asked to name the magazines they thought most deserving of support. After this survey the smaller panel would review the results and recommend a list of not more than eight magazines. These magazines would be asked to apply for support to raise rates to contributors. The smaller panel would assist the officers in making the final selections. Throughout the evaluation process, both panels and the funding source would remain unidentified to the public.

The small panel reflected the crucial constituencies of the emerging postwar consensus: Richard Blackmur at Princeton for the New Critics, Lionel Trilling at Columbia for the New York intellectuals (thus, both for the elite universities), and Malcolm Cowley for his independent advocacy of Faulkner and the other "good" contemporary American writers. Marshall, it should be noted, also discussed with Blackmur an August meeting between Stevens and Ransom concerning a proposed five-year plan to create a summer institute of critical studies at Kenyon College. Ransom was suggesting the establishment of a faculty of fifteen to eighteen critics, with some six to teach each summer at the institute. He apparently had commitments to such a project from Trilling, Warren, Tate, Matthiessen, Brooks, Blackmur, and Harry Levin.[5]

Blackmur, Cowley and Trilling met on 24 October at the Foundation offices in New York and drafted a letter to nineteen critics. But members of this larger group were hardly an independent panel. The little magazines were for most of them the primary outlet for their own work. And, of course, many of them had well-established professional and/or personal relationships with one another. The nineteen critics were: W.H. Auden, Kenneth Burke, Eric Bentley, Louise Bogan, Van Wyck Brooks, Granville Hicks, Frederick Hoffman, Alfred Kazin, Randall Jarrell, F.O. Matthiessen, George Mayberry, Marianne Moore, Wallace Stevens, Allen Tate, Robert Penn Warren, William Carlos Williams, Edmund Wilson, Yvor Winters, and Morton Zabel.

The letter was carefully worded with no reference to the Rockefeller Foundation, but it was apparent that Blackmur, Cowley, and Trilling were working under the auspices of an organization ready to provide money. Of the fourteen who responded in time for the report to Marshall, there was a clear consensus that *Partisan Review, Kenyon Review, Sewanee Review, Accent,* and *Poetry,* in rank order, deserved support. (Responses were not received from Bogan, Brooks, Mayberry, Winters, and Zabel.) There was obvious diversity in their individual analyses, but the critics were in agreement that such magazines were necessary for the health of literature and were worthy of support.

Perhaps the most idiosyncratic and harsh judgment came from Edmund Wilson:

> In reply to your mysterious letter: you may quote me to the effect that magazines of the type of *The Dial, The Little Review,* and *Partisan Review,* have done an immensely valuable service in printing the work of important writers who were rejected or had not yet been discovered by the commercial publications, and in keeping the discussion of literature and art on a high level of seriousness. . . . The *Kenyon Review* is indescribably awful. Allen Tate, before he left *Sewanee,* never succeeded lifting the shadow of influence of J.C. Ransom of not being able to refuse filling up its space with the writings of cousins and aunts. *Accent* is perfectly piffling; and *Poetry,* except when, with obvious and ignominious timidity, it recently tried to do something for Pound, has been as dead as Hull House for years.

Tate, who knew perfectly well that this letter was prompted by the Foundation, wrote for the record. He said the little magazines were crucial and had been the only defense against the commercialization of culture. With Eliot as his major example, he claimed that the *best* writers were published in these journals. In fact, Tate noted that he preferred to have his own work appear first in these journals. They were, in his opinion, the only literary conscience in America. And, perhaps most importantly, he claimed that what was now called "the new criticism" could not have developed outside of these literary quarterlies: the essays that appeared in these journals had been *the only criticism.*[6]

Trilling was especially pleased with *Partisan Review*'s top rating because it was in a relatively weak position with respect to the Foundation: *Partisan Review* was not tied to the academy (and the editors, of course, were proud of that); it was not a non-profit corporation which would make for difficulties under the tax codes; it was not free from the taint of "socialist" politics, even though the editors had long since repudiated Marxism in favor of democratic liberalism. In addition to Trilling's participation on the small panel, his introduction to *The Partisan Reader* (1946), published that autumn, was carefully crafted to conform to the Foundation's new interest in American literary culture. It seems safe to suggest that he highlighted *Partisan Review*'s special cultural contributions specifically to build a case for *Partisan Review* and to help secure the Foundation's support.

In this introductory essay, Trilling explored one of his favorite themes: the dialectical relationship between literary modernism and political "liberalism"—namely, that the best modern writers were very far from "democratic liberals," while the intellectual elite who promoted that literature were self-proclaimed "liberals." Trilling made the point that a "discrepancy . . . exists between the political beliefs of our educated class and the literature that, by its merits should properly belong to that class." According to Trilling, the editors of *Partisan Review* created a "union between our political ideas and our imaginations." Furthermore, *Partisan Review* was concerned with "serious" ideas, and its importance as a journal must be measured, he said, by the level of its seriousness and commitment to imagination and politics. Trilling also differentiated *Partisan Re-*

view's wide-ranging concern with cultural issues from the narrower technical analyses that appeared in *Kenyon Review* and *Sewanee Review.*

In short, Trilling argued that *Partisan Review* appealed to a coterie, rather than a large audience, but this was not a failing, because "literature has always been carried on within small limits and under great difficulties." He suggested that Shelley's comment was an appropriate measure of the influence of journals such as *Partisan Review:* " 'it exceeds all imagination to conceive of the world' if literature did not continue in existence with its appeal to its limited group. . . ."[7]

The editors were also aware that Foundation support would come only if the journal was perceived as literary, not political. In their retrospective in *The Partisan Reader,* the editors argued that the value of the *Review* was its merger of the radical tradition with modern literature.

> It is precisely from this union of sensibility with a radical temper that *Partisan Review* has derived its tone and quality. In the realm of action, priorities may be inescapable, but in the realm of thought it is not always necessary to submit to them. . . . That the specific emphasis of the magazine has not been without influence among its literary contributors, in that it has led some of them to modify their previous attitudes of superiority or indifference to political issues; and in the same way, some of the readers of the magazine who were first drawn to it on political grounds have been led to realize that the claims of the imagination cannot be subordinated to the utilitarian demands of the political mind.[8]

However, the political emphasis at *Partisan Review* was clearly outlined in Randall Jarrell's remarkably candid response to the survey by Blackmur, Trilling, and Cowley. He did not seem to know of the Rockefeller connection and wrote a long, honest analysis of the little magazine "scene." He placed *Partisan Review* at the top, with *Kenyon Review* and *Sewanee Review* close behind. *Partisan Review* was the strongest because the editors had, with their very cosmopolitan orientation, an accurate sense of the literary marketplace. They published good literary analyses and probably the best short stories.

However, he also offered rather pointed and honest criticisms of *Partisan Review.* Jarrell said the editors viewed the world from an anti-Stalinist, quasi-Marxist, and semibohemian perspective (believing New York City to be Paris in America). He explained that a significant *Partisan Review* limitation was its one-sided representation of the New York writer and its lack of imagination toward other groups. It was starting to publish a wider variety of authors, he said, and consciously excluded only "Stalinists." Thus, at *Partisan Review* the advocacy of avant-garde modernism was intimately tied to an attack on 1930s Communist politics and literary social realism.

In short, these responses to the Foundation's panel reflected the new literary ambiance in support of avant-garde modernism, an attack on the naturalist tradition, and the aesthetic formalism of the New Critics. And in late November, Blackmur, Cowley, and Trilling submitted their report to Marshall for grants to literary journals. Their priority list included ten journals: *Partisan Review, Kenyon Review, Sewanee Review, Accent, Poetry, Western Review, Chimera, View, Furioso,* and *Yale Poetry Review.*

II

Clearly, the critics on both panels, despite Wilson's animosity toward Ransom and *Kenyon Review,* wanted to find ways to guarantee the survival of the three journals. Raising rates was one way to protect them and to help the best writers avoid watering down material to suit the commercial publishers. At the beginning of January 1947, Marshall summarized the work of the Blackmur, Cowley, and Trilling panel for Stevens. Marshall explained that an increase in payment rates to contributors would make it possible to support the kinds of writers who would influence the future of literary development in the United States but would relieve the Foundation of the responsibility of having to make direct selection of specific writers. Marshall viewed the proposed program as a process: the rates are raised to encourage writers to publish in these journals, which, in turn, raises the reputation of the journals and increases their circulation. And increased circulation leads to self-sufficiency. For example, he pointed to *Partisan Review,* which had secured its current high reputation and increased circulation, in part, because T.S. Eliot chose to have first United States publication of much of his recent work appear in it. As an example, there was the publication of Eliot's "Notes toward a Definition of Culture" (1944), which argued for literary elites to clearly define and defend what is valuable in culture—"to inculcate the right values of what is worth achieving."[9]

Marshall thus advanced a "theory" about how an agency like the Foundation could help the "growth in contemporary literature" through aid to literary magazines:

> Growth in literature is, fundamentally, growth in sensibility first on the part of writers, and, by appreciation of their work in the minds of their readers. Such growth in sensibility . . . occurs as writers become aware of aspects of experience which their predecessors have not sufficiently treated, and discover ways of treating that experience which makes its significance appreciable . . . for readers of their time. This phenomenon in literary history has been most striking when it took the form of "revolt" from a prevailing tradition. . . . Such "revolts" are, however, only striking instances of a constant process of growth in literature, which in its less dramatic forms merely reflects an extension in the sensibility of this or that writer, or group of writers. Such a less dramatic instance is now well recognized in what writers of the French existentialist group drew from American writers of the inter-war period, notably, in their estimation, from Faulkner. In short, in its constant operation the process may be one of extension rather than the more striking occurrence of 'revolt.'[10]

Furthermore, Marshall believed that such growth in sensibility was initially only the concern of a small group of writers and critics—hardly of interest to a large audience. That this process existed must be acknowledged even if it could not be defined precisely at a given instant. The process, he believed, was reflected in the writers and critics who actively read and critiqued such new work, and who struggled to understand it. In the United States, the small and proper audience for such literary advance was in the little magazines. They really were the only "vehicles" for such work, he concluded. And in the United States the need for support of such efforts was necessary because "official" sponsorship was unavailable.

In consultation with the small panel, Marshall wanted to invite applications from *Partisan Review, Kenyon Review,* and *Sewanee Review.* If the trustees supported grants to all three journals for the five-year experiment, the cost would be only $60,000. In short, Marshall believed that the magazines were a significant cultural resource and the editors were the best brokers for the advance of writing:

> Almost by definition, in this "theory," to encourage the work of writers and critics whose work is published in them, is to encourage whatever growth is in process. Acceptance for publication in them constitutes a kind of natural selection of the writers and critics on whom growth depends.[11]

After reviewing the applications, including complete financial data, Marshall consulted with Blackmur, Cowley, and Trilling to set an order for presentation to the executive committee of the trustees.[12] They proposed *Kenyon Review, Partisan Review,* and *Sewanee Review* (although the larger panel had ordered them: *Partisan Review, Kenyon Review,* and *Sewanee Review),* giving first position to Ransom's journal because of its established position with the Foundation. However, they were confident that support would be available for all three.

On April 2, the trustees approved a five-year grant of $22,500 for *Kenyon Review* to raise rates to its contributors. Marshall prepared a brief in support of the grant. He told the trustees that, with the revival of interest in literature after the war, *Kenyon Review* and similar journals had a chance to win a larger audience and much greater recognition for recent developments in literature. To keep up with contemporary literature, it was already required reading. If the present circulation of 2,400 could be raised to 10,000, then it probably could "live comfortably" and pay reasonable rates to writers.

Marshall presented the rationale for raising rates in terms of improving the quality of *Kenyon Review* to attract potential readers.

First, the editors could solicit material from writers who previously could not afford to submit material to *Kenyon Review;* second, it would be easier for the editors to ask the most competent critics to devote attention to subjects they thought important; and third, it could raise the standards for book reviewing, an important and time-consuming literary task.

Marshall argued that these journals were the outlets for important younger poets, critics, and writers. Citing *The Little Magazine,* he noted that historically in the United States all of the important contemporary writers saw their first publication in such journals— Sherwood Anderson, Ernest Hemingway, William Faulkner, Erskine Caldwell, and T.S. Eliot. The five-year grant to *Kenyon Review* was to commence July 1, 1947.[13]

However, with respect to the other journals Marshall found that there were still problems. Stevens reported that the trustees' executive committee would not support grants to all three journals. Since the Foundation had never been involved with such activity, there was resistance to a large scheme. It seemed money would be available only to *Kenyon Review,* mainly because of Ransom's reputation and the previous Foundation award. As for *Sewanee Review,* it was turned down because Tate was no longer editor, and there was too much uncertainty about John Palmer's ability to maintain Tate's editorial direction.

Apparently, *Partisan Review* was still perceived as controversial, especially given its roots in the Communist movement of the 1930s. Even though the editors had repudiated their political radicalism, *Partisan Review* was too much involved with politics for the trustees. Ironically it was the former fellow-traveler, Malcolm Cowley, who contributed to the negative vote. Stevens cited Malcolm Cowley's essay, "Ten Little Magazines," in the *New Republic* (March 10, 1947), which criticized *Partisan Review* for its heavy-handed emphasis on political matters. Specifically, Cowley pointed to the 1946 editorial, " 'Liberal' Fifth Column," as particularly inappropriate for a magazine supposedly concerned with literary values, though the editors believed this statement to be a significant analysis of the postwar political and cultural environment (see chapter 3.) But Cowley was not alone in his attack. Schorer, also writing in the *New Republic,* reviewed *The Partisan Reader,* and disagreed with Trilling's assessment that *Partisan Review*'s contribution was to create a healthy union between politics and imagination. Schorer thought the journal was too dogmatic in its anti-Stalinist politics, which tended to overshadow the more important functions of a literary magazine. Schorer claimed that the magazine was at its best when it was "apolitical, even asocial." Schorer advised the editors to concentrate on encouraging avant-garde modernists, shift away from naturalism, and avoid politics.[14]

Trilling was particularly disturbed and disappointed when he learned that only *Kenyon* would be funded. He had hoped for far more from the Foundation, and saw *Kenyon Review* now at a distinct advantage over *Partisan Review* and *Sewanee Review.* Stevens told him that the venture to support writers was new to the Foundation, and a small step now was all that could be done, while Marshall explained that the Foundation was still open to a review of this decision.[15]

In June, Rahv and Phillips announced a reorganization of *Partisan Review.* They had found a private benefactor, Allan Dowling, a New York real estate entrepreneur, who was prepared to donate $50,000 per year to subsidize publication of *Partisan Review.* He was willing to contribute money without substantially interfering in editorial functions. Now *Partisan Review* could both raise rates to contributors and become a monthly.[16] For the first time in its ten-year history, the magazine was free from financial worries. Clearly, with *Partisan Review* now generously endowed, and *Kenyon Review* the recipient of a Foundation grant, *Sewanee Review* was at a disadvantage.

Tate arranged a meeting between John Palmer, *Sewanee's* editor, and David Stevens in New York in July 1947. The plan was to ask the officers to reconsider *Sewanee Review*'s position, and to make a grant that would give the magazine equivalency. Palmer told Stevens that the three journals were truly the cornerstones of contemporary writing and criticism in the United States, each with a slightly different slant and audience, though all joined together on the matter of maintaining the highest critical standards. Palmer suggested that there existed a friendly competitive environment in which the editors vied to publish the best writing and selected the most competent critics to evaluate literary problems. In short, the three journals constituted American literary culture, and Palmer did not want to see *Sewanee Review* diminished because it could not offer the same rates.[17]

The officers agreed. They arranged for a five-year, $27,600 grant for *Sewanee Review* on the same basis as the April grant to *Kenyon Review*. The trustees approved the grant on January 16, 1948. The resolution, in support of the grant, prepared by Marshall noted:

> With the grant now proposed, three leading literary magazines in three sections of the country . . . will share this opportunity to give recognition due to contemporary work of genuine literary importance. Such recognition opens the way to a wider recognition for writers, critics, and university and college teachers concerned with literary studies. The proposed grant thus rounds out an effort on the Foundation's part to strengthen these journals as an independent force in American literary and academic life.[18]

In what has been called the "age of criticism," the three journals flourished in the late 1940s and through the 1950s. It was such a robust period that, in the summer of 1947, three Princeton graduates and disciples of Tate and Blackmur—Frederick Morgan, Joseph Bennett, and William Arrowsmith—decided that New Criticism needed a New York voice. In close consultation with Tate, they created the *Hudson Review,* which began publishing in January 1948 and quickly achieved parity with the other three journals.

Marshall's hypothesis about the profound cultural influence of these journals was certainly correct. But he was wrong about their potential for self-sufficiency. The increase in readership was never able to create a strong enough financial base, and, in 1952, the Foundation dropped the program for increased payments to contributors, shifting to decentralized fellowships that included direct subsidies to the journals to pay for administrative costs.

III

The editors of, and principal contributors to, the three important literary journals continued to lobby for even more substantial commitments by the Foundation toward modernist literary culture and formalist criticism. In January 1947, Marshall had discussions with both Blackmur and Ransom concerning the direction of critical studies in American colleges and the relationship between the teaching of literature and training of critics. Blackmur met with Marshall to consider possible ways to get the Foundation involved in moving literary critics onto the faculty at Princeton.

While Blackmur believed that the university was a necessary connection for critics because the audience and market for serious criticism were so small, he doubted that literature could readily find a "home" at the university. Real literary advance and development occurred in the journals, but critics, if they were mature, established, and discriminating, might very well flourish in the academy. The essential point he made to Marshall was that there were now really just a few able critics on university faculties: Matthiessen, Levin, and Richards at Harvard, Newton Arvin at Smith, Ransom at Kenyon, Bentley at Minnesota, Winters at Stanford, and Trilling at Columbia. Most faculty who dealt with criticism were third- and fourth-rate critics, he claimed.

Once a new director for the Institute of Advanced Study was named, Blackmur planned to open discussions about a program in critical studies.[19] However, for now, he offered no specific proposal to the Foundation because Ransom, Trilling, and Matthiessen had applied to Marshall for formal consideration of a Kenyon School of Criticism. The proposal asked the Foundation to help set up a summer school in literary criticism for advanced graduate students taught by the leading critics, who would offer formal courses and seminars. The New Critics had already revolutionized the teaching of literature in the undergraduate curriculum with textbooks such as Brooks and Warren, *Understanding Poetry* (1938) and *Understanding Fiction* (1943).

The goal was nothing less than to change the nature of graduate study in literature in the United States. For years, Ransom had believed that advanced work in English was too scholastic, emphasizing philology, "denotative" history, and biography. There seemed to be no place for the study of a single work. It was an appropriate time to begin such a school because there existed a new substantial body of original criticism which had moved well beyond the usual form of academic scholasticism.[20].

The plan said the school would create a public forum for the discussion of criticism and begin training the next generation of critics and teachers. Given the postwar expansion in higher education, an important change in English graduate education could and should occur quickly. Furthermore, such a public institute would be evidence of the importance of critical values and modern literature. In addition to Ransom, Trilling, and Matthiessen, the faculty was to be drawn from a group of leading critics such as: Auden, Barzun, Bentley, Brooks, Blackmur, Davidson, Fergusson, Levin, Mizener, Rahv, Rice, Richards, Tate, Vivas, Austin Warren, Robert Penn Warren, Wellek and Zabel.[21] Before its final approval in October 1947, the Ransom, Trilling, Matthiessen plan took several months of study at the Foundation and required several revisions.

In August 1947, Ransom wrote to Marshall summarizing, from his perspective, the importance of the Foundation grants to *Kenyon Review*. Ransom claimed that the literary standards of the journal continued to rise, and that *Kenyon Review* was now recognized as offering perhaps the finest examples of literary criticism. He noted that one of the benefits of the relationship to the Foundation was that it helped younger writers to establish their careers under the guidance of "mature" critics. He cited particularly Eric Bentley's development. Ransom felt that this evidence of success was sufficient grounds for asking the Foundation, once again, to consider the proposal for the School of English. Ransom repeated his belief that there was an urgent need to train the next generation of instructors, and a summer school taught by the leading critics was the appropriate method.[22]

However, Edward F. D'Arms, an assistant director in the Humanities Division assigned to review the Ransom summer school proposal, had serious reservations about the project. D'Arms thought
the premise was valid—strengthening interest in criticism at the graduate level. But it seemed to him to be too much of a one-man show.
D'Arms was concerned that, with so much attention devoted to Kenyon College, the impression would be given that the Foundation was
sanctioning it as the "ideal" for liberal arts education. D'Arms
suggested that the Foundation support the school, but at a "neutral"
campus. Marshall agreed, but Stevens was willing to give Ransom a
three-year trial project.[23]

The resolution in support of a $40,000 grant to Kenyon College
(for three summers starting in 1948) adopted much of Ransom's
language and rationale. Courses in literary criticism had entered into
the academy, but the rate of change was too slow to be of value to the
next group of college and university teachers. The school would help
create a new approach to criticism for younger teachers, which
would replace the emphasis on language study in graduate schools of
English.

According to the formal description of the School issued in No-
vember, the summer program, taught by distinguished critics and
teachers to selected, advanced students, was to concentrate on the
methodology of criticism. Named as senior fellows were Ransom,
Trilling, and Matthiessen. Named as fellows were Arvin, Bentley,
Blackmur, Brooks, Burke, Chase, Empson, Kazin, Knights, Lowell,
Mizener, Rahv, Read, Rice, Schorer, Schwartz, Tate, Warren, Penn
Warren, Wellek, Willey, Winters, and Zabel.[24]

Perhaps the most elaborate expression of what these critics
planned was found in the essay, "The Study of Literature in the
Graduate School: Diagnosis and Prescription," by Austin Warren
and René Wellek, published as part of a *Sewanee Review* symposium
on the teaching of literature. They wanted to reform graduate training
to produce a doctoral candidate who would not be "a specialist in a
period but a professional man of letters, a man who, in addition to
English and American literature, knows literary theory, modes of

scholarship and criticism; who without recourse to impressionism and 'appreciation,' can analyze and discuss books with his classes. . . ."

They wanted the universities to provide leadership for setting of new values and models and for creating a sound theory which could be the basis for producing humanists with a dedication to literature as art. Essentially, they argued for a university system that treated literary criticism as the central task of the professor; they wanted to create professors of literature rather than professors of English; and they believed doctoral candidates ought to view literature as an international movement, should be conversant with both contemporary and classical literature, and fluent in at least two modern languages. The theoretical basis for this approach to literature was articulated in Wellek and Warren's influential *Theory of Literature* (1949), which became the centerpiece for the new graduate programs. Not surprisingly, the authors received, in April 1945, a two-year grant-in-aid to permit them to complete the manuscript. The Rockefeller Foundation and the State University of Iowa cosponsored the project.[25]

But just as the first Kenyon session began in the summer of 1948, Blackmur published "A Burden for Criticism" which, in part, was a mild attack on New Criticism. The essay was, of course, both disturbing and puzzling to Ransom and Tate. Blackmur argued that New Criticism was at bottom "facile." It seemed to be adequate for Eliot and Yeats and some older poetry "but less because of the nature of the poetry than because of the limitation of the modern reader. . . . It is useless for Dante, Chaucer, Goethe, or Racine. Applied to drama it is disfiguring, as it is to the late seventeenth and all the eighteenth-century poetry. . . ." Blackmur claimed that it was invoked because "there has seemed no other way for creating—in the absence of a positive culture outside of poetry—a verbal sensibility capable of coping with poetry at all." He seemed to feel that New Criticism had not been judgmental enough with respect to literature in its larger cultural context. He wanted criticism to push art to a more complete elucidation of society and experience, to act as a surrogate theological conscience.

Almost the whole job of culture, as it has formerly been understood, has been dumped into the hands of the writer. . . . Those who seem to be the chief writers of our time have found their subjects in attempting to dramatize at once both the culture and the turbulence it was meant to control, and in doing so they have had practically to create—as it happens, to recreate—the terms, the very symbolic substance, of the culture as they went along.[26]

According to Blackmur, writers now had to interpret an irrational world, and critics had to offer a bridge between artists and audience, especially helping the audience recover the "lost skill of symbolic thinking." In an unstable and chaotic era the critic had an unprecedented burden, equal to that of the artist.

In large measure, Blackmur published the essay as a way to revive discussions with the Foundation about creating a school of criticism at Princeton. He wanted to bring literary criticism into the Princeton curriculum through a series of advanced seminars, involving both the Institute for Advanced Study (IAS) and the university departments. When Blackmur met with Marshall in July 1948, he suggested that it was now necessary for the critic to find support from the major institutions, in this case the Rockefeller Foundation and Princeton University. The group would not have an agenda other than a common dedication to understanding how literature helps to transmit cultural values and meanings. Blackmur's idea was to make Princeton the center of discourse on literary criticism, to help the invited critics advance their own work, to stimulate the faculty, and to train advanced students. Marshall made no promise of support but told him that such a plan would get a serious hearing at the Foundation.[27]

Blackmur envisioned a group of about eight critics: there would be two distinguished critics at the IAS, continuing the established sequence. Two would be appointed as permanent faculty at the university; he suggested, not surprisingly, his own appointment in English and Francis Fergusson's in modern languages. Two or three critics who were actively engaged in their own serious projects would be invited to explain and discuss their work. And, finally, there would be the appointment of one fellow in creative writing. Blackmur also suggested to Marshall that, perhaps, several of the critics could be Europeans who were being brought to the United States as part of the Foundation's postwar efforts to relocate refugee scholars.[28]

The Foundation officers were very much interested in and supportive of Blackmur's plan. It was a way to move criticism into a prestigious graduate program and to guarantee that contemporary literature would begin to be studied and fused to a traditional program in English. Stevens, Marshall, and D'Arms worked with Blackmur, Stewart, and Harold W. Dodds (Princeton University president and Rockefeller Foundation trustee) to formulate a plan that could get both Foundation and university support.[29] On February 18, 1949, the trustees of the Foundation approved a three-year, $30,000 grant (to run from July 1949 to June 1952) for an interdepartmental program in literary criticism. It was a demonstration project to show that the traditionally compartmentalized structure of graduate programs in English could be expanded to include modern criticism of contemporary literature. In the first year, for example, seminars were offered by Erich Auerbach, (on his *Mimesis)*, Fergusson (on Dante), Delmore Schwartz (on Eliot), and Mark Schorer (on technique in the modern novel). This support for Princeton University opened the next phase of Foundation work in criticism and contemporary literature. The goal was to gain wider appreciation for contemporary literature, while assuring the maintenance of rigorous literary values.[30]

The sharpest manifestation of the shift to a new phase was the decision, in the winter of 1950, *not* to continue support for the Kenyon School. It had served as a symbol for rigorous literary criticism, but it was not associated with a major graduate program in English. In addition there were institutional difficulties. When Kenyon College could not continue its partial subsidy, the School's option was picked up by Indiana University—certainly not education at the top. And, furthermore, Ransom admitted that they had not drawn the best students from Princeton, Yale, Harvard, or Minnesota. In short, the Foundation had agreed to support the first three years of the Kenyon School of English more as a gesture toward Ransom's personal, lifetime commitment to literary excellence than a whole-hearted endorsement of the project. The officers believed that revision of graduate education in literature should occur at elite universities, and Blackmur was quick to understand this philosophy, to the benefit of Princeton and his own career.

Interestingly, when the future of the Kenyon School was in doubt, Tate resurrected Ransom's 1936 idea of an elite American Academy. Working with Fergusson, Rice, and Austin Warren, Tate wanted Ransom to send a proposal to the Ford Foundation to support an institute to set standards, appoint fellows, and make awards. This time it was Ransom who hesitated. He thought such a powerful organization might come under the control of the "wrong" group. Furthermore, Ransom believed the right standards could be maintained because New Criticism had become so pervasive in graduate schools.[31]

Thus, Princeton University and Richard Blackmur were fortunate beneficiaries of the new emphasis. Then in the summer of 1951, Harold Dodds had the pleasant duty of directing members of his humanities faculty to "rethink" the entire program. The university was about to receive a $1.5 million private donation to restructure the humanities program. Dodds and Blackmur wanted to incorporate the seminar program into the new plans. The seminars would be retitled, "The Christian Gauss Seminars in Criticism" (named for the influential professor of literature who died in November 1951). Dodds and Blackmur asked the Foundation for a five-year, $100,000 grant to fund the seminars, which would be one element of a new four-part program in the humanities to make the university the leading center of literary study in the country. In April 1952, the Foundation approved the grant.[32]

The first year's seminar focused on the novel, with Edmund Wilson, Ralph Ellison, John Berryman, Leon Edel, and Irving Howe presiding; also John Aldridge held the one-year fellowship for his study of contemporary writers, *After the Lost Generation.* In short, the Princeton program was very much enlightened patronage, and, combined with support for the important literary journals, the Foundation acknowledged the vital significance of critical interpretation of culture.

IV

What concerned the Rockefeller Foundation officers, who clearly recognized the international importance of American literature, was the extent to which it remained on the fringe of culture in the United States, never finding a mass audience. The Foundation had wanted to stimulate and encourage new writing, writing which could be at once "good" and popular. The goal was to have the editors of the literary journals identify young writers of promise and quickly bring them to a reading public.

In 1952, at the end of the five-year experiment of making grants to *Kenyon Review* and *Sewanee Review,* the officers decided that raising rates to contributors had not resulted in sharp gains in readership and certainly had not placed the journals nearer to self-sufficiency, though without question high standards had been maintained. Also the officers had difficulty in justifying the program in two further respects. First, it provided support to writers in one part of the humanities when no similar payments were available to professionals in other disciplines. Second, the increased payments rewarded both the talented and the mediocre.

The officers still wanted to help create a larger audience for contemporary literature and to support promising writers, but this format had proved unsatisfactory. It was replaced by a program of decentralized fellowships which Marshall and Blackmur had devised in 1946. Grants were to be given by the editors to younger writers of high promise, while the journals would receive payments for editorial expenses. The Foundation was not so much interested in establishing the careers of specific writers as it was in guaranteeing a robust American literary culture.

Kenyon Review's grant was the first to expire, and the fellowship program was started immediately, in October 1952, with an appropriation to Ransom of $41,400 for three years. Each year there would be three fellowships, one each in fiction, poetry, and criticism. Married fellows would receive $3,000 per year (unmarried fellows, $2,000), and the journal would receive $4,800 per year for general editorial expenses and administrative costs. Ransom was also clearly informed that the program was *not* to be an open competition.[33]

In the fall of 1952, Monroe K. Spears, then editor of *Sewanee Review,* prepared a request for a similar fellowship program, but with a decidedly southern literary slant. Spears argued that *Sewanee Review* served two invaluable functions: first, it was an important international journal (citing a recent letter from T.S. Eliot which proclaimed its cultural value); and second, it provided a special avenue to publication for southern writers. Given the fact that American literature had been dominated by the southern writer for the past twenty-five years (Faulkner, Porter, Warren, Tate, Welty, etc.), Spears wanted to create a fellowship program that would identify the next generation of southern writers or support established writers who wanted to try out new ideas. The panel of selection would include Spears, Tate, Fergusson, and Andrew Lytle. The Foundation also accepted this proposal and granted $45,000 for three years (1953–56): $10,000 per year for fellowships and a generous $5,000 per year for editorial expenses.[34]

However, the case of the *Partisan Review* was particularly nettlesome for the officers, especially for John Marshall, who had always been sympathetic to the journal. In November 1950, Marshall had met with William Barrett and Delmore Schwartz to discuss the possibilities of a Foundation grant, since they were once again confronted with financial problems. The editors explained that Allan Dowling was planning at least a $10,000 per year reduction in support. They also wanted Marshall to know that the journal had been reorganized as the Foundation For Cultural Projects, a non-profit, tax-exempt corporation, but Marshall said that nothing could be done until the expiration of the grants to *Kenyon Review* and *Sewanee Review* in 1952.[35]

As the officers were considering *Sewanee Review*'s proposal for fellowships, Charles B. Fahs, successor to David Stevens as director, met with Phillips, Rahv, and Trilling. With Dowling's subvention coming to an end, the editors were in a more desperate situation. The journal would run a $5,000–6,000 deficit for the year. They needed help. In autumn 1952, Marshall prepared a confidential report on *Partisan Review* with respect to a possible fellowship grant. Marshall, citing Trilling's introduction to the *Partisan Reader* (1946), noted its cultural importance. *Partisan Review* had the largest circulation of the small literary magazines and a wide readership in Europe as well. Marshall acknowledged that the journal was still often criticized for its faddishness and "New York cosmopolitan cliquishness."[36] But nevertheless he favored a fellowship program for the journal.

The journal's Marxist roots were still a consideration, but, in the covering note to his report, Marshall told Fahs that *Partisan Review* had made a clean separation from its Communist past. The journal was now, without question, consistently anti-Communist. As Marshall noted, a check for Communist affiliation in the indices of congressional investigating committees (the routine procedure for the Foundation since 1948) showed no ties to subversive organizations. In fact, he reported several positive citations for anti-Communist activity on the part of members of the advisory board, James Burnham and Sidney Hook in particular, for their congressional testimony and organizational activities in the Congress for Cultural Freedom and Americans for Intellectual Freedom. (Of course, Rahv and Phillips were also members of the Congress for Cultural Freedom.) The editors, he believed, had no present political affiliations, and the magazine really could be characterized as a journal of independent radicalism, though recently even its "radicalism" had become merely political commentary.[37]

Of course, at the height of the Cold War, the Communist issue was no small matter, and for board of trustee members such as John Foster Dulles and Dean Rusk it was particularly significant. The trustees established a policy of reasonable vigilance whereby the officers made routine screenings of all prospective individuals and organizations. The goal was to proceed with the Foundation's work to "promote the well-being of mankind" without having its programs too much distorted by the politics of the Cold War, because the only way to guarantee that money would not find its way to Communists or subversives was to stop all grants, which was beyond consideration. After all, as Dean Rusk said, they all knew on which side of the struggle the Foundation worked.[38]

In the fall of 1953, Marshall asked the editors at *Partisan Review* to prepare a fellowship proposal. They submitted an extremely detailed analysis entitled, "The Problem of Democratic Culture and the Granting of Fellowships." The essential thesis was a call, once again, for support of journals such as *Partisan Review,* which attempted to maintain the highest literary standards and struggle against both mediocrity and commercialism. Having a clear understanding of the Foundation philosophy, the editors argued that high culture *did* filter down if the effort by the cultured minority was sufficiently energetic and single-minded. Such vigilance, the editors believed, could result in creating a mass audience for the very best talents.

In particular they cited the effect of paperback publishing on the mass audience for such writers as Thomas Mann and William Faulkner. Their goal as editors had been to push forward, and gain recognition for, the work of the leading artists, scholars, and critics. In their view, the entire process of setting standards, locating new important writers, and struggling to create an intellectual audience was the essence of intellectual freedom in a democracy. This was of course the same cultural elitism advocated by the Foundation, found in the pages of *Kenyon Review* and *Sewanee Review,* and proclaimed by Ransom, Tate, and other New Critics and conservative intellectuals. However, they wanted to distinguish *Partisan Review* from *Kenyon Review* and *Sewanee Review* by suggesting that their critical concerns went well beyond narrow formalist analyses of individual works.[39]

As part of their plan to gain Foundation support, Rahv and Phillips carefully organized a second *Partisan Review* anthology, *The New Partisan Reader: 1945–53,* mainly a collection of fiction and

literary criticism, with no essays on politics and only a few dealing
with the politics of culture. For the editors, literature was now the
centerpiece of cultural sensibility. As they claimed in the foreword to
the anthology, while the magazine had been from its origins interested in politics, its focus was really on the larger issues of ideology
and movements, not on the advocacy of a party: "The magazine was
both anti-fascist and anti-communist long before it became commonplace to identify the two forms of totalitarianism and to regard them
with equal repugnance."[40]

It seems safe to suggest that both the proposal and the introduction
to the anthology were formulated to match the guidelines for the new
round of fellowship grants and to match the programs submitted by
the other reviews. At the beginning of December, Marshall prepared
the resolution in support of the grant to *Partisan Review*, and made
the presentation to the trustees. But on December 9, 1953, Dean
Rusk, writing on behalf of the Foundation, told Phillips that after an
excellent presentation by the officers and considerable discussion it
was clear the trustees would not support the application. He claimed
that the major problem was the journal's tax status, though the sensitivity to the Communist issue was, obviously, still strong.[41]

When the fellowship program was reviewed in December 1955,
the officers thought that it had been beneficial to the selected writers
and to the journals but was little more than a remedial effort to raise
the overall cultural level or to change the market for good writing.
However, it still seemed ironic to the officers that in a country with
160 million people there was not enough interest in contemporary
writing to support advanced literary journals and new writers. Yet,
the Rockefeller Foundation was not terribly successful in creating a
wider audience for contemporary literature. By supporting the elitist
and esoteric journals, the Foundation encouraged critics who had
little concern with a large-public audience. The critics who held
power in these journals were not at all interested in popular fiction
with a mass appeal, unless it was overtly antitotalitarian.

Marshall was particularly impressed with the work of Flannery
O'Conner, recipient of two *Kenyon* awards. In his view, she was the

kind of literary discovery that justified the program. Marshall was also enthusiastic about the other Kenyon Fellows as well: Irving Howe on Faulkner and politics and the novel; Richard Ellmann on Yeats, and R.W.B. Lewis on the literary tradition of nineteenth-century American literature. After the 1955 review, the officers decided to expand the program by inviting both *Hudson Review* and *Partisan Review* to participate; thus, the four leading reviews would offer some forty-eight fellowships over the next three years. Each journal would receive $52,200, with $12,000 set aside for editorial expenses.[42]

By 1950, it was clear to the officers at the Foundation, especially Marshall, that the postwar revival of interest in literature and the already manifest tensions of the Cold War were part of a new cultural era. The Foundation had created excellent connections to the leading critics through which initiatives were carried out, and there was consensus. All were agreed that preservation of cultural values required support for these individuals whose commitment was to both modern literature and "high" culture.

V

When Charles B. Fahs succeeded David Stevens (who retired in December 1949) as director, he continued to interpret the Foundation charter in broad internationalist terms, though with somewhat more awareness of the importance of cultural Cold War. This meant increasing efforts at home and overseas in the traditional humane fields of philosophy, religion, history, and literature which were "essential to moral and spiritual welfare." As his 1951 summary made clear, the Foundation was active in defending cultural values and vigilant in its anti-Communism.

> Any activity by the RF in these fields, however, inevitably raises questions of freedom of thought. The communists have demonstrated that original writing, under authoritarian control, can be made an effective means whereby a few can manipulate the subconscious attitudes and beliefs of a nation. In every country the original writer has been one of

the first targets of communist infiltration. What is the answer for the democracies. Surely it is not the same kind of authoritarian control merely for different ends. . . . The question for the RF is whether it is possible to find means whereby creative activity in philosophy, religion, history, literature, and drama can be made more vigorous, mature, and effective without interference with its freedom. We believe that such means can be found through direct aid to new *original work,* through the further development of *criticism* of original work new and old, and through broadening of opportunities for its *experience.*[43]

In the next few years, this was converted in the United States into the program of fellowships for writers through the literary journals, but it also reflected a more serious role for criticism as an interpreter of cultural values. Fahs explained that support of Leavis in England and of the Kenyon School and Princeton seminars had offered a good start: "Building on what has thus far been gained, we should like now to move in the direction of criticism which will be more deeply concerned with the effect of original works on individuals and in society." He believed that this was an area not adequately supported in the past but "of crucial importance for the freedom of arts in a democratic society":

If opportunities for work of this kind can be discovered, several benefits should result. First, writers would be helped to understand how their work has its effect, and so to become aware of the responsibility implied in the freedom to create afforded them by society. Second, readers would be helped to be more discriminating in their selection of reading material. Third, both we and the public would gain a clearer idea as to the functions which both original writing and criticism serve in the well being of the individual and of society. . . . Widespread, independent, cogent criticism seems to us to be the necessary counterpart and safeguard to freedom for original work in a democracy, the best protection against abuses of freedom which might lead to control.[44]

The ideological component of this struggle was, and continues to be, anti-Communism. Its literary form was a repudiation of the heritage of naturalism and realism. The critics and writers involved with this shift in cultural emphasis put forward a formalist aesthetic that became the dominant mode of criticism in the postwar era, and advocated a solipsistic literary modernism that repudiated 1930s realism. It was not enough for literature to make social and historical connections. In these terms, important literature had to explain the uncertainties and nightmares of a world at the abyss, to assimilate the existential world of the problematic, and to interpret the psychic world of the irrational. The postwar art-for-art's-sake formalism was a way to evade the world and, in the guise of avoiding the explicitly political, to give the appearance that there were no underlying political criteria for literature.

By war's end the literary community of New Critics and New York intellectuals had begun to dominate contemporary literature. There evolved a cohesive and powerful literary movement, one with palpable cultural authority. According to Alexander Bloom in his history of *Partisan Review,* the shift in aesthetic emphasis had been made, "the completion of a cultural crusade begun in the 1930s." As Leslie Fiedler explained, in a 1948 survey of American culture published in *Partisan Review,* many writers who once were part of the radical movement were looking for an alternative to naturalism and the "dead-end" of the Proletarian novel:

> . . . [W]hen we were kids becoming a writer seemed if not synonymous with, at least an aspect of becoming a Communist; abandoning oneself to the proletariat and finding oneself as an artist seemed a single act. . . . Our awakening was gradual, though a little faster than our political disenchantment toward a realization of the enormous *contempt* for art just below the culture-vulturish surface of the John Reed Clubs."

And by the end of the decade Clement Greenburg believed, as he stated in the 1948 *Partisan* survey, "The most pervasive event in American letters over the last ten years is the stabilization of the avant-garde, accompanied by its growing acceptance by official and commercial culture."[45]

The several literary elites realized that the literary nationalism of the war years, which in turn had its roots in the democratized social fiction of the 1930s, was not the way to guarantee the preservation of high culture or to ensure American leadership in setting cultural values. As Jacques Barzun noted:

> In short, by 1945, America having won a war on both the oceans, and finding herself involved in the four quarters of the earth, was quite simply *the* world power, which means: the center of world awareness: it was Europe that was provincial.[46]

Also, as these last three chapters have shown, the intelligentsia understood that the defense of culture was part of a larger economic and political struggle with the Soviet Union in which the United States represented Western values and traditions. The editors' introduction to the pivotal *Partisan Review* symposium "Our Country and Our Culture," made this explicit:

> . . . The wheel has come full circle, and now America has become the protector of Western civilization at least in a military and economic sense.
> Obviously, this overwhelming change involves a new image of America politically. There is a recognition that the kind of democracy which exists in America has an intrinsic and positive value: it is not merely a capitalist myth but a reality which must be defended against Russian totalitarianism.[47]

In sum, the Rockefeller Foundation supported the promulgation of very specific critical values which proved, in their own way, to be extremely valuable for American culture in the postwar period. And what has often been viewed, in the 1940s, as antagonism between New Critics on the right and New York intellectuals on the left was really a far more seamless and consistent relation, because by the early 1950s "literary radicalism" had nothing at all to do with dissident politics. It is clear that starting early in the 1940s both groups supported the same aesthetic values and were searching to find a way to bring contemporary literature into the modernist tradition. The New Critics and the New York intellectuals were very consciously cultivating the Foundation. They worked together to provide money for their journals, schools, separate literary projects, textbooks, and graduate programs. It is difficult to imagine a more comprehensive effort in cultural planning. The value and authority of this movement was recognized a few years later when the federal government began subsidizing cultural programs both openly and secretly.

The specific way that this aesthetic shift affected the interpretation of Faulkner still remains to be analyzed in detail. However, when the war began, the literary elites saw no American equal in stature to the great European novelists. By 1950, it was said that Faulkner had that stature. Faulkner became a writer who could resonate with the whole dialectic of a culture as Trilling and Tate would suggest; he was not a southern regionalist at all but a writer with universal appeal. The elites wanted literature to reflect an ideology, and Faulkner came to serve that purpose. But such a dramatic shift in judgment was made in the name of elitism (in the literary journals and the graduate programs in literature), not egalitarianism. This confluence of elitism and ideology was clearly demonstrated in the way Cowley's transition affected his view of Faulkner and in turn how that revision influenced the novelist's larger reputation.

For example, after the Nobel Prize was awarded to Faulkner, even Alfred Kazin had to drop much of his antagonism. In a February 1951 lecture at Harvard, Kazin suggested that Faulkner's difficult style and technical innovation were really a way of knowing the common ground of our humanity.

> It is an attempt to realize continuity with all our genesis, our "progenitors" . . . with all we have touched, known, loved. *This* is why he needs those long parentheses. . . . They exemplify the chain of human succession. The greatest horror his characters know is to feel they have been dropped out of his stream of being, to think of themselves as "self-progenitive" or "sourceless."[48]

The last step in understanding the rediscovery of Faulkner is to set the developments in high culture and the marketplace into the context of actual literary criticism. It seems safe to suggest that complete literary fame in the modern era cannot be achieved without commercial success and advocacy by the literary elite. The next two chapters show how the critics made the case for Faulkner from Cowley's *Portable* in 1946 to the Nobel Prize in 1950, and beyond.

The Triumph of the New Literary Consensus: Literary Elitism and Liberal Anti-Communism

The commonplace is to argue that with Cowley in the lead it simply took time to create a context in which Faulkner's fiction could be assimilated and appreciated—an evolution in understanding. The critics had to learn to read Faulkner, as they had had to learn to read other difficult modern novelists. By the time of Faulkner's death, the outpouring of critical studies, including Cleanth Brooks's complete formalist synthesis, *William Faulkner: The Yoknapatawpha Country* (1963), had identified the novelist as a special genius who had created an imaginary world with universal significance. In his eulogy, Allen Tate praised Faulkner as a master writer equal in stature to the great European novelists, one who should be accorded a central role in the international evolution of modern letters.

> From Stendhal through Flaubert and Joyce there is a direct line to Faulkner, and it is not a mere question of influence. Faulkner's great subject, as it was Flaubert's and Proust's, is passive suffering, the victim being destroyed either by society or by the dark forces within himself. Faulkner is one of the great exemplars of the international school of fiction which for more than a century has reversed the Aristotelian doctrine that tragedy is an action not a quality.[1]

For Tate and Ransom, the attempt to elevate Faulkner was part of their long-term struggle to assert the larger significance of southern literature. This began in the mid-1930s when first Ransom and then Tate drew away from radical Agrarianism, as they came to understand that for their literary movement to have authority it needed to be perceived both as ideologically "pure" and as divorced, as much as possible, from a specific social cause (see chapter 3). But in the late 1920s and early 1930s, along with the other Southern Agrarians, they had hoped to find a southern writer equal to Ernest Hemingway in stylistic power. Tate wanted to identify a novelist who could represent the conservative philosophy of radical Agrarianism.

> We cannot afford to admire only those writers who explicitly support our thesis. Now, as a matter of fact, if you look closely enough, Hemingway really supports it. . . . Hemingway, in fact, has that sense of a stable world, of a total sufficiency of character, which we miss in modern life. He is one of the most irreconcilable reactionaries I have ever met; he hates everything we hate. . . . [I]f Hemingway were a Southerner he would be just the novelist we are looking for—he would present us without any theses at all. In other words, the ideal Southern novelist is the ideal novelist anywhere. . . .
>
> PS: This could almost be made into a principle—that all great, or really good writers, must have a simple homogenous sense of values, which incidentally are the kind of values we wish to restore.[2]

Tate and Ransom well understood the contradictory nature of having a literature created by politically conservative writers who possessed a deep historical and philosophical sense but who appeared to write as if they had no explicitly philosophical purpose. After the war Faulkner would come to represent these literary values now transformed from Agrarianism to New Criticism and modernism, from American provincial to international avant-garde.

One of the first attempts to explain, in general terms, the new international importance of contemporary American literature appeared in the summer of 1947. It was an essay written by Yale French professor, Henri Peyre: "American Literature through French Eyes."[3] It was far from a profound technical analysis, but rather a popularized summary of French literary trends interpreted for the culturally aware audience of the *Virginia Quarterly Review.* Peyre argued that the best French critics (Sartre, Camus, Claude-Edmonde Magny, and Maurice Blanchot) had devoted careful attention to such writers as Hemingway, Faulkner, Steinbeck, and Dos Passos—attention not given by American critics (see chapter 1).

Essentially, he was trying to interpret Sartre's claim that these Americans had initiated a new literary movement equal in importance to that prompted by publication of Joyce's *Ulysses*. Peyre thought that the rise in prestige of American literature during the past twenty years was one of the most remarkable artistic revolutions in history. And within this general movement, the literature of the American South was of special interest.

> Such is the magic of literary creation. The South, vanquished in the Civil War, left behind in the economic struggle, the depressed area of the United States. . . . [I]t has won the literary battle of America. Through the South, the immense continent seems to have gained a consciousness of tradition and sense of history. . . . [I]t has acquired a sense of tragedy. . . . Faulkner, like Hardy in England and Mauriac in France, has tapped the richest sources of fictional themes for a novelist: the excessive concentration of life in a restricted provincial environment, the jealous spying of family upon family. The bitter struggle between dispossessed traditional heroes and brutal newcomers. Above all this, he has conjured up the ghost of slavery. . . .[4]

Peyre made it clear that French interest in American books was not strictly a function of the revised position of the United States at the end of the war. After all, he noted, there was no comparable involvement with contemporary Soviet writers. French readers had been drawn to American literature in the 1930s because they understood the exaggeration of American novelists toward violence, drink, and sexuality. They saw it, according to Peyre, as "a healthy if brutal reaction against the monotony and standardization of conditions in America." In short, the work of Steinbeck, Caldwell, Faulkner, and others offered a different vision of the United States, at odds with its supposed efficiency, cleanliness, and conformity. The vigor and vitality of American literature drew in the French reader, a vitality in sharp contrast to the stolid intellectualism of the European novel. French writers wanted to break away from the tradition-bound *roman d'analyse,* as Peyre noted.

> For the literature of Europe, however expert in technique and subtle in psychological dissection, lacks vigor and knows it. Kafka and Proust,

Huxley and Gide, Auden and Rilke are supremely endowed in intelligence and in sensitiveness: but they lack imaginative power to recreate life, that is, an intense grasp of the concrete.[5]

In fact, Peyre suggested that, given the French wartime experience of Fascism and invasion, the American novelists were extremely prophetic. In these terms, the pessimism in the modern novel had its roots in the distance that existed between artists and a social life dominated by money and commerce, and in which individuals were powerless to control their own lives. Modern French writers, trying to find a way to attract a wider audience, latched onto the "hard-boiled" Americans, whose intense pessimism and nightmare violence were seen as a new form of classic tragedy.

For Peyre, the American novel had risen to prominence at a crucial moment when the other historically important literatures—Russian, German, Italian, Spanish, and South American—had lost their audience and influence. He suggested that perhaps only the French (with Malraux, Giono, Saint-Exupery, and the existentialists) still had a world-wide force. England, Peyre claimed, now had a watered-down tradition with no contemporary replacements for Joyce, Lawrence, and Woolf—even Eliot might be overrated![6]

Peyre's view of the French interest in American literature was corroborated in Simone De Beauvoir's *New York Times Book Review* essay, "An American Renaissance in France." She focused on the importance of the technical innovations:

What struck us in the great American novelists was their effort to bring into their books life that was still throbbing; to describe it, they employed a living language, and they invented daring and flexible techniques to preserve the freshness of the events described.

De Beauvoir also suggested, in the language of the Resistance and existentialism, that embedded in this literature was an implied moralism. American novelists of the first rank, she said, were able to depict life in its most dramatic form where "reality is invested with the concreteness of an experience in which an individual consciousness and an individual liberty have been staked." It was literature's true mission:

> . . . to describe in dramatic form the relationship of the individual to the world in which he stakes his freedom. What we found in the great contemporary American writers was not so much riches of language or even skilled technique, as this authentic sense of the function of literature.[7]

While Malraux, Camus, Sartre, and De Beauvoir, to name the better-known French writers, were all interested in Faulkner, it was Claude-Edmonde Magny, a young disciple of Sartre's, who, in 1948, argued for his supremacy over the other American novelists. In general, the rise to prominence in France of the American writers and especially Faulkner was attributable to their efforts on behalf of a style which "opened up the novel to a variety of social types, and created characters with 'souls.' "

> Through its masterpieces we glimpse the province of a new humanism. If its major importance is its content, however, why is it its technique that is most imitated? To use Sartre's apt phrase, it is because the technique is pregnant with a whole metaphysic. Even more, it is a means of communicating this metaphysic directly to the reader by addressing itself to the 'sensitive' part of his soul.[8]

Magny suggested that Faulkner's writing offered "the conditions for salvation" in the postwar world.

> If Faulkner's work so surpasses that of all his contemporaries, it is not by virtue of its literary graces, technical perfection, or psychological acuity. It is because he is the only one to show us, in *Sanctuary, Pylon, Light in August* (to take three novels in which it is most obvious), the reconstitution of a community that can be truly called sacred. . . . [H]e is the only one among them to have acted out, in all its fullness the literary drama of the age—the reconstructions of a Church.[9]

Taking up the themes of Cowley, Warren, and the French existentialists, Magny tried to determine what was special in Faulkner. She found in the novelist's poetic voice the dislocations of consciousness played back against the past. Faulkner, she argued, "is sure that a person's true reality does not reside, as common sense would have it, in actions he is completing or the feeling he is experiencing *now,* but that it is completely situated in the past. . . ." In her view, Faulkner's work held mythic qualities—a "sorcery" of language so deliberately difficult and alienating that it forced the reader to feel life not see it. He solved the problem of how to create an image that conveyed the deepest human emotions without having words get in the way. It was ". . . an art that will restore to us, without recourse to pointless chatter, the brief incandescence of the supreme moment of existence." His art had the power to mesmerize, "the dream of a speech that would no longer speak, but simply *be.'"*[10]

In short, Magny argued in Kantian terms that Faulkner "makes a transcendent use of what is only the transcendental form of knowledge. He gives us *legend* as sole *truth.''* Thus she claimed that Faulkner was concerned with humanity's forging ties to an "Eternal" community by communion through its past. This was not very far from Eliot, the New Critics, or even the New York intellectuals, as represented by Trilling's notion of an artist who held in suspension, within his work, the dialectic of society.[11]

Because Magny was, in part, carrying forward the wartime existentialism of the French Resistance intellectual, it is worth noting that French existentialism was apparently the culmination of the Resistance and not a breaking out into something new. Existentialism was shaped by the Resistance experience during the war and retained a cultural legacy best understood as politically conservative, ethically moral, and aesthetically formalistic. Within the Resistance, according to the recent work of historian James Wilkinson, there was a pervasive belief that the Continent could not sustain further disruption. In the immediate postwar era, Resistance intellectuals worked to encompass in their writing traditional ideals such as "humanism and individualism, freedom and justice. They were preservers rather than innovators. . . ." They wrote about "personal commitment" in work that announced "the author's own conversion to an ethic of social responsibility."

. . . the notion that armed force might be required to impose the "revo-lution," once the Resistance had triumphed, the intellectuals never seri-ously entertained. Instead, they believed they could secure popular support through persuasion. . . .

The literature of "unveiling," to use Sartre's term, was thus a prime tool for the intellectuals' attempt at persuasion. Their desire to act di-rectly on the conscience of their readers was one reason for the conserva-tive style of these writers during the 1940s. . . .[12]

Wilkinson's judgment was that the Resistance's "greatest contri-bution remained a moral one: the defeat of nihilism and the creation of an ethical consensus based on the principle of human dignity." The Resistance intellectuals were part of a movement that struggled against nihilism, despair, and skepticism.

The Resistance spirit was a blend of defiance and idealism. . . . The Resistance offered a model for the social order to be erected after the war—one in which individual freedom would coexist with social justice, human dignity would be accorded new respect. . . .[13]

What was needed after the war, according to Magny, Malraux, Sartre, Camus, and De Beauvoir, was a literature that was simultane-ously moralistic, serious, and technically innovative. Ironically, while the French writers and critics were trying to find in Americans such as Hemingway, Faulkner, and Dos Passos a fresh, less over-bearing approach to literature, American critics were struggling to find a way to bring the American writer into the European literary tradition, to an art form in which "ideas" mattered.

II

By the mid-1950s, New Criticism was safely in control of aca-demia, the New York intellectuals had advanced the cause of literary modernism with Faulkner as the central American novelist, and his Nobel Prize had created the necessary public awareness to guarantee his commercial and critical success. However, in the crucible years of cultural Cold War (1948–50), Faulkner and the new literary con-sensus, a coalition of New Critics and New York intellectuals, struggled to acquire a recognizable *public* image. *Intruder in the Dust* helped to reestablish the novelist's presence with a mass audience, while the major literary controversy of the period, the Bollingen Prize to Ezra Pound, provided the literary elites with the opportunity to assert a consistent public voice. This unusual mass exposure helped make both Faulkner and aesthetic formalism part of the literary mainstream.

In 1949, the messy and splenetic literary dispute over the award to Pound turned out to be the first *public* demonstration in Cold War America of the extraordinary reconciliation of New Critics and New York intellectuals. While there was significant disagreement over the propriety of honoring an indicted traitor whose poetry was tainted with Fascist and anti-Semitic lyrics, there was, in both the public pronouncements and private discussions, rather complete agreement that competent literary professionals had to be responsible for making assessments, setting standards, and defending cultural values. The Pound controversy was a measure of how tight an allegiance to the same cultural and political values there was between the New York intellectuals and the New Critics—an allegiance to aesthetic formalism and liberal anti-Communism. The positive reception of Faulkner's polemical new novel also revealed the solidarity of the emerging literary consensus just prior to the author's Nobel Prize.[14]

Faulkner wrote *Intruder in the Dust* in a concentrated four-month period from January to April, 1948 to prove to himself that he could still write a complete book, to show his publishers that he could produce a money-making book, and to comment on the rise in postwar civil rights tensions. At the beginning of February 1948, he wrote to his agent, Harold Ober, saying that the manuscript was at the halfway mark:

> The story is a mystery-murder though the theme is more relationship between Negro and white, specifically or rather the premise being that the white people in the South, before the North or the government or anyone else, owe and must pay a responsibility to the Negro. But it's a story; nobody preaches in it. . . .[15]

But as the book moved to completion it changed, becoming much more of a social and political commentary than anything Faulkner had published before: "It started out to be a simple quick 150 page who dunit but jumped the traces, strikes me as being a pretty good study of a 16 year old boy who overnight becomes a man." Because it was a mystery story and deliberately provocative in its racial message, *Intruder* was the kind of book Faulkner knew could be successful.[16]

Faulkner's commercial revival was tied to *Intruder in the Dust*. Random House published the novel on the fall list, with a careful build-up of publicity to get the important reviewers, sold the movie rights prior to trade publication, and contracted the reprint rights to have the paperback publication coincide with the release of the movie. It was one of the first modern-day publicity campaigns. Faulkner and his new book were thus guaranteed a full year of fanfare, publicity, and media attention.[17] The early work by Cowley on the need for a reinterpretation and rereading, and the admiration of the French critics helped to justify the interest in Faulkner. A highbrow reputation is not a necessary, much less a sufficient prerequisite to commercial success. But to insure a presence in the contemporary dialogues about fiction and culture, an author must have both critical acceptance and a general audience.

Upon publication in the fall of 1948, *Intruder in the Dust* received generally favorable reviews in the *New York Times Book Review*, the *Saturday Review of Literature*, the *New Yorker*, the *New Republic*, and the *Nation*, to name the most influential. In the *NYTBR*, Harvey Breit, a *Times* reviewer and personal friend of Faulkner's, was emphatic, in what was less a review than a statement: Faulkner was an important artistic genius equal to the great nineteenth-century Americans and the best of the European writers. Breit claimed that Faulkner was a distinctive stylist who was difficult but worth the effort because his language was poetic. The Marxist critics of the 1930s had been wrong and narrow-visioned to merely isolate Faulkner's Gothic, violent themes. Faulkner was a prose virtuoso. This was not Faulkner's best book, he explained, but better than almost anything recently published.

Breit's main purpose in the review was to amplify Cowley's plea for a rereading of Faulkner. Breit acknowledged that he was a difficult novelist and had contributed to his own separation from a mass audience; but he was a genius, Breit believed, an American genius, isolated, introspective, and compulsive.

> He writes without concession, in his own time, out of his own cadence, through his own syntax. . . . For sheer virtuosity in prose Faulkner has no American rival since Melville and James. It is this talent, more than any other in Faulkner's possession that has given him the reputation of a "writer's writer."[18]

In short, Breit argued that Faulkner was important because of his distinctive use of language. His style made him hard but the best way to see Faulkner was as a poet who was "making language act creatively."

Harrison Smith, Faulkner's friend and former publisher, and soon to be at the epicenter of the Pound debate, introduced Maxwell Geismar's review in almost homiletic tones, and Geismar's review itself was rather positive as well, calling Faulkner the best novelist of his generation.

> The addition of another novel of William Faulkner's to his Tragedie Humaine of the South which he has labored to create for over twenty years marks a red-letter day in American literature. Whether or not "Intruder in the Dust" will win him the wide audience in his own country to which his somber genius entitle him, he is fast becoming in the minds of intellectuals here and abroad America's premier novelist. He is not always easy to read and is difficult to translate, but his exalted place in the minds of European critics is nevertheless secure. . . . Faulkner's absorption in human beings caught, as in other countries, in the ancient patterns of communal guilt and expiation, will be studied and comprehended, as we read and proclaim Dostoyevsky today.[19]

But the most important and influential review in the mass circulation journals was Edmund Wilson's in the *New Yorker*. He read the book carefully and was much impressed. He conceded that it was flawed, like most of Faulkner's fiction, but praised Faulkner's special voice, poetic genius, and humanistic morality (despite the Dixiecrat southern nationalism).

> The earlier Faulkner of *Sanctuary* was often accused of misanthropy and despair, but the truth is that, from *Pylon* on, at any rate one of the most striking features of his work, and one that sets it off from that of many of his American contemporaries, has been a kind of romantic morality that allows you the thrills of melodrama without making you ashamed. . . . [H]is chivalry, which constitutes his morality, is a part of his Southern heritage, and it appears in Faulkner's work as a force more humane and more positive than . . . even those writers . . . who have set out to defend human rights.

Wilson did not see the novelist as the technical equal of Conrad, Proust, or Joyce—Faulkner was too inconsistent; but he was certainly closer to those Europeans and their highly complex fiction than to Hemingway and Anderson. Yet Faulkner's immersion in his southern subject was valuable, Wilson explained, a kind of Shakespearean connection between images, social implications, and distinctive "human meanings." Despite the segregationism inherent in Faulkner's stance on civil rights, Wilson saw Faulkner as a poetic genius. This talent "produced the book, which sustains, like its predecessors, the polymorphous polychromatic vitality, the poetic truth to experience of Faulkner's Balzacian chronicle of Yoknapatawpha County. . . ."[20]

In fact, Faulkner's extreme southern nationalism was sharply at odds with the existential moralism that many critics had claimed for his work. Cowley, in the *New Republic,* wrote a review that was intended to deflect attention away from the overt southern nationalism of the novel, a specific criticism directed at Faulkner by Elizabeth Hardwick in *Partisan Review.* He claimed that Faulkner must be seen as a writer with a deep commitment to humanity and social equality and that it should be understood that the novelist was caught between deeply felt but contending beliefs: "The tragedy of intelligent Southerners like Faulkner is that their two fundamental beliefs, in human equality and in Southern independence, are now in violent conflict."[21]

Meanwhile in *Sewanee Review,* Andrew Lytle defended Faulkner's southern nationalism by rejecting claims that the novel was didactic or flawed. Relying on the technical analysis offered by literary formalists, Lytle asserted that Faulkner "has achieved a oneness of style and point of view which is the first order of literary distinction. It is all effortless and . . . fused." Its value as art was reflected in the conversion of the boy to the man which offered a way to justice and expiation for the South; it was not propaganda because Faulkner's vision was tied to the "moral destiny of a boy" and the South. The novel must be compared to the social commentary offered by Dickens in *Bleak House,* Lytle argued. In fact, it want beyond Dickens's concern with a single institution to confront "the complex and fundamental involvement of a whole society."[22]

No matter whether *Intruder in the Dust* was considered more tract than novel, Faulkner was now being treated in the popular literary journals as a serious and important writer. As Paolo Milano explained in the *Nation,* Faulkner was best seen as two writers: "One is an American regionalist, the hermit leader of a new school in Southern fiction and the dissident heir of a tradition. The other is almost a European writer, a master of the metaphysical novel. . . ." Milano was also troubled by Faulkner's southern nationalism which held overtones of Fascist solutions to class and race difference. But, for Milano, the book was important because for the first time Faulkner tried "to provide his fable explicitly with a moral and social dimension."

> For once, Faulkner may be profitably compared to Dostoyevsky; he is a "Slavophile" of the deep South. . . . Faulkner's insight into social evil is not half so keen as Dostoyevsky's; but his revulsion from what is usually called "progress" has a comparable intensity. Our materialism appalls Faulkner. He dreams of "homogeneity," meaning, I suppose a social cohesiveness less inimical to life than the profit motive.[23]

In short, in the fall of 1948, Faulkner's friends and admirers made a plea not so much for his novel, though they believed it to be worthy, but for Faulkner as the great neglected contemporary writer, a writer to be considered on the same basis as the great Europeans and nineteenth-century Americans. This was, of course, a vital part of

Cowley's and Warren's arguments. And with the efforts at Random House to make sure that *Intruder* was a publishing "event," Faulkner was assured of a mass audience as well.

III

Although the major literary dispute of the period, the controversy surrounding the Bollingen Prize to Ezra Pound, did not involve Faulkner directly, there emerged, in the course of the defense of the award, a public assertion on the part of leading critics of a commitment to the same kinds of literary values also invoked on behalf of the novelist. The defense of Pound was the planned and conscious effort of Allen Tate. In orchestrating the battles to preserve the honor of the jury that made the award to Pound, Tate relied on the literary coalition of New Critics and New York intellectuals to fight an important battle for the validity of formalist aesthetics and for the cultural significance of contemporary writing. The new aesthetic direction for the literary elite in the United States, at the end of the decade, is nowhere more fully revealed than in the machinations to defend the award to Pound.

The Ezra Pound-Bollingen Prize imbroglio lasted for almost two years, beginning in the summer of 1948 when plans were set to give Pound an award. The prize was announced in late February, but the controversy really flared in June 1949, in the *Saturday Review of Literature*, when its publisher, Harrison Smith, and editor, Norman Cousins, printed and endorsed Robert Hillyer's sweeping indictment of the award. The two notorious articles, "Treason's Strange Fruit: The Case of Ezra Pound and the Bollingen Award" (June 11, 1949), and "Poetry's New Priesthood" (June 18, 1949), baldly stated that Ezra Pound was a traitor and that the *Pisan Cantos* was an obscene and grossly anti-Semitic book. Hillyer also suggested in sweeping, condemnatory terms that there were intimate ties to Fascism which bound together members of the jury of award, Paul Mellon and his Bollingen Foundation, and Carl Jung. Hillyer's attack rested on 1930s "popular front" cultural patriotism and literary social realism, which argued that obscure poetry which ordinary people could not understand was undemocratic: "It is appropriate that an award named after Dr. Jung's headquarters should be given to Ezra Pound. But it is extraordinary that it should be awarded by a committee of Americans sponsored by the Library of Congress."[24]

Furthermore, Hillyer argued that Eliot was the key figure in the award to Pound. With half the jury made up of disciples of Pound and Eliot, the award was the work of a "cabal" which had established the hegemony of art-for-art's-sake formalism. He charged the poet, the poem, the jury, and the benefactor with Fascist tendencies and with creating a conspiracy within an agency of the United States government:

> What I have been leading up to in this sketch of the new estheticism is that its sterile pedantry . . . results in a blurring of judgment both esthetic and moral. I have said that in the Bollingen Award to Pound the clouds of an intellectual neo-Fascism and the new estheticism have perceptibly met. . . .
>
> Nothing can be salvaged from the disgrace of the Bollingen Award of 1949. Nothing can be atoned for. . . . It is not genteel authoritarianism or the desire for order in a disordered world, as polite critics called it. It is the mystical and cultural preparation for a new authoritarianism.[25]

In response, eighty-four writers, critics, and academics issued a protest letter, in the fall of 1949, addressed to the editors of the *SRL*, which, after it was refused by *SRL*, appeared in the *Nation* (December 17, 1949). Margaret Marshall, the book page editor, introduced the letter by noting that Hillyer's articles were presented as "a righteous attack in the name of patriotism," but she believed that it was more accurate to see the campaign as a "philistine attack on modern literature." The letter of protest was written by Allen Tate and Karl Shapiro, and circulated by Tate and the New York-connected poet John Berryman. It called Hillyer's articles and *SRL* editorial support "reprehensible," an attack which "has violated the standards of responsible literary controversy, and thus has dealt a blow to American culture. . . . [Y]our campaign was conducted in a dangerous and unprincipled manner."[26]

It was signed by key representatives of the New Critics and the New York intellectuals: Agee, Arvin, Blackmur, Breit, Brooks, Burnham, Chase, Cowley, Fergusson, Greenberg, Hyman, Jarrell, Macdonald, Mizener, Nemerov, Rahv, Schwartz, Wescott, Winters, and Zabel. Tate organized the publication of a rebuttal to Hillyer and the *SRL,* which *Poetry* published that fall as a pamphlet, *The Case against The Saturday Review of Literature.* For Tate, the pamphlet and letter were necessary to demonstrate that art and aesthetics must be treated with proper respect, dignity, and civil behavior. But they served another function. He believed it was important to show philanthropists, such as Paul Mellon, and the officers and trustees of foundations, such as Bollingen and Rockefeller, that "legitimate" critical opinion resided with the Fellows and their supporters in the literary community.[27] In short, by year's end the New Critics, the New York intellectuals, and independent academics had joined together to condemn Hillyer and *SRL.* And more remarkably, Smith and Cousins had admitted that their editorial support for Hillyer was a ploy to boost circulation—a promotion to "hype" the controversy![28]

As Robert Corrigan has suggested in his review of the controversy, it was the most public debate about literary values in a generation, spilling out of the literary journals and involving the press, the public, and the politicians:

> For although, the Pound-Bollingen controversy is provocative on a number of levels, perhaps the most intriguing aspect is how quickly Pound himself was pushed into the background and the emphasis shifted to T.S. Eliot, the new poetry, and the Higher Criticism.[29]

With respect to the ascendency of aesthetic formalism and the power of the New Critics, Hillyer's polemical essays were on target. But the views Hillyer opposed were no longer those of the New Critics alone. Hillyer's call to promote socially conscious literature and criticism was a program that would not be defended by the New York intellectuals who had adopted the politics of "vital center" liberal anti-Communism. As one historian of the controversy explained:

> . . . [T]his dispute was literary only in a narrow sense, for its political and institutional dynamics reflected a broader and deeper cultural

crisis . . . a prime example of Cold War America's method of achieving social cohesion. In particular, it marked the emergence of a conservative cultural consensus in which intellectual and social values were closely identified.[30]

What is valuable about this controversy for an understanding of the cases of both Faulkner and Pound is not that it demonstrates equivalency between the two artists but that it reveals the extent to which New Critical standards had come to be accepted by the cultural elites. The Pound controversy brought to the surface the underlying ideology whereby what mattered in great art seemed to be technical virtuosity, not content, and such art was to be judged by "men of letters" and with political disinterest.

Poet Leonie Adams was the nominal chair of the Bollingen Prize Committee for the Fellows in American Letters, but it was clear that Allen Tate held the non-public role as organizer of the public defense of the Pound award.[31] By the late-1940s, Tate was perfectly situated to take on the job because he was both an important American poet and an international intellectual figure, significantly influential within the intelligentsia, the artistic community, academia, and the elite foundations.[32]

In 1948, Tate thought that such a prize, offered by a prestigious jury including a Nobel laureate (Eliot) and working under the aegis of the Library of Congress, would be a dramatic, bold plea for a reconsideration of the Pound case. Five years before, in 1943, while working with MacLeish at the Library of Congress, he helped to create a "sanity" defense for Pound. Tate, MacLeish, Hemingway, and others were worried that Pound, indicted for treason *in absentia,* would be executed once captured. The group devised a plan to save his life. They would claim that he was "crazy."[33]

When Pound was captured in 1945 and returned to the United States for trial, the sanity defense was invoked by this group of self-appointed literary guardians (also including Dudley Fitts, James Laughlin, and Merrill Moore), by Julien Cornell, Pound's attorney, and in collusion with Dr. Winfred Overholser, the superintendent of St. Elizabeths Hospital.

Nobody thought he was really "crazy." As E. Fuller Torrey notes in his recent provocative book about the medical ethics of the case, there were many myths about Ezra Pound; "the biggest myth, however, was that he was insane." Overholser, according to Torrey, was determined to protect a poet whom he considered to be a genius and a literary treasure. By 1948, Torrey asserted, Overholser managed to create a literary salon within the hospital for Pound in which the poet seemed to flourish. With Pound safe, protected, and comfortable in St. Elizabeths, the literary coterie began to work on a plan for his release.

According to Torrey, they met in the summer of 1948 to begin a publicity campaign to help restore Pound's literary reputation as a way to pressure the government into granting clemency, and at this meeting it was decided that the Bollingen Prize for poetry was to be the first major step. As MacLeish has explained, friends "conceived the idea of a new national prize for poetry to be awarded by the Library of Congress through a jury of notables who would select Pound as the first recipient, thus dramatizing his situation and putting the government, and particularly the Department of Justice, in an awkward if not untenable position."[34]

Torrey claimed that although MacLeish was not present at the summer meeting, he took charge of the campaign. This was not correct. Rather, Allen Tate became the chief organizer, because MacLeish was, at the time, opposed to the award. In private, MacLeish disagreed thoroughly with the judgment of the jury and with the tactics devised by Tate to fight against Hillyer and the *SRL*. But, in public, he would not betray his friends or the Library or the cultural interests of the nation by repudiating the aesthetic decision of a distinguished panel of his literary coequals and friends. Indeed, his later analysis of the award offered a complete defense for the relevance of apolitical literary criteria and the authority of the new literary consensus.[35]

Given Tate's early work on the planning of the sanity defense, and his subsequent involvement, in the summer of 1948, with the preliminary planning for Pound's Bollingen Prize, he could not easily assume public leadership of the Pound award, and maintain the appearance of decorum, civility, and professional disinterest. Furthermore, Tate had created the Fellows in American Letters for the Library of Congress during his tenure as Chair of Poetry. The Fellows involved in 1949 almost all had personal ties to Tate: Leonie Adams, Conrad Aiken, W.H. Auden, Louise Bogan, Katherine Garrison Chapin, T.S. Eliot, Paul Green, Robert Lowell, Katherine Anne Porter, Karl Shapiro, Theodore Spencer (died in January 1949), Tate, and Willard Thorp—with MacLeish and William Carlos Williams added after the award to Pound.

The Fellows met in November 1948 and voted for Pound, with the award to be announced in February 1949.[36] But by late January, Tate knew that the plan to help Pound would backfire. His good friend Karl Shapiro, a Pulitzer Prize poet and the only Jewish member of the jury, decided to change his vote—Adams, Shapiro, and Lowell formed the Bollingen Prize subcommittee and were to meet at the beginning of February to review Tate's draft of the award statement to be issued by the Library. Shapiro said that he could not support the award to Pound and was planning a public statement. Shapiro explained that he could no longer ignore the pressure of the poet's anti-Semitism. He was in full support of Pound, the poet, but could not in good conscience vote an award, even though he believed *Pisan Cantos* was the best book of 1948. He resisted raising these matters in November during the initial balloting because he did not believe anti-Semitic issues were involved in the decision, though in retrospect he felt that the ramifications of the award should have been discussed. In Shapiro's view, the vote went through without discussion or debate because there was such deep-seated sympathy for the man.[37]

Several days later, Tate received a long, disquieting letter from Leonie Adams reporting Shapiro's decision and summarizing other difficulties: Katherine Chapin's husband Francis Biddle, attorney general at the time of Pound's prosecution, was warning of reactions in the Justice Department and Congress. Also Adams had been warned by members of the Library of Congress staff that the award would almost certainly invite fierce attacks by such powerful columnists as Walter Winchell; this alone could prompt a congressional investigation which would reflect poorly on the Library and be harmful to Pound. Adams felt under terrific pressure and suggested to Tate that perhaps the best move would be to drop the award.[38]

On the last day of January, Tate wrote to Shapiro and Adams explaining his own position, acknowledging that the award could no longer help Pound, and outlining a new strategy to defend, not Pound, but the award. With great tact and sympathy, Tate asked Shapiro to return to his November position of support, because such a stand would be a way of launching the most direct assault on anti-Semitism while simultaneously affirming the value of the artist. Tate wanted Shapiro to believe that the vote for Pound was certainly not prearranged or given in sympathy with his opinions. Tate asserted that he almost voted against Pound because he despised the politics and anti-Semitism, which could not be easily ignored; he also felt that Pound was, perhaps, not a great poet. But in the end he voted for the book, not because the *Pisan Cantos* were great poems but because the work was the best book under the terms of the award. Of course, if he had been convinced of Pound's greatness the political questions would have no bearing at all, he said.[39]

Shapiro responded with a contrite and explanatory letter. But he wouldn't change his mind, and planned to have his statement printed in *Partisan Review* (May 1949). Shapiro asked Adams to tell the other Fellows that he "voted against Pound in the belief that the poet's political and moral philosophy ultimately vitiates his poetry and lowers its standard as literary work." If Pound were Jewish or a Communist, Shapiro said, he would take the same stand. Shapiro apologized for any suggestion that Tate had Fascist sympathies. He felt guilty for his November vote. Finally, it was decided to poll the Fellows once more in a secret ballot. The vote for Pound was reaffirmed, and the award announced in February. Of course, Shapiro's argument about anti-Semitism and a conspiracy for Pound was not very far removed from the attack Hillyer was to make in June.[40]

But several days later, just prior to publication of the statement in *Partisan Review,* Shapiro wrote to Tate again apologizing for any implied suggestion of Fascist sympathies. He was sick of the whole affair. The issue, he tried to explain, was not how conservatives can be used by Fascists, or liberals by Communists, because that happened all the time—as a liberal, Shapiro said he realized he had been misused and suggested that both Tate and Eliot must have had similar experiences with forces from the right. The central problem for Shapiro occurred when an artist's politics affected the poetics of his work. For example, he could not vote, hypothetically, for Pablo Neruda because of the Stalinist politics reflected in his poetry, and he could not even vote for MacLeish because of the latter's narrow nationalism. In short, the art of Neruda, MacLeish, and Pound had been "vitiated" by their politics. Shapiro saw a vote for Pound's art as an acceptance of his politics.[41]

Tate simply asked that Shapiro make public his belief that the jurors had acted in good conscience. Shapiro agreed and, in mid-May, sent Tate a copy of the follow-up statement for *Partisan Review* (which appeared in July). More importantly for Tate, Shapiro pledged that he would issue no further public statements. This guaranteed the secrecy of the deliberations and ended the prospect of future embarrassments. This statement returned Shapiro to the family, and, after Hillyer's attacks in June, he accepted the legitimacy of Tate's arguments and helped to organize the public defense of the Fellows.[42]

At the beginning of June, Tate received from MacLeish prepublication copies of the Hillyer essays and realized that the large aesthetic and cultural questions would move dramatically into the public arena. Tate decided to offer a much more forceful defense of the jury. He would argue for the protection of true artists, even if they had Fascist sympathies and created art obscure to the point of incoherence.

He would make the case for aesthetic autonomy. He would build on the argument he made to Shapiro: Even though there were deeply felt social and political questions, it was necessary to agree to the autonomy of the arts and intellect. Tate suggested that Shapiro's own Pulitzer could have been denied on the same grounds as Shapiro's rejection of Pound. Shapiro's position was too narrow because he refused to acknowledge the possibility of a great art deriving from an unpopular minority position. One must be ready, Tate believed, to make exceptions for what might be important art. A vote for Pound was not a vote for his politics or his anti-Semitism. It was a vote for artistic independence and for themselves, the cultural elite, those who placed aesthetic matters ahead of extrinsic concerns.

IV

With an attack by *SRL* inevitable, Tate constructed his first complete public defense of the award. He now understood that, in the current political environment, Pound could not be helped by activities such as the Bollingen Prize. At a time when the Democrats were being accused of "softness" on Communism, clemency for a man accused of supporting Fascism would make it appear that the administration was yielding to the totalitarianism of both the right and the left. Tate turned away from any attempt to defend Pound and took the view that the award to Pound was a principled defense of cultural values, not an affirmation of a particular critical school, as some suggested. In a subtle and masterful way he began to make the dispute over the award into a referendum on the nature of art in a "democratic" society. He argued that, in a civilized culture, the defense of artists and their art was an assertion of moral commitment.

As it appeared in the June issue of *Partisan Review,* Tate's statement was addressed to the intelligentsia, to all those who claimed to be concerned about serious literature in an anarchic world. It was a call to defend, not Pound, but modernist art and vitality in culture, not content, but language and vision. Tate explained his vote for Pound:

> The specific task of the man of letters is to attend to the health of society *not at large* but through literature—that is, he must be constantly aware of the condition of language of his age. . . . I had become convinced that he had done more than any other man to regenerate the language, if not

the imaginative forms, of English verse. I had to face the disagreeable fact that he had done this even in passages of verse in which opinions . . . ranged from the childish to the detestable.

Tate claimed that he easily could have voted against the *Pisan Cantos* because their incoherence suggested that the poems might not be truly great art. He explained, "the work to which I helped give the Bollingen Prize is formless, eccentric, and personal. The Cantos are now, as I said then [1931], 'about nothing at all.' They have a voice but no subject." In fact Tate argued that Pound was ". . . incapable of sustained thought in either prose or verse. . . . But if there is any poetry of our age which may be said to be totally lacking in the historical sense, the sense of how ideas move in history, it is Pound's *Cantos.*" The essential question was one of language and the protection of high art, even if incomprehensible and vile:

> I have little sympathy with the view that holds that Pound's irresponsible opinions merely lie alongside the poetry, which remains uncontaminated. The disagreeable opinions are right in the middle of the poetry. And they have got to be seen for what they are: they are personal, willful, and unrelated; and thus are not brought together under a mature conception of life as it is or ever was. I infer the absence of such a mature view in the man from the incoherence of the form; but it is only the latter that concerns me."[43]

Throughout the summer, in the wake of Hillyer's attacks and the congressional decision to remove the award from the Library of Congress, Tate rallied, to the defense of poetry and criticism, members of the jury, poets, critics, and writers. Essentially, those defending the award charged Hillyer with both aesthetic totalitarianism and criticism by defamation. For example, Cleanth Brooks was disgusted by the entire spectacle of Hillyer and the *SRL* editors; however, he told Tate that there was, perhaps, an important positive value to the Hillyer distortions. Brooks believed that the Hillyer articles merely carried out to their logical and vulgar conclusions the antiliterary values inherent in the Marxist or "social" approaches to art. This, he told Tate, made Hillyer an easier target.[44]

In August, Tate drafted the "Statement of the Committee of the Fellows of the Library of Congress in American Letters," which Adams, Bogan, Shapiro, and Thorp had revised and then signed. This statement was then issued by the Library as a press release. The statement asserted that the jury had acted in good faith as an advisory panel of competent professionals, and in that capacity had served the best interests of the country. The *Pisan Cantos* was selected as the best book available under the terms of the award, and selected not in disregard of the poet's treason indictment or objectionable opinions but by relevant literary criteria.

> This charge of irresponsible aestheticism was leveled against a great many critics, among them several of the jurors, by Marxist-dominated criticism in the thirties. Now, by an odd turn of Fate, this charge is being made, not by Communists, but by the *Saturday Review of Literature*. Some correspondents in the *Saturday Review* have expressed fears that a similar authoritarianism is suggested in the *Saturday Review*'s attack: that of standard-brand positive Americanism as a test for literary worth.[45]

In September, Tate met with Bogan, Shapiro, Adams, and Thorp in New York to organize the pamphlet and to draft the letter of protest. Tate had worked out an arrangement with Carruth to have *Poetry* act as the publisher. The pamphlet was to be released at the end of October. Its centerpieces were to be the Fellows' own statement and the reprint of Malcolm Cowley's forthcoming essay "The Battle over Ezra Pound," which was to appear in the *New Republic* (October 3, 1949).

Cowley's analysis was carefully crafted, offering a clear summary of the controversy, a mild criticism of the award, and a sharp denunciation of Hillyer's sweeping accusations. Cowley said that he spoke to many of the members of the jury, individuals he had known for years. To suggest that their decision was prompted by sympathy to Pound's politics or anti-Semitism was "ridiculous."

> . . . the Fellows have been accused of advancing the false principle that art is entirely separated from life. Those with whom I talked insisted that they had no such intention. To paraphrase what some of them said . . .

they felt that too many second-rate authors had been given prizes for expressing the right opinions. We criticize the Russians—and rightly— for making their poets follow the party line; yet recently some American critics have been treating our own poets in the same fashion, demanding that they be wholesome, popular, and patriotic. The Fellows insisted that there are other virtues in literary works. . . . Originality, learning, sharpness of image, purity of phrase, and strict literary conscience: these are virtues, too, and they are present in Pound's work along with his contemptible politics.[46]

Cowley's own judgment was that *Pisan Cantos* was Pound's weakest work and a poor choice for an award, given other stronger books in 1948. His personal grievance with the Fellows was "that by giving a prize to Pound they forced him back into the limelight, thus destroying the symmetry and perfect justice of his fate." But his grievance against Hillyer was far more cutting. Cowley said that writers have a duty to both the public and their profession and Hillyer betrayed both:

He has misled the public about the nature of an argument among poets and critics, while he has harmed all writers in his attempt to punish a few. Today there is a war in which the battle over Ezra Pound is merely an episode. The little American republic of letters is under attack by pretty much the same forces as those which the Russian writers have already yielded: that is, by the people who prefer slogans to poetry and national self-flattery to honest writing. Hillyer has gone over to the enemy, like Pound in another war. Worsted in a struggle among his colleagues and compatriots, he has appealed over their heads and under false colors to the great hostile empire of the Philistines.[47]

Of Eliot, who was Hillyer's central target, Cowley wrote that his "political convictions are conservative, traditional, and not in the least totalitarian. He is a pluralist who believes that we owe our loyalties, not to the state alone, but also to church, class, region, family, and profession." This was a rather remarkable statement from a former Marxist fellow-traveler, but Cowley had dropped his politics, as we have seen, becoming an important advocate of contemporary writing, and working, behind the scenes, to help gain foundation support for the influential literary quarterlies. His attack on Hillyer was comparable to his rejection of the myopic interpretations of Faulkner that such critics as Hicks, Geismar, and Kazin had offered prior to the war.

The New York intellectuals were remarkably restrained in their criticism of the award to Pound. Despite their proclaimed interest in literature's social and historical web, they found little basis for an attack on Eliot, Pound, or formalist aesthetics. They had already affirmed the same principles of "autonomy" in aesthetic judgments and had defended the same cultural values and institutions. Essentially, they supported Tate and his attack on Hillyer, though they certainly did not like public praise for art that promoted Fascist ideas.

The April 1949 issue of *Partisan Review* contained a long essay by John Berryman in praise of Pound's *Cantos* and a mildly critical editorial written by William Barrett. Barrett felt that the jury's statement of "the validity of that objective perception of value" was an evasion of judgment about Pound's deeply "hideous, ugly, and vicious" anti-human attitudes. Barrett questioned whether it was possible "in a lyric poem, for technical embellishment to transform vicious and ugly matter into beautiful poetry?" He applauded the judges for reaffirming "the validity of aesthetic principles," but he believed in this case that Pound's politics could not be ignored. The jury, he said, should have made a more direct comment about the poem's content. Between Barrett and Berryman, the magazine seemed deliberately ambiguous about the whole affair.[48]

While in Leslie Fiedler's response to the Pound controversy for the May 1949 issue of *Commentary,* "What Can We Do about Fagin? The Jew-Villain in Western Tradition," he claimed that the myth of the Jew as monster, a "symbol of darkness," was pervasive in Western high culture. This must be accepted, he stated, but Jewish artists had already started to build a rival myth. He saw this new response emerging in contemporary literary culture where Jews were moving into more central positions. In an alienated and apocalyptic world, he argued, Jewish experience was more like every man's. But what was to be done about literary anti-Semitism in the English literary tradition?

It is ridiculous to attempt to censor a whole culture, even if what we know is a palpable and terrible evil. As we permit to art, for the sake of values real though difficult to define, blasphemy, scurrility . . . so we must permit . . . anti-Semitism. I would myself be unwilling to give up, even in a self-imposed boycott, *The Merchant of Venice* or the poems of Ezra Pound because they contain evil doctrine; beside the corruption, there is beauty and a degree of true vision that we cannot afford to sacrifice.[49]

For the September and October issues, the editors of *Commentary* organized a symposium, "The Jewish Writer and the English Literary Tradition," asking Jewish writers to comment on Fiedler's argument that anti-Semitism ran through the entire English literary tradition from Chaucer to Eliot. The editors also solicited reactions to the Pound controversy. The respondents included William Phillips, Paul Goodman, Louis Kronenberger, David Daiches, Isaac Rosenfield, Stanley Hyman, Diana Trilling, Howard Nemerov, Stephen Spender, Philip Rahv, James Grossman, Martin Greenberg, Harry Levin, Irving Howe, William Poster, Saul Bellow, Alfred Kazin, Lionel Trilling, and Karl Shapiro.[50] Not surprisingly, given the fact that *Commentary* was the leading American journal of Jewish opinion, the respondents all argued the position that, as conscious Jews surviving in the post-holocaust world, it was necessary to actively oppose anti-Semitism. And almost all supported Fiedler's prescient defense of modernism and aesthetic formalism. There was very little direct criticism of Eliot and almost no concern with the Bollingen Prize as symptomatic of Fascism or anti-Semitism. Howe and Phillips presented the sharpest attacks, but their comments constituted no support for Hillyer.

William Phillips argued that literary anti-Semitism should be fought, though he believed that it was often not taken seriously. He saw a prevailing "cult of literature" which proposed the sacredness of "any 'created' object." He advocated a cosmopolitan literary tradition that was more humane and universal. Thus, he was very much opposed to the elevation of Eliot and the celebration of the English tradition, a literature too genteel, aristocratic, and anti-urban.[51]

Howe argued that modern anti-Semitism was far more reprehen-

sible than the historical anti-Semitism of Chaucer and Shakespeare
and that one should not acquiesce in it:

> The important thing is not to let any notions about the inviolability of
> literature or the sacredness of art sway us from expressing our spontane-
> ous passionate feelings about these contemporary writers who succumb,
> willingly or not, to anti-Semitism. . . . It is not only necessary but *right*
> that we say exactly what we feel about the anti-Semitic remarks or
> passages of even the greatest modern writer. Indignation is often in-
> sufficient but sometimes it is the only condition of dignity.[52]

Holding a middle course were Rahv, Trilling, and Kazin, all of
whom personally detested all forms of anti-Semitism but realized
that the object of the critic was to judge the work. But Kazin also saw
an important reciprocal relationship of shared experiences.

> If we wrote of Pound as he writes of us, who would pass judgment on
> anyone and give him a prize? No, we and the Eliots are all in this
> together, as he has virtually acknowledged, and we must show the others
> exactly why this is so. We must read them and endure—angrily so, of
> course; without toadying; not afraid to call ignorance and heartlessness
> by their right names, even if they do come from our literary dictators,
> those on whom we have modelled ourselves. . . .[53]

In short, the New York intellectuals agreed with Tate that a competent jury of award had to have the freedom to make an aesthetic
judgment without considering Pound's politics or the political reper-
cussions of honoring him through a semi-official award given by the
Library of Congress, though obviously such a stance would never be
presented in defense of writers with Communist sympathies. This
was also a pragmatic decision since it focused attention on aesthetic
standards, helping to protect Pound from more adverse publicity and
from the real possibility of a new trial. The key to Tate's strategy was
to demonstrate that *SRL* practiced methods of literary criticism associated with Nazi Germany and Stalinist Russia. In his view the
defense of the award was a clear protest against politicized art,
and clear evidence of artistic freedom in the United States. This
was echoed by Dwight Macdonald, one of the more independent-
minded New York intellectuals: "[T]he award is indeed . . . a poli-

tical act—and one which should demonstrate to many parts of our world that at least some Americans have a right to oppose Soviet totalitarianism."[54]

Finally, MacLeish had devoted the summer to studying the *Pisan Cantos* and preparing *Poetry and Opinion: The Pisan Cantos of Ezra Pound; A Dialog on the Role of Poetry.* MacLeish argued that perhaps the true "liberals" were those who could find an aesthetic basis for support of the poem. He had nothing but contempt for Hillyer and *SRL* because their attack rested on defamatory assertions. It was based on no theory of aesthetics, but on the dangerous proposition "that the jury had given a great and semi-official prize to a poem containing 'bad' opinions and written by a 'bad' man."

In MacLeish's view, to measure poetry against social or political criteria was to abet its destruction. His analysis of the controversy showed a significant shift for a poet who had for years argued for a socially responsible, nationalist literature. Yet, in 1949, those who did not oppose the imposition of external standards were seen as helping to corrupt literature. MacLeish claimed that the central issue in the dispute was the "function of poetry." For MacLeish the complete defense was the loyalty of the poet to his own vision, even if the vision were evil and perverse, i.e., the poem remains art if the poet is loyal to his own perceptions. MacLeish's position on the nature of "totalitarian" interference in the arts was clear:

> If it is true that poetry is an instrument of intuitive knowledge, does it not follow that the presence of opinions in a poem destroys the poem only when the opinions predetermine the intuitions—when they, and not the poet's sensibility, supply the insights? No one would trust the insights of a Communist poet or a Franco-fascist. With them the opinions come first and the poetry—if you can call it that—comes after. But it is possible, as Dante proves, for the most dogmatic opinions—opinions hateful to multitudes of human beings—to live in a poem beside the most profound and enduring insights, where the poet's overriding loyalty is to his poet's perception of the world. With Pound, as this poem itself demonstrates and as the earlier Cantos make abundantly clear, the loyalty is not to dogmas of fascism but to the poet's vision of a tragic disorder which lies far deeper in our lives and in our time.[55]

If it was art, then the jury was justified in honoring the poet even if his vision was contemptible.

In the end, Tate had incorporated, into the overall defense, refutations of Hillyer's slurs about conspiracy, Fascist politics, and anti-Semitism. But the real goal was to denounce any attempt to make "great" art answer a political test. Pound's work was idiosyncratic, obscure, and impenetrable, but the best readers of the day had recognized in it an unswerving dedication to craft and an underlying morality and vision. As one of Pound's supporters stated at the height of the controversy, *The Cantos,* and *Pisan Cantos* represented the best examples of "aesthetic morality" in contemporary verse.[56]

The award to Pound was made and justified because of his formal skills as a poet despite his Fascist sympathies. In Tate's view "men of letters" had to be prepared to defend and protect even the most obnoxious artistic creations. Paradoxically, the defense of Pound's politicized poetry was presented as the application of apolitical aesthetic principles, while Hillyer's attack was labeled as politicized corruption of poetry.

> Pound's language remains our particular concern. If he were a convicted traitor, I should still think that, in another direction which complicates the problem ultimately beyond our comprehension, he had performed an indispensable duty to society.[57]

This was what the New Critics and New York intellectuals upheld against Hillyer. Hillyer was attacked and "redbaited" for defending democratic values in art. Thus, under the influence of the Cold War and operating with formalist aesthetic criteria, the signal was clear. A Fascist could be an excellent poet, but a communist or naturalist could not. In the postwar era important literature would be judged without the contamination of the extrinsic concerns of literary naturalism. In these terms, a vote for Pound was worth the risks because it was a vote for language and an affirmation of the value of modern, living literature as a vital part of the cultural heritage.

Faulkner was certainly not a Fascist. In fact, he was uninvolved in the radical political upheavals of either the right or the left in the

1930s, which helped to simplify matters a great deal since he could be presented as a pure example of an apolitical artist. But beyond the technical innovations in form and the unique imaginative vision, he did share with Pound an aristocratic outlook, an antidemocratic stance, and a respect for tradition. Faulkner was important, it was claimed, because he understood the reconstituted moral duty of the artist, and because he maintained the purity of an individualistic vision and style. As we have seen, this was the basis on which Faulkner was being presented for reconsideration—by Cowley, Warren, the French existentialists, and in the reviews of *Intruder in the Dust.* It was a position that would be more fully developed in the next few years, as more critics came over to Faulkner.

CHAPTER SEVEN

Faulkner's Postwar Reputation: The Cultural Politics of a New Aesthetics

To what extent beyond the circumstantial did the Rockefeller Foundation's concern with contemporary literature and its ties to the leading critics and editors strengthen the efforts to rehabilitate Faulkner's reputation? Cowley's essays and research on Faulkner were well known to Tate, Warren, Ransom, Gordon, and others. In a certain sense, they worked together to help highlight Faulkner's significance. Tate had made Cowley's essay, "William Faulkner's Legend of the South," the prize-winning centerpiece of *A Southern Vanguard*. According to George Mayberry, then literary editor of the *New Republic,* after Cowley's resignation, Warren's review/essay ("Cowley's Faulkner," August 12 and 26, 1946) was published in the magazine at Cowley's own insistence; he was then a nonresident editor.[1]

Warren wrote this very important essay while at Kenyon College in the summer of 1946 during the early Rockefeller subvention to Ransom and the *Kenyon Review*. The review made the case for Faulkner's universality, symbolic complexity, and bold experimental style. Warren was particularly vehement about the previous critical misreading and careless scholarly attention. Until Cowley's analysis, the critique of Faulkner had presented, for the most part, a horribly distorted picture, "a combination of Thomas Nelson Page, a fascist and a psychopath, gnawing his nails." Warren asserted Faulkner's world required much more consideration than "a grudging remark about genius." (By contrast, Warren's 1941 review of *The Hamlet* in

Kenyon Review had contained nothing at all about Faulkner's larger significance. Until 1942 Warren had rated him as an occasionally first-rate short-story writer in a lesser category with Willa Cather, John Peale Bishop, Caroline Gordon, and Delmore Schwartz.[2])

> The study of Faulkner is the most challenging single task in contemporary American literature for criticism to undertake. Here is a novelist who, in mass of work, in scope of material, in range of effect, in reportorial accuracy and symbolic subtlety, in philosophical weight can be put beside the masters of our own literature. Yet this accomplishment has been effected in what almost amounts to critical isolation and silence, and when the silence has been broken it has usually been by someone (sometimes one of our better critics) whose reading has been hasty, whose analysis unscholarly and whose judgments superficial.[3]

Warren's analysis also reassessed the novelist's moral imperative, and was, perhaps, the catalyst for converting Faulkner's status to that of existential modernist. Warren believed that at the center of Yoknapatawpha County's "traditional order" there was a "notion of truth . . . which allowed the traditional man to define himself as human by setting up codes, concepts of virtue, obligations, and by accepting the risks of his humanity." The terror, evil, and violence were not the central message, according to Warren:

> The human effort is what is important, the capacity to make the effort to rise above the mechanical process of life, the pride to endure, for in endurance there is a kind of self conquest.
> When it is said, as it is often said, that Faulkner's work is "backward looking," the answer is that the constant ethical center is to be found in the glorification of the human effort and of human endurance, which are not in time, even though in modernity they seem to persist most surely among the despised and rejected.[4]

In short, Faulkner's fictive world was important "both ethically and artistically" because of its "symbolic function." Warren would not yet make Faulkner equal to the European masters—Dostoyevsky, Kafka, Conrad, or Proust, for example—but he was certainly the most important American novelist, and the logical successor, given the *angst* of the Atomic Age, to Hemingway.

In order to help make the case for Faulkner, Warren and Ransom decided at this time to organize a special issue of the *Kenyon Review* to celebrate the novelist on the occasion of his fiftieth birthday in 1947. They planned a number that would include a new story by Faulkner, several essays by American critics, several essays by Europeans (perhaps one each by an English, French, and Italian critic), one short biographical piece, and a bibliographical summary. Ransom wrote to Tate in mid-July outlining the plan and asking him to consider either writing an essay himself or editing the number; he also needed Tate's advice on which European critics to approach. Ransom hoped also to convince Warren and Katherine Anne Porter to produce essays, and, to avoid too heavy a southern emphasis, Blackmur to represent the "Yankees." And of course, Cowley was to be included because he now had the best direct ties to the novelist.

None of the Agrarians had ever liked Faulkner personally or been able to build a friendship with him. While they admired his work and believed he was one of the best contemporary novelists in English, they had felt powerless in the early 1940s to alter his diminished reputation in the United States. In 1947, they hoped a special number of *Kenyon Review,* including material by non-southerners, might begin to alter the critical perception. However, Ransom's prescient judgment that Faulkner would not be fully honored at home until there was some substantial public recognition from Europe was to prove accurate. The New York critics, especially, were not yet prepared to consider Faulkner on the same terms as Proust, Joyce, Kafka, or Mann.[5]

Tate's immediate reaction to the plan for a special issue of *Kenyon Review* was positive and supportive, but he did not want to write an essay on Faulkner, having decided not to concentrate on direct literary criticism of individual writers. Tate suggested that Caroline Gordon be invited to participate; he thought that her book review of the *Portable* had been watered down for a general audience and that much of what she really wanted to say remained in her notes. Tate had no immediate suggestions for a French critic, though he definitely wanted to avoid the existentialists; he thought that Maurice Coindreau, Faulkner's French translator, might be a good candidate.[6]

As for Tate's decision not to do the central Faulkner essay, it seems safe to say that, given the war and his image as a "man of letters," he tried in this period to encompass a more complete view of culture and to assert more universalist values for the literature he admired. By the mid-1940s Tate had dropped his radical Agrarianism, reflecting the high status already achieved by so many of the writers and critics in that movement.

Tate never did take on a thoroughgoing analysis of Faulkner, or of any contemporary novelist for that matter. As a critic, he seemed uncomfortable with criticism of the novel form. His position on the novel was reflected in his 1944 essay, "Techniques of Fiction," where he took up Flaubert's *Madame Bovary* to explore what was to him a basic paradox in criticism of the novel: the critic had trouble apprehending the entirety of the novel, because he never knew as much as the novelist.

According to Tate, Flaubert showed how to infuse fiction with the entirety of imagination. He did not force the reader or critic to take the imaginative leap, to imagine details of scene or character or action; it was all merged. He did "the complete imaginative job himself," and, in these terms, Tate claimed that "the novel has at last caught up with poetry." Furthermore, Tate argued that critics took too short a view of fiction by focusing on the overall form, style, or structure. He believed that the key was to look into the individual scenes that made up the whole to find out why and how they worked. For him, Dreiser, Faulkner, and Hemingway were the only American novelists, but it was Flaubert who "created the modern novel." A scene in *Madame Bovary* in which Emma thinks briefly about suicide was for Tate exemplary of Flaubert's power, a standard against which to measure a novelist's skill:

We are not looking at this scene through Emma's eyes. We occupy a position slightly above and to one side, where we see her against the full setting; yet observe that at the same time we see nothing that she does not see, hear nothing she does not hear. It is one of the amazing paradoxes of the modern novel, whose great subject is man alone in society or even against society, almost never with society, that out of this view of man isolated we see developed the highest possible point of virtuosity and power, a technique of putting man wholly into his physical setting. The action is not stated from the point of view of the author; it is rendered in terms of situation and scene. To have made this the viable property of the art of fiction was to have virtually made the art of fiction.[7]

Despite Ransom's several requests, Tate was not prepared to write an essay on Faulkner's singular significance. His essay on technique was suggestive with respect to Faulkner's style and form, but Tate was not ready, in 1944, to make him equal to Flaubert. In August 1946, confident of Rockefeller support, Ransom met with Tate and Gordon, and then Ransom wrote Tate to encourage him to edit the number and to solicit essays from Gordon, Warren, and Cowley. Katherine Anne Porter remained a possible contributor, along with Francis Fergusson, William Troy, and perhaps F.O. Matthiessen. Ransom did not really have a lead on English critics but believed Auden was a possibility. Both Warren and Ransom thought it would be advantageous to try to get a piece by either Camus or Sartre, but Ransom favored Jean Hytier, who was more conservative. He also reported that Cowley suggested contacting Harold Ober to see if an unpublished Faulkner story was available. Finally, Ransom had two suggestions with respect to the New York publishers. First, he thought that it might be helpful to time the appearance of the issue with publication of Faulkner's next book as a way to publicize Faulkner and the *Review;* and second, he suggested that Tate consider having Holt publish the special issue as a book.[8]

At the end of August, Tate agreed to take on the editorship. Tate thought Auden would charge too much for an essay, but was willing to ask him. If not, he was considering B.S. Savage, Geoffrey Grigson, or Herbert Read. He preferred Hytier to either Camus or Sartre (not wanting to encourage leftist and existential interpretations of the novelist), and perhaps Malraux if Hytier declined. Tate wanted a very distinctive issue of the highest quality, reflecting both American and European appreciation of Faulkner and avoiding a merely southern invocation of the novelist's greatness. In September, he wrote to both Auden and Hytier. Auden scribbled a short reply on a postcard saying he was not really qualified. Hytier was flattered but claimed that only seven novels had been translated, not enough, in his estimation, to write an overview of the French perspective.[9]

In late October, Tate received a query letter from Warren Beck, who had heard about the special issue from Warren. Beck asked whether he could contribute an essay on forms in Faulkner novels. Beck was an early Faulkner admirer who had written several appreciative essays in the early 1940s. Tate was interested, but cautious; he thought Beck's essay "Faulkner and the South" (*Antioch Review*) was too "sociological," another northerner misreading the South. Tate would accept an essay if its concern was restricted to literary criticism. He also approached two New York critics, Alfred Kazin and Richard Chase, the latter a disciple of Trilling's also at Columbia. Kazin initially agreed to write an article connecting Faulkner and Melville, but then quickly backed out.[10]

By the end of the year Tate had not received commitments from prominent critics or writers outside of the southern family. There was little interest in Faulkner among "top critics." With Tate opposed to securing material from the French existentialists, the only influential literary group actively interested in Faulkner, the entire project was suspended for a year. In September 1947, after the year's suspension, Tate and Ransom agreed to drop the plan for a special Faulkner number. They saw no reason to proceed when material was available only from critics of the second rank.[11] Without the best critics, it was hardly possible to argue persuasively for Faulkner's elevation. Tate and Ransom believed that anything short of the finest in critical commentary would only serve to retard any reconsideration of Faulkner by emphasizing the novelist's limited audience.

In fact, Tate and Ransom had only two new essays in hand, both addressing rather narrow topics: the one promised by Richard Chase, "The Stone and the Crucifixion: Faulkner's *Light in August*," and the other by Laurence Bowling, "Faulkner: The Technique of *The Sound and the Fury*." Ransom held these papers until the fall of 1948, when they were published in planned coordination with the appearance of Faulkner's new novel, *Intruder in the Dust*. This guaranteed some presence for the New Critics, balancing a few of the negative views while still helping to add a bit more momentum to the critical reconsideration after 1948. Bowling's piece was a technical discussion of the kind that would come to dominate Faulkner criticism in the 1950s.[12] Chase's essay, while also narrow, did try to place the novelist in a more general context and took up the several themes raised by Warren and Cowley. For Chase, Faulkner was most certainly the equal of Hemingway in the twentieth-century and, perhaps, even equal to the nineteenth-century giants, Melville and Hawthorne:

> Mr. Warren suggests that we ought not to think of Faulkner as an exclusively Southern writer but as a writer concerned with modern times in general. To this, one might add that Faulkner has many affinities with both Hemingway and Melville. As Malcolm Cowley said, the myth of a Southern society which emerges from Faulkner's works as a whole can be compared with Hawthorne's myth of New England.

Chase suggested that Faulkner's affinity to Hemingway could be seen in his concern with the absence of codes, values, and rules in the modern world, and in his belief that without such guides people failed to see their own humanity. Faulkner was also similar to Melville in that he worked with "American folk-literary consciousness"—i.e., the folk proverb. Chase blamed the tepid state of Faulkner criticism on "Northern" critics who, too much influenced by the radical politics of the 1930s, had misread a "great" novelist:

> Like the author of *Moby Dick* Faulkner might say of himself, "I try everything; I achieve what I can." In these bad times, a seriousness must count heavily with us. But it is also a sense of Faulkner's achievement which makes me think him the equal of any American novelist of his generation. Perhaps *The Great Gatsby* is the only novel of the time which can be defended as superior to Faulkner's best work.
>
> In the nineteen-thirties the liberal-progressive culture turned away from Faulkner for many of the same bad reasons which caused it, eighty years before, to turn away from Melville. If our liberal thought now begins to return from its disastrous wanderings of the last decades—that era of the great rejections—and to recover its vitality, it is because it

grows capable of coming to terms with Faulkner, as it already learns again to come to terms with Hawthorne and Melville.[13]

Caroline Gordon's essay for the planned special issue in 1947 also did not see print until 1948. In "Notes on Faulkner and Flaubert," which appeared in the *Hudson Review,* she elaborated Tate's earlier discussion of Flaubert by arguing that the challenge to all modern writers came from Flaubert and James. Faulkner was the writer who accepted that challenge and created fiction that rendered both a complete vision (Flaubert) and a full illusion (James) of life. Working with "Spotted Horses," she argued that perhaps Faulkner was more like Flaubert than like James. Faulkner accomplished, she said, what "Flaubert himself longed to accomplish, the union of concrete historical detail with lyricism. . . ." His literary power came from poetic images which added detail and commentary to the "thing observed" so that it "causes a further revolution of the thing observed, contributing powerfully to the illusion of life, of *"action."* For Gordon, Faulkner's genius, which had been too long ignored, was the way in which mastery of detail became incorporated into a larger scheme—"the result of a lifelong devotion to a particular scene."[14]

In short, with the tensions of the Cold War just beginning to be felt in 1946, the direction of literary culture was ambiguous, but clearly Faulkner did not hold much appeal as a literary subject or as a symbol for a new era. Ransom and Tate assumed, incorrectly, that Cowley's work and Warren's essay represented broader acceptance of Faulkner's significance. Their efforts, however, were not enough to push him into the mainstream. The *Portable* had prompted Faulkner to write the valuable Appendix to *The Sound and the Fury,* but without a new novel there was little to stimulate renewed critical or public interest. It would take two more years for aesthetic formalism and avant-garde modernism to thoroughly dominate literary culture and, with some bit of help from the world of commercial publishing, to shape Faulkner's role as postwar moralist.

Finally, not only could Tate not find outside critics to work on Faulkner, but Robert Penn Warren, instead of producing a piece on "nature" in Faulkner (one of the sub-themes in his commentary on the *Portable),* wrote a long, somewhat existential analysis of nature in Hemingway for the Winter 1947 issue of *Kenyon Review.* Here Warren interpreted Hemingway's importance in much the same terms as he argued for Faulkner's, and his analysis is worth reviewing. First, he suggested that Hemingway's vision of nothingness was part of a literary trend that coursed through the worlds of Zola, Dreiser, Conrad, and Faulkner: "It is the God-abandoned world, the world of Nature-as-all." In Hemingway, there was a purity in the depiction of nature that rivaled both Thoreau in the nineteenth-century and Faulkner. This purity and the inner strength of the individual—the Hemingway hero's code—was all that remained to be salvaged from the catastrophe of the First World War.

> The code and discipline are important because they can give meaning to life which otherwise seems to have no meaning or justification. In other words, in a world without supernatural sanctions, in the God-abandoned world of modernity, man can realize an ideal meaning only in so far as he can diffuse and maintain the code.

What Warren saw in Hemingway was a writer who condemned the "general community" by creating characters whose survival was predicated on their resignation from it.

Second, Warren focused on an analysis of *A Farewell to Arms* to counter the argument that Hemingway was an author without values whose work was immoral, or dirty, or without meaning. For Warren that novel was fraught with moral and philosophical substance: ". . . [T]he book, even if it does not end with a solution which is generally acceptable, still embodies a moral effort and is another document of the human will to achieve ideal values." This was exactly the same argument he made for Faulkner. Hemingway too, like Conrad, James, and Faulkner, was often attacked for being too exotic, too far from the mainstream. But Warren argued that Hemingway went beyond "economic" or "political" man. He was a *moralist,* concerned with "love, death, courage, the point of honor. . . . A man does not only have to live with other men in terms of economic and political arrangements; he has to live with them in terms of moral arrangements, and he has to live with himself, he has to define himself."

Third, like other lyric writers of great power, his genius, according to Warren, was his capacity to write intensely about a small and specific group:

> We have said that Hemingway is concerned with the scruple of honor, that this is a basic idea in his work. But we find that he applies this idea to a relatively small area of experience. In fact, we never see a story in which the issue involves the problem of definition of the scruple, or we never see a story in which honor calls for a slow, grinding, day-to-day conquest of nagging difficulties.[15]

Warren believed that Hemingway had given not a diagnosis but a compelling symbol for an age. The problem now was that the offered symbol was not effective enough to transcend the net of social and political connections of the interwar period. In Warren's view, by the end of World War II Hemingway was a writer of a past era, a different literary tradition. This judgment was reinforced when Hemingway's first novel in a decade, *Across the River and into the Trees* (1950), was generally called a literary disaster. In Warren's terms, Faulkner said the same things, but with a symbolism more appropriate for the postwar era, and he was a man without previous political or cultural ties to the 1930s literature of social protest. In a certain sense, the repudiation of Hemingway made space for Faulkner, just as the post-1948 critiques of Faulkner quickly accepted Warren's argument that Faulkner was at least Hemingway's equal, perhaps even his superior.

Warren, Ransom, and Tate were frustrated and disappointed in their failure to produce a distinctive Faulkner commemorative, but they were pleased by the achievements and successes of their literary community. In addition to institutional support for the important literary journals and the start up of the *Hudson Review,* there were

significant personal honors which contributed to a heightened public
awareness of contemporary letters. Robert Lowell and Robert Penn
Warren both won Pulitzer Prizes (with Warren also receiving a Guggenheim grant). Warren's *All the King's Men* had been sold to Hollywood for a reported $200,000, guaranteeing Warren financial
independence. With solid financial support from the Rockefeller
Foundation and strong links to New York, the prospects for high-
level literary criticism of the right kind never looked brighter.[16]

II

Ironically, the claim that Faulkner's work performed a special
moral function was made most completely by one of the more politically minded New York intellectuals. In the first postwar, book-
length synthesis of the fictive world of William Faulkner, Irving
Howe wrote:

> He has grappled with the inherited biases of his tradition, breaking
> through to a tragic realization that, at least in part, they are inadequate
> and wrong. He has dramatized, as have few other American novelists,
> the problem of living in a historical moment suspended between a dead
> past and an unavailable future; dramatized it in his own terms, as a clash
> between traditional mores no longer valued or relevant and a time of
> moral uncertainty and opportunism. . . . An authentic moralist when not
> moralizing, he has tried to reach, in images of character, the meaning of
> human virtue: of pride and forbearance, of humility and brotherhood, of
> truth and charity.[17]

Irving Howe argued, in his close reading of Faulkner's fiction and
in his careful synthesis of Faulkner criticism from Cowley's work in
1945 to the novelist's own Nobel Prize speech, that here was an
American writer who could be set into the continuing literary tradition and made into the conscience of an entire literary generation.
Howe was the first critic to offer a fully developed critique of Faulkner's work, and one that also attempted to delineate his role as the
American writer who satisfied the requirements of the postwar consensus.

Howe's involvement with Faulkner and the literature of the South started in 1948 when he began working more systematically on the place of American moderns in contemporary literature. His first book was on Sherwood Anderson and his second on Faulkner.[18] For example, in his review of the reissued *Wild Palms* (1949), Howe argued that Faulkner was essentially a modernist who tried to show the insurmountable distance between "man's aspirations and realizations," between "rebellion and acceptance." This novel, in particular, and Faulkner, in general, Howe believed, were worthy of far more consideration and praise. The complexity and dissonance in *The Wild Palms* represented existential tensions of the modern world.

> Always emotion must exceed possibility, response must exceed situation. This is the source of the fury and strain behind Faulkner's vision of life and the agonized prose expressing that vision; it is the source of his preoccupation with the word that seems dominant in his writing— *outrage.*

Howe also made the case for the sanctity of artistic creation and individualistic vision by arguing that the role of critic and reader was to understand why "important" artists choose a structure and pattern. "Whoever tampers with a work of art," Howe stated, does so "at his own moral peril, and in the eyes of people who care about such things that is a very great peril indeed."[19]

Howe finished his study of Faulkner after the Nobel announcement and was in a most advantageous position to capitalize on the publicity surrounding the award, placing the study with Faulkner's own publisher, Random House. He offered four major themes that were crucial to the postwar elevation of the novelist. First, Faulkner was the equivalent of the "twentieth-century European masters," and a contemporary writer who spoke to the new moral requirements of a chaotic, dangerous, and threatened world. According to Howe, "Faulkner has filled out a complex world of imagination in which we recognize the moral lineaments of our time; a world that reappears, enlarged and replenished, from book to book."[20]

Second, the moral message was offered within a complete imaginary world, thus meeting a significant requirement for "great" literature, technical virtuosity fused to serious content: "Though of great fascination simply as a spectacle of drama and event, this world is also the setting for an ambitious moral chronicle in which a popular myth and an almost legendary past provide dimension—and thereby contrast—for the present." While Howe was certainly not a New Critic, his strategy in this book was to offer a detailed description of Faulkner's world and in that process reveal the novelist's social and moral meaning. Howe claimed that the particularities of the world of Yoknapatawpha should be seen more as "a chronicle than a group of novels: . . . through its history of the clans it elaborates a moral fable of which the materials derive from Southern life but the meanings at Faulkner's best—are quite without geographical reference or limit."[21] This was simply formalist criticism set in a social context.

Third, Howe also worked to elevate Faulkner's involvement with the Southern Legend into a more universal commentary. He relied on Tate's argument, which claimed that the Southern Legend was not merely a provincial myth, but a commentary on the defects of the modern world.

> It is therefore insufficient to say, as some critics do, that Faulkner is a traditional moralist drawing his creative strength from the Southern myth; the truth is that he writes in opposition to his tradition as well as in acceptance, that he struggles with the Southern myth even as he acknowledges and celebrates it.

While Tate believed that the Southern myth was historically valid, Howe would not go that far:

> The Southern myth, like any other, is less an attempt at historical description than a voicing of the collective imagination, perhaps of the collective will. The old South over which it chants in threnody is an ideal image—a buried city, Allen Tate has called it. . . . Such myths form the raw material of literature.[22]

According to Howe, Faulkner worked with this myth in a contra-
puntal scheme that "set his pride in the past against his despair over
the present. This testing of the myth, though by no means the only
important activity in Faulkner's work, is basic to the Yoknapatawpha
novels and stories; and from it comes his growing vision as an
artist." Furthermore, Howe claimed that perhaps one way to explain
Faulkner's difficult and obscure style may be to connect it to his deep
involvement with this myth. According to Howe, Faulkner "is working with the decayed fragments of a myth, the somewhat soured
pieties of regional memory, and that is why his language is so often
tortured, forced and even incoherent."[23]

And finally, echoing Faulkner's Nobel speech, Howe believed that
the novelist should be seen as a writer who returned human emotion
and feeling to American literature:

> . . . anger and grief and fear and violent love and pity. He tells us that
> life is bitter and misery assails us; turning to "the human heart in conflict
> with itself," he speaks in the words of his Nobel speech, for "the old
> universal truths lacking which any story is ephemeral and doomed—love
> and honor and pity and pride and compassion and sacrifice."[24]

What a few critics were tentatively suggesting in 1948, Howe and
others now asserted with full authority as Faulkner's "unique" contribution. In his Faulkner book, Howe took up the postwar challenge
to engage in criticism of the text, to understand the value of tradition,
and to argue for the universal substance underlying the regional
consciousness and myth. Howe's acceptance of a fused past and
present that makes history subjective and nostalgic, best understood
by artistic imagination, not by systematic "rational" inquiry, was *not*
far removed from the arguments of Eliot, Tate, and the other New
Critics. In a 1951 *Kenyon Review* essay, R.W.B. Lewis claimed
without qualification that Faulkner's fiction could do "as much as
literature may with propriety try to do: it enacts for us, by means of
human individuals in a local habitation, the miracle of moral regeneration."[25]

III

In the late 1940s, prior to the appearance of the authoritative *Theory of Literature* by René Wellek and Austin Warren, the most important New Critical statement regarding the novel and aesthetic formalism was Mark Schorer's essay "Technique as Discovery," which appeared in the inaugural issue of *Hudson Review*. That Schorer's piece was an important contribution to the reinterpretation of the modern novel in the postwar period was not lost on his mentor, Allen Tate, or his colleagues. Tate had read an early draft of the essay and suggested that Schorer send it to John Palmer, *Sewanee Review* editor. Also Schorer had been asked by both William Van O'Connor and Robert Stallman for permission to include "Technique as Discovery" in forthcoming anthologies on literary criticism. Schorer's plan was to have the piece published first in a journal and then in a book. With O'Connor's collection going to press in the spring of 1948, Schorer wanted the essay published in the winter or spring to precede the book. He presented it to Palmer, who wanted it but could not promise quick publication. In January 1948, Schorer wrote to Tate and asked that Tate arrange to have the editors at *Hudson Review* invite Schorer to submit it for the first number, where it appeared.[26]

Schorer argued, in an explicitly anti-Marxist analysis, that in fiction, as in poetry, technique must be considered as primary. If technique was adequate to the novel's purpose then it elevated the work to the level of true art. Essentially, he believed that highly developed technique ultimately yielded works with "satisfying and rich content." For example, he claimed that *Moll Flanders* was weak because it had no technique, though it was valuable for describing the social conventions of the mercantile class, while *Wuthering Heights* was an obvious experiment with technique to tell a complex, though not very believable, story. Modern British writers represented by H.G. Wells, for example, were good storytellers but not great writers. Without concern for technique there could be no greatness. In short, Schorer argued, the only way to create art was to master technique: "Technique alone objectifies the materials of art; hence technique alone evaluates those materials." In the modern novel, this concern with technique forced writers to confront important new subjects.

> Under the "immense" preoccupation with James and Conrad and Joyce, the form of the novel changed, and with the technical change, analogous changes took place in substance, in point of view, in the whole conception of fiction. . . . [T]echnique is not the secondary thing that it seemed to Wells . . . but a deep and primary operation; not only that technique *contains* intellectual and moral implications but that it *discovers* them. . . . [T]he order of intellectual and the order of morality do not exist at all, in art, except as they are organized in the order of art.[27]

Thus, style became the measure of greatness. Lawrence's *Sons and Lovers* failed because its style was inappropriate to the author's intention, whereas *Ulysses* was a brilliant achievement: "[I]ts author held an attitude toward technique and the technical scrutiny of subject matter which enabled him to order, within a single work and with superb coherence, the greatest amount of our experience." Or perhaps the ideal effort was *Finnegan's Wake,* because there, for Schorer, was the pristine indivisibility of technique and subject.[28]

In America, according to Schorer, the best Americans were those who transcended the limitations of naturalism. Thomas Wolfe and James T. Farrell failed as novelists because they never went beyond the surface reality which, according to Schorer, had always seriously limited naturalist fiction. Farrell the realist showed only environment, and Wolfe the subjectivist showed only bewilderment. Hemingway and Faulkner were the great stylists, Schorer explained, and he elaborated on the themes laid out by New Critics such as Warren.

> The contribution of his [Hemingway's] prose was to his subject, and the terseness of style for which his early work is justly celebrated is not more valuable, as an end in itself, than the baroque involutedness of Faulkner's prose. . . . Hemingway's early subject, the exhaustion of values, was perfectly investigated and invested by his style . . . no meaning at all is to be inferred from the fiction except as the style itself suggests that there is no meaning in life. . . .

> The involutions of Faulkner's style are a perfect equivalent of his involved structures, and the two together are the perfect representation of the moral labyrinth he explores, and of the ruined world which his novels repeatedly invoke and in which these labyrinths exist.[29]

For Schorer there was a clear, necessary turning away from the tradition of naturalism/realism in the novel. His conclusion made that clear: "Elizabeth Bowen, writing of Lawrence, said of modern fiction, 'We want the naturalistic surface, but with a kind of internal burning. In Lawrence, every bush burns.' " But Schorer wrote that fiction burned brightest "when a passionate private vision finds its objectification in exacting technical search. . . ." Thus realists, he added, "deny the resources of art for the sake of life. . . ."[30]

Schorer synthesized formalist aesthetics with European moralism and created a basis for reconsidering Faulkner:

> The technique of modern fiction, at once greedy and fastidious, achieves as its subject matter not some singleness, some topic or thesis, but the whole of the modern consciousness. It discovers the complexity of the modern spirit, the difficulty of personal morality, and the fact of evil. . . . [W]hile it puts its hard light on our environment, it penetrates, with its sharp weapons, the depths of our bewilderment. These are not two things, but only an adequate technique can show them as one.[31]

Schorer's argument in this essay was a complete reversal from his prewar analysis in which he had criticized these same modernists for their total preoccupation with technique.[32] Before 1945, the literary situation had not offered up a writer of "genius" from the younger generation to represent a new era in American civilization. However, as William Barrett argued in his essay, "American Fiction and American Values," the new democratic emphasis was a radical break with the past and traditionalism:

> [W]hat has happened in America is that democracy has become, more than a mere political form, a positive *ethos* permeating the whole society, from the bottom up, and therefore has also come to involve a bold experimentation with life itself and with the traditional human norms in which the life of the past sought to concern itself.[33]

If the era of realism was at an end, as Schorer suggested, what was to follow? This was certainly a question at the center of much of the work of the New York intellectuals. Throughout the 1940s Lionel Trilling had been treating the same questions, as was made plain with the appearance of his most important essays in *The Liberal Imagination*—a collection of studies on culture and psychology. It was Trilling who created the bridge between New York intellectuals and the New Critics. As he explained to Tate in the early 1940s, what he wanted to explore was cultural criticism, but not the tendentious sort. It should be written on specific themes or works, and out of a devotion to literature. He was unhappy with the trend toward avant-garde criticism. Like Tate and Blackmur, he thought that there needed to be a close fraternity of the best critics, who could carry culture forward and provide an ideology for a difficult period.[34]

Perhaps the central essay in *The Liberal Imagination* with respect to postwar literary culture was "The Meaning of a Literary Idea." In it Trilling argued that there was a common ground in literature for both emotion and thought, and for content and technique. He explained:

> Say what we will as critics and teachers trying to defend the province of art from the dogged tendency of our time to ideolize all things into grayness. . . . [W]e as readers know that we demand of our literature some of the virtues which we define in a successful work of systematic thought . . . the authority, the cogency, the completeness, the brilliance, the *hardness* of systematic thought.[35]

Trilling believed that the power of literature must in some measure derive from the force of its ideas. This explained for him the strength of European fiction and in some measure the weakness of American literature, which somehow seemed passive and not quite serious enough. But for Trilling literature was not merely another system of thought; it still retained its own devices for "absorbing and disturbing us in secret ways."

> Intellectual assent in literature is not quite the same thing as agreement. We can take pleasure in literature where we do not agree, respond-

ing to the power and grace of a mind without admitting the rightness of its intention or conclusion—we can take pure pleasure from an intellect's *cogency,* without making a final judgment on the correctness or adaptability of what it says.[36]

Great or important literature must somehow be infused with both emotional and intellectual power. American writers like O'Neill, Dos Passos, or Wolfe, in Trilling's view, created large works of high emotional intensity, but they were not engaged with ideas. However, Hemingway and Faulkner, despite their public stance of anti-intellectualism, must be considered in a separate category. These two writers, Trilling argued, "hold out to me the possibility of a living reciprocal relationship with their work. . . ."

> [I]t will bring us back more dramatically because Hemingway and Faulkner have insisted on their indifference to the conscious intellectual tradition of our time and have acquired the reputation of achieving their effects by means that have the least possible connection with any sort of intellectuality or even with intelligence.
>
> The aesthetic effect which I have in mind can be suggested by a word that I have used before—activity. We feel that Hemingway and Faulkner are intensely at work upon the recalcitrant stuff of life. . . . We seldom have the sense that they have deceived themselves, that they have misrepresented to themselves the nature and the difficulty of the matter they work on. . . .[37]

Trilling argued that these two writers seemed to be involved with something serious and almost total—so that there was the appearance that they were engaged in telling us something about "life." To connect the emotional power of these two novelists to intellectual achievement, Trilling suggested (negating an extreme rationalist position which permits the unconscious no influence) that when two emotions confront one another and have a relationship with one another, then you have an "idea." But given their conscious disavowal of intellectualism, how was it that these writers became masters of ideas? Trilling offered this solution:

> Ideas may also be said to be generated in the opposition of ideals, and in the felt awareness of the impact of new circumstances upon old forms of

feeling and estimation, in the response to the conflict between new exigencies and old pieties. . . . In Hemingway's stories a strongly charged piety toward the ideals and attachments of boyhood and the lusts of maturity is in conflict not only with the imagination of death but also with that imagination as it is peculiarly modified by the dark negation of the modern world. Faulkner as a Southerner . . . deeply implicated in the pieties of his tradition, is of course at the very heart of an exigent historical event which thrusts upon him the awareness of the inadequacy and wrongness of the very tradition he loves. In the work of both men the cogency is a function not of their conscious but of their unconscious minds.[38]

While Faulkner in particular represented a complete immersion in the traditionalism of the past and its pieties, neither writer was part of the "liberal tradition." In the important European writers and these two Americans, Trilling saw the necessary literary qualities of greatness at odds with liberal social and political beliefs. This pointed to the main thesis of this essay and a central tenet of Trilling's ideology:

> For it is in general true that the modern European literature to which we can have an active, reciprocal relationship, which is the right relationship to have, has been written by men who are indifferent to, or even hostile to, the tradition of democratic liberalism as we know it. Yeats and Eliot, Proust and Joyce, Lawrence and Gide—these men do not seem to confirm us in the social and political ideas we hold.
>
> If we now turn and consider the contemporary literature of America, we see that wherever we can describe it as patently liberal and democratic, we must say that it is not of lasting interest. . . . The sense of largeness, of cogency, of the transcendence which largeness and cogency can give, the sense of gain reached in our secret and primitive minds—this we virtually never get from writers of the liberal democratic tradition at the present time.[39]

In essence Trilling argued that for literature to be important it had to confront the important ideas and intellectual dilemmas and questions of its time. He well understood, in terms not unlike those evoked by Schorer, that the problem was both a matter of style and content. For example, in his earlier essay, "The Life of the Novel,"

Trilling agreed with other critics who saw literary naturalism coming
to an end and the need for a new method that could balance the
necessary social aspects of realism with the awareness of an inner,
mystical, consciousness. The question of Faulkner's moral conscience was important to the several reinterpretations (Cowley, Warren, and the French existentialists) just after the war, when the first
arguments in favor of the novelist's high value were made.[40]

Trilling believed that, for fiction to be of the first order, there had
to be an interplay between nightmare and anxiety, on the one hand,
and a depiction of the real world, on the other. He wanted novels to
include more of the fantasy of possibility (more of James's potential-
ity of being) and less of the art of "what is." This was also part of his
message in the introduction to *The Partisan Reader* (1946), where he
claimed that the social realism of the 1930s was too superficial and
artistically inadequate to modern needs.[41]

The theme of "The Life of the Novel" was reworked in his widely
read essay, "Manners, Morals, and the Novel" (1948), which first
appeared in the *Kenyon Review* and then was included in *The Liberal
Imagination*. Here he invoked the term "moral realism" and said:
"We have no books that raise questions in our minds not only about
conditions but about ourselves, that lead us to refine our motives and
ask what might lie behind our good impulses." The writers of the
present day had immersed themselves too deeply in social fact, and
their novels, concerned with only one element of reality, were incomplete: "The novel . . . is a perpetual quest for reality, the field of
its research being always the social world, the material of its analysis
being always manners as the indication of the direction of man's
soul." Questions of morality had always been the central concerns of
the novel, and of contemporary writers "perhaps only William
Faulkner deals with society as the field of tragic reality. . . ."[42]

Essentially, in *The Liberal Imagination,* it must be understood
that Trilling's central assertion about liberal ideology was addressed
as a challenge to the inherent conservatism of modern literature. "In
the United States at this time," he claimed, "liberalism is not only
the dominant but even the sole intellectual tradition. For it is the

plain fact that nowadays there are no conservative or reactionary ideas in general circulation." In its antagonism to liberalism, literature functioned as a "loyal opposition":

> To the carrying out of the job of criticizing the liberal imagination, literature has a unique relevance, not merely because so much of modern literature has explicitly directed itself upon politics, but more importantly because literature is the human activity that takes the fullest and most precise account of variousness, possibility, complexity, and difficulty.[43]

In short, according to Trilling, because contemporary literature did not appeal to a mass audience, it was the special responsibility of the "limited" critical audience to consciously undertake the aesthetic evaluation, even if the work did not fall within the boundaries of liberal ideas. But in 1946 there was no American who could be elevated to the intellectual level of the great Europeans, though by 1948 Trilling altered that judgment, as we have seen. Faulkner became that moral realist for New York intellectuals such as Howe and Trilling, and New Critics such as Schorer and Warren.

IV

The affinity between Schorer and Trilling was quickly recognized, both in general ideological terms and with specific reference to Faulkner. In a most cogent review of *The Liberal Imagination*, Stephen Spender, representing the Tory wing of the New Critics, argued that Trilling, while trying to deny the existence of a conservative orthodoxy, was reading literature in a way not very far removed from the formalists. What Spender perceived was a postwar fusion with the reconstituted liberalism, and he identified it with remarkable clarity and precision:

> In effect, the conservative-liberal opposition should wither away in a living democracy and be superseded by a kind of revolutionary traditionalism; that is to say to a determination to improve conditions, inseparably

fused with a determination that the most valuable characteristics of tradition should be reborn within the future.[44]

Through the cultural institutions which they influenced or controlled, Tate, Ransom, Warren, and the other New Critics were closely and personally allied with Trilling, Rahv, and the other New York intellectuals, this despite many public differences.

These ties were clearly noted by Cleanth Brooks in his contribution to the "My Credo" symposium in *Kenyon Review:* "The Formalist Critic." Brooks believed that Trilling was not nearly so much in opposition to New Criticism as commonly perceived. In Brooks's terms, a critic must evaluate and judge. What is relevant to literary criticism must be determined by the principles of criticism, but articulating such principles did "not constitute a method for carrying out the criticism." Brooks argued that Trilling's compatibility with the formalists rested with his good judgment that literature could not be called upon to "produce" or represent ideas in some neat formula or patent. Trilling, he said, clearly rejected "any simple one-to-one relation between the truth of the idea and the value of the literary work in which it is embodied." For Trilling, the critic's work was directed at exploring the intellectual process in literature, i.e., the production of an "aesthetic effect."

Brooks argued that Trilling was right to choose Faulkner and Hemingway as American examples of writers who reflected the power of ideas in literature.

> Suppose, then, that we tried to state Mr. Trilling's point, not in terms of the effort of the artist, but in terms of the structure of the work itself. Should we not get something very like the terms used by the formalist critics? A description in terms of "tensions," or symbolic development, or ironies and their resolution? In short, is not the formalist critic trying to describe in terms of the dynamic form of the work itself how the recalcitrancy of the material is acknowledged and dealt with?[45]

Of course, for Brooks, the case of Faulkner was the most revealing. The critics had misread the novelist because they failed to address his work as *literature.* Trilling, like the formalists, understood this requirement.

But consider the misreadings of Faulkner now current, some of them the work of the most brilliant critics that we have, some of them quite wrong-headed, and demonstrably so. . . . Literature has many "uses"—critics propose new uses, some of them exciting and spectacular. But all the multiform uses to which literature can be put rest finally upon our knowing what a given work "means." That knowledge is basic.[46]

However, the analysis that converted Faulkner's traditional morality into Cold War social conscience had already been presented, in December 1949, in reaction to publication of *Intruder in the Dust*. Dayton Kohler's essay, "William Faulkner and the Social Conscience," argued that the novelist had to be read for his vision of the ancestral southern past and of the prospect of a moral future. He informed the present world with the morality of the southern legend. Kohler claimed that Faulkner was not simply "another elegist of the Confederacy. . . . His function has been to restore causal tragedy and a sense of the irrational cruelty of things to the dissolving outlines of southern myth."

What is important is the fact that the traditional order established sanctions and defined virtues and obligations by which men could assume the social and moral responsibilities of their humanity.

In these terms, Faulkner would continue to be misinterpreted if readers did not understand the relationship of history to myth: "His Yoknapatawpha County is a part of the present world, his Jefferson the geographical center of a moral universe."

Because his fiction reflects a land and a people fallen into social confusion and moral sterility, it touches also upon the greater problems of our time. . . . Unless I am greatly mistaken, Faulkner is writing about the disorders of our time, an age marked by social collapse and the decay of traditional morality. His Yoknapatawpha County is more than a microcosm of the South; it is a compass point in the geography of man's fate.[47]

Just one month before the Nobel Prize announcement Leslie Fiedler wrote an essay in *Commentary* calling for a rereading of Faulkner. A careful review of both his popular and esoteric work showed Fiedler that Faulkner had appeal and value for both a mass audience and intellectuals.

No one can write about William Faulkner without committing himself to the weary task of trying to disengage the author and his work from the misconceptions that surround them. It has taken me ten years of wary reading to distinguish the actual writer of *The Sound and the Fury* from a synthetic Faulkner, compounded of sub-Marxian stereotypes (Negro-hater, nostalgic and pessimistic proto-fascist, etc.); and I am aware that there is yet another pseudo-Faulkner, derived mostly from the potboiling *Sanctuary,* a more elaborate and chaotic Erskine Caldwell. . . . [A]nd equally confusing are the less hysterical academic partial glimpses which make Faulkner primarily a historian of Southern culture, or a canny technician whose evocations of terror are secondary to Jamesian experiments with "point of view."[48]

Fiedler argued that here was a writer who for some twenty-five years had managed to attract both a mass audience (referring to the short stories in the mass circulation magazines after publication of *Sanctuary)* and comparisons to the great European writers. He had been badly misread by the Communists, and now the distortions of 1930s politicized criticism must be set aside in order to do justice to Faulkner's pure literary power. That was the challenge for postwar intellectuals and critics. The Nobel Prize forced critics to respond quickly to Fiedler's invitation.

In late summer 1950, with strong rumors of a Nobel Prize in the offing for Faulkner, Harry Sylvester reviewed the *Collected Stories of William Faulkner* for the front page of the *New York Times Book Review.* There he argued for the recognition of Faulkner as a "great" writer, a literary resource as profound as James or Melville. Sylvester demanded that readers struggle to understand Faulkner, and his review reflected the degree to which the academic claims for Faulkner's universality had penetrated the cultural mainstream.

Still, for the serious reader, for the reader not yet lost from the world of literature, Faulkner can be a deep and continuous source of wisdom. For this kind of reader Faulkner reveals the laws of existence and the conditions of survival—and how people behave under them.[49]

Yet, because so much written about Faulkner was still directed toward an academic audience, the Nobel Prize appeared in somewhat of a popular void. The important mass circulation journals scrambled to present general analyses to explain the apparent sudden elevation of the novelist. One such effort was underway at the *Atlantic* in the spring of 1951, where its editor, Edward Weeks, was organizing a special Faulkner issue. Weeks arranged for Harvey Breit—whose laudatory review of *Intruder in the Dust* in the *NYTBR,* as we have seen, helped that novel achieve remarkable success—to write the introduction.[50] In the *Atlantic,* Breit's essay was intended primarily to suggest that Faulkner deserved a rereading and reconsideration even though his style was so difficult.

Breit said Faulkner was worth the effort: "He helps us to remember and to understand the human situation in its particularity, and thus in its universality, and he helps us to become more human." This novelist was, following Melville and James, America's "greatest prose virtuoso:"

> There is more to Faulkner's prose than brilliant architectonics, as there is more to his content than violence and sex. For all the magnificence, the language is minutely and infinitely flexible, capable of registering, and transforming into art, the bloom's bouquet or the corpse's smell, the most rudimentary instinct or the most conscious moral act. For all the brutality and frenzy in Faulkner's work, outweighing them are gentleness and love, courage and idealism, ethical concern and moral decision.[51]

However, Breit's essay also interpreted, for a mass audience, the new direction in formalist criticism and Cold War ideology. He called Faulkner's unraveling of the "tragedy of progress" his most important literary contribution. Breit saw in the novelist's most recent work, *Requiem for a Nun,* a further tallying of the cost of progress on the human spirit: "It is no longer easy, as it once was in the thirties, to scorn such a nonpolitical, or apolitical, vision. We learn each day that gain is expensive, that each step advanced is as well a retreat."[52] Breit asked readers to see Faulkner as the "bardic chronicler" of our humanism, and as the supreme moralist of the contemporary era. Breit carried forward into the mass circulation magazines the argument of the formalists and the modernists that what mattered in the postwar era was a literary elitism that elevated Faulkner and repudiated the radicalism of the 1930s which had tied literature to a Communist movement.

Finally, it may be suggested that during the Cold War, when it was possible for former Marxists to agree with Tate, Ransom, and Eliot that only the elite, whose vocation was the dedication to high culture, could be entrusted with the work of setting standards, then the autonomy of art was assured, and the debate between the materialists and idealists over content and form virtually ended. In such terms, the great writer was responsible to art, and the true critic to the obligation to protect this rarest of creations. Art had to be judged with political disinterest; and the setting of standards became the business of "men of letters" who "truly" understood social responsibility and the power of culture. As Irving Howe noted in his reminiscences, the unity of New York intellectuals and New Critics was represented by the common agreement that Leon Trotsky had been correct: *art has its own laws.*

> [C]riticism mattered because it could serve as open-ended humanist discourse. Precisely what made it tempting also made it treacherous: the endlessness of possibility. The best critics of all schools took for granted that a literary text merited respect for its integrity, but saw no reason to stop there, neither the *Partisan* critics in principle nor the New Critics in practice. Obeying the command of limit, they realized that it also signified there were stretches of perception beyond that limit, which one might yet bring to bear upon the literary work. . . . Indeed scorn for political contamination of critical judgment was an idea shared by all writers near *Partisan Review.* I'm not saying this value was never violated in the magazine; of course it was. But the fact that everyone from Rahv to Troy, Shapiro to Trilling, Rosenberg to Kazin would have found common ground at least in this belief represented a major step in shaking off the rubbish of the thirties.[53]

After the war, the new literary coalition had to fight an important battle for the validity of formalist aesthetics and for the cultural value of contemporary writing. According to Tate, the guiding premise in the struggle was Eliot's dictum: "The greatness of literature cannot be determined solely by literary standards; though we must remember that whether it is literature or not can be determined only by literary standards."[54] The coalition came to re-value Faulkner, at once denying the significance of the political dimension in "great" art, and arguing that the denial was not politics, but morality. With the publication of *Intruder in the Dust,* Faulkner was read anew. His elevation would reflect a commitment to these same traditional and elitist principles. To set aside the political dimensions of art was, of course, a supreme political statement, but one which helped to make the case for Faulkner, and for formalism as well.

Given the treatment of Faulkner in the literary journals from 1947 to 1950, as he was incorporated into the literary avant-garde and became identified with postwar modernism and formalist aesthetics, the novelist's new status was guaranteed—even without the Nobel Prize. It appears that the inherent textual difficulties made his prose even more valuable in the Cold War, as a symbol of resistance to Fascism and to delimited individual freedom, and as a symbol of the importance of stylistic innovation and personal perceptions over socially conscious art. When the dominant ethos of the postwar period was the moral superiority of the United States, it was not surprising that Faulkner came to be regarded as its most important literary voice.

CHAPTER EIGHT

Conclusion

The rise in Faulkner's critical standing can be attributed to a change in aesthetic sensibility (a new cultural *Zeitgeist*) during and after the war. This shift in aesthetic emphasis, which saw Faulkner replace Hemingway as the most important American novelist, is best understood in the context of the intelligentsia's accommodation to a changed political order. Faulkner was part of the American literary revolution that had enraptured and captivated the European, and, especially, the French, intellectuals during the 1930s and 1940s. As Harvard's Perry Miller noted during a 1949 lecture tour in Europe, there existed a "tremendous vogue" for American writers.

> In the intellectual history of Europe the impact of these writers during the last two decades is comparable to the domination of the *philosophes* in the eighteenth century, to the contagion of the German romantics in the early nineteenth, or to the later influence of Turgenev, Tolstoy, and Chekhov.[1]

Justification for Faulkner's elevation was provided in the United States by the ascendant literary elites. The New Critics and their younger disciples located in the elite universities praised Faulkner's technical virtuosity and his concern for the "eternal" human issues of honor, pride, justice, and courage. The New York intellectuals raised the novelist into the heroic corps of an international avant-garde (Joyce, Kafka, Dostoyevsky, James, and Proust) who, they said, offered persuasive psychoanalytical and existential interpretations of modern culture.

This postwar *Zeitgeist* evolved within the cold War on the cultural front, when the aesthetics of formalism and modernism not only reflected a political ideology but helped to legitimize it as well. Literary modernism, with "individualism" adopted as its symbol of artistic freedom, became an instrument of anti-Communism and an ideological weapon with which to battle the "totalitarianism" of the Soviet Union. In the arts, so the argument went, the United States encouraged individual expression and experimentation, while the Soviet Union accepted only the monolithic, the banal, and the propagandistic. The United States represented freedom, democratic institutions, and an open society promoting diversity and tolerating dissent; but the Soviet Union stood for fanatical authoritarianism, unquestioning obedience, and stupefying bureaucratic control. The demands of the Cold War required a cultural politics which promoted new literary and artistic voices as evidence of a "true" allegiance to the arts, and which also appeared to be an aesthetics without political content or motivation. In the morality play of the Cold War, American "liberalism" represented democracy; and its literature and art, cultural freedom.[2]

After the war, the New Critics and the New York intellectuals embraced the new formalism in a protean coalition unified by elitism and art-for-art's-sake aestheticism. In this movement there was room for both the traditional and the avant-garde, provided the aesthetic "quality" was high and the content apolitical, or, if literary excellence was lacking, at least a clear anti-Communist message would do—as in Koestler, Silone, or Orwell, for example. In terms of American literature, which was institutionalized within university English departments during the Cold War era, the nineteenth-century "classic" writers formed the common base, with the New Critics supporting the southern renaissance and traditionalism, and the New York intellectuals adopting European existentialism and modernism. The former group would have Eliot and Faulkner as a Nobel laureates, and the latter, in time, Saul Bellow. Thus, there was a clear shift in literary culture away from social concerns and from any criticism that tended to weaken or thwart United States interests.

Of course, the aesthetics of realism/naturalism were repudiated, having been tainted in the 1930s by an overt political orientation and ties to international Communism and support of the Soviet Union.[3]

Thus, with the ascendency of formalist aesthetics and avant-garde experimentalism and individualism as central literary and ideological elements of the cultural Cold War, Faulkner's previous liabilities turned into crucial assets. Because Faulkner's difficult style was tied to complex, exotic, and macabre themes, critics in the prewar years generally deemed his fiction curiously interesting, but inaccessible and remote; his personal rewards, of course, were obscurity and economic hardship. Yet, after the war, Faulkner more than any other writer was seen as the "supreme" individualist. He was dedicated, aloof, and isolated, a creative genius stubbornly committed to his personal vision. Faulkner's sacrifice and struggle to survive as an artist, combined with his concern for the ordinary life of the South, came to symbolize spiritual and moral courage. His provincialism and deep attachment to "human verities" in a traditional setting were now interpreted as a standard by which to measure morality in an increasingly amoral world. His obscurity, southern nationalism, and Gothic mysticism found a new interpretation and value. Uninvolved in the literary radicalism of the 1930s and possessed of a profoundly American literary voice (rural, folksy, and humorous), Faulkner came, while being recast as an ignored genius, to serve an important political function.

Faulkner's reputation in this country was created by the academics and literary critics who integrated him into the modernist tradition, who found in his vast, complex, and difficult work the kind of demanding literature that they had been trained to explicate, and who operated in a closed community of enforced conformity where dissent was suppressed and oppositionist literature and criticism were displaced. Given the cultural politics of the Cold War, which worked to eclipse the rebellious tradition of realism/naturalism, there was a general revival of interest in the classic American writers—Hawthorne, Poe, Melville, and James. After 1945, Faulkner quickly became the modernist representative of that tradition, and the quintessential technical and stylistic revolutionary. In short, he was, I believe, perfectly suited to represent the new conservative liberalism and humanitarianism of American democracy. And analogously, Cowley's rediscovery of Faulkner's "greatness" was perfectly suited to the prevailing formalist aesthetics of the postwar era which claimed, in part, that literature in its fully realized form was universal and apolitical.

After 1950, with a Nobel laureate in the vanguard, American literature would be enlisted, as a symbol of civilization, to defend artistic expression against the rigid, stultifying, state-imposed socialist realism. Faulkner's Nobel Prize was surely an appreciation of a creative literary achievement, but it was just as surely the recognition of the political and economic power of the United States and, at that moment, the preeminence of its ideology. Such a world power required a commensurate culture as well.

II

Of course, it is usually anathema to suggest that aesthetic matters are grounded in the ideological. But in the most recent memoirs, biographies, and commentaries about the rise to power and influence of the New York intellectuals, it has been openly admitted that their anti-Communist ideology played a central role in the advancement of their aesthetic values; without equivocation, they proclaim that this anti-Communism has proven to be the right and correct ideology. According to their view, the historical importance of the anti-Communist left was its early recognition of the malevolence of the Soviet Union and of the relevance of literary modernism. The political analysis was developed in journals such as the *New Leader* and *Commentary,* while the cultural implications were explored in *Partisan Review.*[4]

In the mid-1940s, the New Critics needed no shift in their thinking to adopt official, state-supported anti-Communism. Anti-Marxist and antimaterialist thought had been part of their founding creed, as discussed in chapter 3. The New Critics had apparently disavowed the connection between literature and larger cultural, political, and social issues. Literature that served a social cause was never more than propaganda, and axiomatically, great literature had nothing to do with propaganda. They claimed that Faulkner's work was great literature. As Richard Ohmann cogently argued in *English in America,* New Critics in their refusal to acknowledge the ideological in literature and criticism were, in fact, declaring a political ideology.

> Art is, in brief, a means of freedom from society. And that seems to me the best explanation of the way our criticism has justified literature: as freeing man by setting him above his circumstances. . . . All the schools of criticism argue that literature is a very special and separate thing, whose privileged cultural position needs defending—against science, against politics, against commercialization, against vulgarity, against nearly the whole social process."[5]

It is rare to find the New Criticism discussed as a product of Cold War ideology, and Faulkner is virtually never discussed in such a context. Contemporary analyses focus on the evolution of the southern literary renaissance and examine its connection to New Criticism, literary modernism, and the new South, in an attempt to answer the question of why the renaissance occurred. Faulkner is inevitably presented as the self-conscious modernist who played a central role in the renaissance.[6]

Ohmann recognizes that in the postwar era the New Critics held literary power with an aesthetic method that seemed apolitical but was not. He does not mention the fact that the New York intellectuals, by adjusting their political allegiance, came to share that aesthetic. During the 1940s a reconciliation occurred between the New Critics and the New York intellectuals as both groups came to agree that art must appear to be divorced from politics, and that serious "men of letters" had to stand together in the name of artistic autonomy. In a world of totalitarian threats, the defense of modernism—formal complexity, avant-garde rebelliousness, and artistic detachment—symbolized both intellectual freedom and the defense of culture.

Nathan Glazer, former editor of *Commentary* and a second-generation member of the New York intellectuals, has recently claimed that the intellectual importance of the New York group came from its growing connection to the academy where, as he noted, "Essays that had been wrought with pain and published to a few thousand readers suddenly became part of the canon of literary criticism—discussed, influential." But their *authority,* Glazer says, derived from the "correctness" of the anti-Communist ideology and the combativeness with which they fought the deceptions of the Communists and fellow travelers—the right position then and now. The anti-Communist left had moved dramatically to the right, adopting the same political ideology as the ruling interests of the United States.

> One must add that just as the squabbling intellectuals of New York were right about Communism, they were also right about the importance of Modernism. And just as they had intellectual gifts that enabled them to say something pertinent about great international issues . . . it also turned out they could say something pertinent about literature. . . .
>
> Being right in the large may be more important than being right about details, and about two large things they were right. But being right is hardly enough: History made the rightness relevant, and gave it a market. . . . What they had to say about Communism as a system of ideas and a system of government was right, and it gave them a market in which they wielded a modest influence: what they had to say about literature gave them a larger market.[7]

After the war, the New York intellectuals came to believe that the defense of the United States was necessary to protect political freedom and to guarantee free expression in the arts. The political issue of consequence was Communism. The editors and contributors to the New York cultural and political journals formed the intellectual and cultural center of anti-Communism (well before formal state sponsorship) to fight Stalinists and those liberal fellow-travelers who still defended the Soviet Union. As Sidney Hook said to Philip Rahv, cofounder of *Partisan Review,* in August 1945, "Now that the war is over, I suggest that PR meet the challenge of Stalinist totalitarianism head-on and plan for concentrated fire in each issue on some phase or other of the theme."[8] Communism had replaced Fascism as the essence of totalitarianism, with dramatic implications for culture.

In the new literary consensus, New York intellectuals and New Critics agreed that, when it came to the work of protecting cultural values, their many political differences had to be set aside. The postwar international situation offered intellectuals an influential role in the cultural Cold War. In the late 1940s, with Communists and fellow-travelers attacked, isolated, and repudiated, cultural discussion could proceed along formalist lines without justification of its own ideological implications. Both groups understood that the boundaries of postwar anti-Communist discourse did not include even a minimal defense of the social interpretation of literature. For a new era, literature was to have another direction. It is fruitful, in this context, to reconsider the emergence of Faulkner's reputation, given the dramatic speed with which he was resurrected. As Irving Howe explained in his memoir, *A Margin of Hope,* ". . . *Partisan Review* sanctioned the idea—perhaps the most powerful cultural idea of the century—that there existed an all-but-incomparable generation of modern masters who represented for our time the highest reaches of the imagination."[9]

In 1949 for example, Philip Rahv revised a selection of his essays for the collection *Image and Idea,* which examined, in part, the direction of American writing. For Rahv, the value of the novel as a literary form had always been its power to explain reality through the representation of experience. He was calling for a literature that could account for the irrationality of modern life, but not by repudiating realism. Artists, he believed, must not scrap realism: "[I]t is the most valuable acquisition of the modern mind. It has taught literature how to take in, how to grasp and encompass, the ordinary facts of human existence. . . ."[10] It had made important contributions that opened the way for truly modern fiction; it was a "historical necessity."

However, the world was now simply too uncertain to support a literary technique that evolved from nineteenth-century scientific discovery rooted, as naturalism was, in a stable and understandable reality. It took "inventory" of the world in an effort to tell the truth about reality, but its elevation of the typical to the mythic could not accommodate irrationality, subjectivity, or solipsism. Immersion in the details of ordinary life said almost nothing about psychology, ideas, or inner turmoil. In *Image and Idea,* Rahv suggested that there was a need for a new literature to replace naturalism, a form that was too narrow and tepid and, in modern times, no longer seemed relevant. He proclaimed the end of a literary era:

> The creative power of the cult of experience is almost spent, but what lies beyond it is still unclear. One thing however, is certain: whereas in the past, throughout the nineteenth and well into the twentieth century, the nature of American literary life was largely determined by national forces, now it is international forces that have begun to exert a dominant influence. And in the long run it is in the terms of this historic change that the future course of American writing will define itself.[11]

Ransom's response to Rahv admitted that the New Critics had been primarily concerned with poetry and were not really intimate with the novel. However, he suggested that there was a common ground because the essence of criticism was consideration of the lyricism of any piece of literature. "Let it be proposed to Mr. Rahv," Ransom wrote, ". . . that we should not approve any fictionist who does not possess a prose style. . . . Can we not say that fiction, in being literature, will have style for its essential activity?"[12] By the early 1950s, acceptance of a formalist perspective at *Partisan Review* was apparent, as the magazine adopted an aesthetic stance hardly at odds with that of the New Critics. There was little disagreement between New Critics and the New York intellectuals on the central cultural questions and the need for a new literary direction, as Trilling had made abundantly clear in *The Liberal Imagination.*

It should also be noted that Allen Tate, for example, addressed the American Committee for Cultural Freedom in May 1951 with "To Whom Is the Poet Responsible?" and the Congress for Cultural Freedom at the Paris International Exposition in May 1952 with

"The Man of Letters in the Modern World." In these speeches, Tate reaffirmed the separate values associated with great literature, calling on the poets to write poetry and to stay very far removed from politics. As for the critics, they should study the language of the poem in order to find the truth in literature: "It is the duty of the man of letters to supervise the culture of language, to which the rest of culture is subordinate. . . ."[13] Poets must be responsible only to their own conscience, and critics must immerse themselves in the language of the poem. For Tate, echoing Eliot's thesis in *Notes toward a Definition of Culture* (1949), the crisis of the modern period was an inadequate respect for language as the real "truth" of literature.

By the end of the 1950s with Faulkner's reputation established and secured, Tate could connect Faulkner to modernism without diminishing the contribution of the rest of the southern renaissance. In his 1959 essay, "A Southern Mode of the Imagination," Tate followed Trilling's lead by making Faulkner central to both the avant-garde and the traditional.

> Mr. Lionel Trilling has said somewhere that the great writer, the spokesman of a culture, carries in himself the fundamental dialectic of that culture: the deeper conflicts of which his contemporaries are perhaps only dimly aware. There is a valuable truth in this observation. The inner strains, stresses, tensions, the shocked self-consciousness of a highly differentiated and complex society, issue in the dialectic of the high arts."[14]

Faulkner became the pure example of this dialectical self-consciousness. Both New Critics and New York intellectuals exalted Faulkner's traditionalism and southern nationalism as part of both a new moralism and a new political orthodoxy. However, the sharpest definition of Faulkner's role in the "vital center" of politics and culture came, it should be recalled, from Irving Howe, not from one of the New Critics. He synthesized Cowley's southern legend, the New York intellectuals' concern with the problematic, and the New Critics' belief in the tragedy of tradition into a reading of Faulkner as an artist who made the southern myth into a universal vision of the human condition.

He has grappled with the inherited biases of his tradition, breaking through to a tragic realization that, at least in part, they are inadequate and wrong. He has dramatized . . . the problem of living in a historical moment suspended between a dead past and an unavailable future; dramatized it in his own terms, as a clash between traditional mores no longer valued or relevant and a time of moral uncertainty and opportunism. He has told us again, as every honest creative writer of our day tells us . . . of the devastation of our world, the estrangement of man in an inhuman milieu, the barrenness of commercial culture and a loveless ethos. . . . And he has seen the human enterprise as a risk forever undertaken and forever renewed, a risk in which the true measure is not success but exposure.[15]

Faulkner's elevation provides a key instance of how postwar ideology influenced cultural values, and, by examining the individuals, institutions, and processes that contributed to Faulkner's postwar reputation, this book has tried to illustrate the mechanics of his rise to literary fame in relation to ideology and values. It is at once a case history and an argument for a materialist interpretation of culture. The individuals with cultural power and authority, not surprisingly, did talk to one another, and did, at times, work toward common goals. New Critics and New York intellectuals did, in fact, come together to shape the Cold War cultural agenda. Their conscious activities on Faulkner's behalf, both direct and tangential, were the focus of this study. In exploring these activities, I have tried to trace how Faulkner came to be considered the "great" writer that critics now claim he always was.

Within a few years of the end of World War II the definition of social responsibility in art was radically transformed. The liberal aesthetics traditionally associated with naturalism and socially conscious literature came to be identified with the "totalitarianism" of the Soviet Union and Stalinist politics. Ahistorical art-for-art's-sake formalism was adopted as the aesthetics of postwar America and became redefined as cultural liberalism. Certainly, there were tensions and disagreements within this coalition, but the coalition itself was evidence of the supposed openness and pluralism of American culture.

Once the United States government assumed much of the responsibility for the costs of the Cold War, Faulkner, always the patriot, was enlisted as a state department cultural ambassador and one of Eisenhower's leaders for the "People to People" program. However, much of the intellectual groundwork for this public affirmation of American culture was laid in the period immediately after the war.

In sum, the renewed interest in Faulkner coincided with and was related to the heightened Cold War. The Nobel Prize for Literature, which Faulkner won in 1950, was the keystone of this process. But his re-emergence had its origins in the cultural upheaval immediately after the War, which required a great new American novelist to represent the dominance of Western humanist values. Ultimately, Faulkner's work was championed and canonized because his often supremely individualistic themes and technically difficult prose served an ideological cause. Unintentionally, he produced a commodity of enormous value as a cultural weapon in the early years of the Cold War.

Notes

Frequently cited periodicals have been identified by the following abbreviations:

HR	*Hudson Review*	*SR*	*Sewanee Review*
KR	*Kenyon Review*	*SRL*	*Saturday Review of*
NYTBR	*New York Times Book*		*Literature*
	Review	*VQR*	*Virginia Quarterly Review*
PR	*Partisan Review*		

CHAPTER ONE
Faulkner's Image

1. Cowley, *The Faulkner-Cowley File: Letters and Memories, 1944–1962* (New York, 1966), 5. Cowley's first letter of inquiry is not extant; it was probably written in February 1944. For further discussion of Cowley's significance in the Faulkner revival, see ch. 4.
2. For reports about royalties, income, and book reviews, see Joseph Blotner, *Faulkner: A Biography* (New York, 1974) [hereafter, Blotner], and *Selected Letters of William Faulkner* (New York, 1977) [hereafter, *Letters*].
3. Randall Stewart, "Poetically the Most Accurate Man Alive," *Modern Age* 6 (1962): 82.
4. Cowley, *Faulkner-Cowley File*, 9–10.
5. For discussions of the patterns of Faulkner criticism see the introduction to Frederick J. Hoffman and Olga Vickery, eds., *William Faulkner: Three Decades of Criticism* (New York, 1960), and Robert Penn Warren, ed., *Faulkner: A Collection of Critical Essays* (Englewood Cliffs, N.J., 1966). And for overviews of the changing critical reception of Faulkner, see O.B. Emerson, William Faulkner's Literary Reputation in America," diss., Vanderbilt Univ., 1962, and Gordon Price-Stephens, "The British Reception of

William Faulkner—1929-1962," *Mississippi Quarterly* 18 (Summer 1965): 119-200.

6. Quoted in A. Scott Berg, *Max Perkins: Editor of Genius* (New York, 1978), 530.

7. "Faulkner, Extra Special, Double-Distilled," *New Yorker,* Oct. 31, 1936, 78-80.

8. See Cowley's review of *Absalom, Absalom!, New Republic* 89 (Nov. 4, 1936): 22.

9. Bernard De Voto, "Witchcraft in Mississippi," *Minority Report* (Freeport, N.Y., 1971), 218, originally published *SRL,* in Oct. 31, 1936.

10. Maxwell Geismar, *Writers in Crisis: The American Novel, 1925-1940* (1942; New York, 1971), 167.

11. On Cowley's shift away from 1930s naturalism, see ch. 4.

12. Geismar, *Writers,* 144.

13. Ibid., 182.

14. Ibid., 164, 167, and 163.

15. Ibid., 180.

16. Granville Hicks, "The Past and Future of William Faulkner," *Bookman* 74 (Sept. 1931): 17.

17. Granville Hicks, *The Great Tradition: An Interpretation of American Literature since the Civil War* (New York, 1935), 266.

18. Ibid., 266.

19. Harry Hartwick, *The Foreground of American Fiction* (New York, 1934), 166.

20. Conrad Aiken, "William Faulkner: The Novel As Form," in Hoffman and Vickery, 138 and 139.

21. Ibid., 141.

22. Quoted in Warren, *Faulkner,* 274.

23. "Time in Faulkner: *The Sound and the Fury,*" in Hoffman and Vickery, 232. This essay was first published in 1939.

24. George Marion O'Donnell, "Faulkner's Mythology," in ibid., 84.

25. Ibid., 82.

26. "Introduction," in ibid., 29.

27. Cleanth Brooks, "What Southern Literature Needs," *SRL,* Sept. 19, 1942, 8 and 29.

28. *Time,* Jan. 23, 1939, 47. See also Robert Cantwell, "The Faulkners: Recollections of a Gifted Family," in Hoffman and Vickery.

29. See Blotner, 984-85, 1,000-22, 1,043, 1,056, 1,058, 1,097, 1,102, and 1,137; *Letters,* 104-5, 108, 109, 121-23, 126-55. For further discussion of Faulkner publishing, see ch. 2.

30. *Letters,* 122.

31. *NYTBR*, Oct. 29, 1944, 4. For a detailed discussion of Cowley's work on Faulkner, see Lawrence Schwartz, "Malcolm Cowley's Path to William Faulkner," *Journal of American Studies* 16 (Aug. 1982): 229–42.
32. *NYTBR*, 4.
33. *New Republic* 102 (Apr. 15, 1940): 510.
34. *New Republic* 106 (June 29, 1942): 900. Cowley was referring to his review of *Absalom, Absalom!* (Nov. 4, 1936).
35. *NYTBR*, 4.
36. *Faulkner-Cowley File*, 14–19 (Faulkner's letter is dated Nov. 1944).
37. *SRL*, Apr. 14, 1945, 13.
38. Ibid., 14 and 16.
39. Tate was giving Cowley several months advance notice since the contest was not to be announced publicly until August 1945; Tate also told Cowley that his chances of winning the contest were already excellent. See Tate to Cowley, Dec. 6 and 11, 1944, and Jan. 13, 1945 (Malcolm Cowley Papers at the Newberry Library). As the prize-winning essay in the Prentice-Hall/ *Sewanee Review* contest, it was also published in Allen Tate, ed., *A Southern Vanguard* (New York, 1947), 27. (Also see ch. 4.)
40. *A Southern Vanguard*, 17.
41. *Faulkner-Cowley File*, 27.
42. *Faulkner-Cowley File*, 62 and 20–75. There is yet another essay based on this research, "An Introduction to William Faulkner," in *Critiques and Essays on Modern Fiction 1920–1951*, ed. John Aldridge (New York, 1952), 427–46. For an explanation of the publishing history of the essay and its importance in Cowley's rediscovery of Faulkner, see Cowley to Aldridge, Nov. 28, 1950 (Cowley Papers).
43. Caroline Gordon, "Mr. Faulkner's Southern Saga," *NYTBR*, May 5, 1946, 1. For Cowley's commentary about the early reviews and criticism of the *Portable*, see *Faulkner-Cowley File*, 92–95. See Linscott to Cowley Oct. 31 and Nov. 8, 1944 (Cowley Papers).
44. Robert Penn Warren, "William Faulkner," in Hoffman and Vickery, 112, originally published in the *New Republic* (Aug. 12 and 26, 1946). Warren had been following and applauding Cowley's work on Faulkner. See Warren to Cowley, Mar. 2, and Aug. 29, 1945, and May 2, 1946 (Cowley Papers)— the last written after he had read the *Portable*. Also, Warren had asked Cowley's help in preparing a special issue of *Kenyon Review* on Faulkner to appear in the fall of 1947, though it was never published. See Warren to Cowley, July 18, 1946 (Cowley Papers).
45. Warren, in Hoffman and Vickery, 124.
46. "Introduction: Faulkner: Past and Future," in Warren, *Faulkner*, 2 and 11.
47. Ibid., 11.

48. "Portrait of the Artist as an American," *Horizon* 16 (Oct. 1947): 15 and 19.

49. "The Present Prospects of American Painting and Sculpture," *Horizon* 16 (Oct. 1947): 28.

50. *How New York Stole the Idea of Modern Art: Abstract Expressionism, Freedom, and the Cold War* (Chicago, 1983), 2 and 177. See also Guilbaut's essay "The New Adventures of the Avant-Garde in America: Greenberg, Pollock, or from Trotskyism to the New Liberalism of the 'Vital Center,' " *October,* [a journal published by M.I.T. Press for the Institute for Architecture and Urban Studies] Winter 1980, 61–78.

   On anti-Stalinism, Trotskyism, and art-for-art's-sake formalism, see Irving Howe, "The New York Intellectuals: A Chronicle and a Critique," *Commentary,* Oct. 1968, 29–51.

51. *How New York . . . ,* 174 and 3.

52. Ibid., 172, 3, and 201.

53. *The Vital Center: The Politics of Freedom* (1962; New York, 1949), 170 and 247.

54. Ibid., 248–49 and 255.

55. Faulkner's Nobel speech, "The Stockholm Address," in Hoffman and Vickery, 348.

56. "An American Renaissance in France," *NYTBR,* June 22, 1947, 29.

57. For a discussion of reactions to American novelists in France, see Thelma M. Smith and Ward L. Miner, *Transatlantic Migration: The Contemporary American Novel in France* (Durham, N.C., 1955) 135. (Smith and Miner reported that both Cowley's introduction to the *Portable* and Warren's review had been widely read, both published in *Revue Internationale* in 1946 and 1947.) See also André Malraux, "On American Literature and Civilization," *Horizon,* Oct. 1945, 236–42; and J.P. Sartre, "American Novelists in French Eyes," *Atlantic Monthly* 178 (Aug. 1946): 113–18.

58. "What French Readers Find in William Faulkner's Fiction," *NYTBR,* Dec. 17, 1950, 4.

59. *Atlantic* 188 (Dec. 1951): 56.

60. The historical development of the cultural politics at *Partisan Review* is thoroughly discussed in Alexander Bloom's *Prodigal Sons: The New York Intellectuals and Their World* (New York, 1986). For a reaction to Bloom by the first historian of *Partisan Review,* see James Gilbert's review of *Prodigal Sons* in the *Nation,* Apr. 26, 1986, 589–92.

61. *PR,* 19 (Mar.–Apr. 1952): 284–85.

62. *PR* 19 (July–Aug. 1952): 589–90.

63. *PR* 19 (Mar.–Apr. 1952): 309–10 and 304.

64. Warren, "Introduction," 14–15.

65. Faulkner's Nobel speech in Hoffman and Vickery, 347.

CHAPTER TWO
The Commerce of Culture

1. For a provocative discussion of literature in its "honorific" form in the recent period, see Richard Ohmann, "The Social Definition of Literature," in *What Is Literature?* ed. Paul Hernadi (Bloomington, Ind., 1978), 89–101; Ohmann also discusses the extent of Random House power in the contemporary publishing world. Parts of this chapter appeared in Lawrence Schwartz, "Publishing William Faulkner: *The 1940s*," *Southern Quarterly* 22 (Winter 1984): 70–92.

2. For Faulkner's correspondence with Random House in the 1937 to 1940 period, see *Letters,* 101–18, but for explicit statements of the partners' commitment, see letters from Haas and Klopfer in the Random House files. For example, see Haas to Faulkner, Nov. 15, 1937, and Mar. 17, 1939; and Klopfer to Faulkner, Mar. 31, 1939 (Random House-Faulkner Collection, Univ. of Virginia [hereafter, RH-FC]: 10280, Box 3, Folder 38). Interview with author: D. Klopfer, 25 July 1979. See Blotner, 953–1,022.

3. For Faulkner's money problems in the 1937–39 period, see Blotner, 1,000–22. In 1940, Cerf was still quite optimistic about sales of *The Hamlet;* see Cerf to Faulkner, Apr. 1, 1940 (RH-FC: 10280-A, Box 1, Folder 9).

   During the 1940s, Harold Ober, Faulkner's literary agent, was an important steadying force in the novelist's life and career. Ober played a central role in liberating Faulkner from Hollywood in 1946 and in encouraging him to resume serious fiction writing; see Catherine D. Bowen, "Harold Ober, Literary Agent," *Atlantic Monthly,* July 1960, 35–43.

4. Faulkner to Haas, Apr. 28, 1940 (*Letters,* 121–22). Ober had sold "A Point of Law" to *Colliers* in February for $1,000.

5. Haas reported that, by the end of April, *The Hamlet* had sold 6,780 copies, earning the novelist about $2,500, and that the firm had little interest in a collection of related stories similar in format to *The Unvanquished* which, he reminded Faulkner, sold only 6,000 copies (his least successful book). See *Letters,* 122–24, and Blotner, 1,043.

6. Faulkner to Haas, June 7, 1940 (*Letters,* 124–26) and Blotner, 1,047–49.

7. In order to negotiate freely with a new publisher for a larger advance, Faulkner realized that the contract would probably cover several books. As part of their "gentleman's" code, he was fully prepared to buy back the recently signed contract for the "unnamed" novel. Haas to Faulkner, June 10, 1940 (RH-FC: 10280, Box 3, Folder 39), and Faulkner to Haas, June 12, 1940 (*Letters,* 129–30). See also Blotner, 1,049–50.

8. Faulkner's letter to Guinzburg is not extant, but Cerf mentioned the $6,000

amount in his letter to the author, July 8, 1940 (RH-FC: 10280, Box 3, Folder 39).

9. Cerf to Faulkner, June 19, 1940 (RH-FC: 10280, Box 3, Folder 39). See also Blotner, 1,051, and *Letters,* 130–36. Faulkner traveled to New York in late June in an unsuccessful attempt to settle the new contract. First, he met with Guinzburg and then Haas, receiving, at that meeting, $1,000 from Random House as final payment of the advance.

10. According to Cerf the plates cost $1,162 and the firm held 2,700 copies costing 40 cents/copy and 101 copies of a limited edition (60 cents/copy). Cerf asked Guinzburg for $1,500 to take over the novel. Cerf to Guinzburg, June 24 (RH-FC: 10280-A, Box 3, Folder 42).

11. Guinzburg to Faulkner, July 3, 1940 [copy of letter] (RH-FC: 10280, Box 3, Folder 39). See also Cerf to Guinzburg, July 8, 1940, and Guinzburg to Cerf, July 11, 1940 (RH-FC: 10280-A, Box 3, Folder 42). Cerf contended that *The Hamlet* was always part of the discussion for Faulkner's release.

12. Faulkner to Cerf, July 28, 1940 (*Letters,* 134–35).

13. Cerf to Faulkner, July 8, 26, and 31, 1940 (RH-FC: 10280, Box 3, Folder 39). See also Blotner, 1,066 and 1,051–60, and *Letters,* 134–39. During this period, as a way to help Faulkner, Ober refused to collect his usual 10 percent fee.

14. On Faulkner in particular and publishing in general in the 1940s, see both Cerf, *At Random: The Reminiscences of Bennett Cerf* (New York, 1977), and "Trade Winds," *Saturday Review,* (July 12, 1947, 12–13.

    The Hamlet provided a dramatic illustration of the marketplace constraints on Faulkner publishing: The novel was printed in an edition of 10,000 copies to be sold at $2.50; with an average discount of 40 percent, Random House received about $1.50 per copy. The novel sold about 6,800 copies upon publication, returning $10,000 to the firm. Associated costs were $1,162 for plates, $4,000 for printing, $2,500 for Faulkner's advance, and about $3,000 for related expenses. The total cost was $10,500. The firm could just expect to cover expenses.

    There was one other element to the publishing story of *The Hamlet* in this period. In January 1941, Klopfer tried to arrange with Grosset and Dunlap to issue the novel as a hard-cover reprint. When the salesmen at Grosset and Dunlap were queried about adding Faulkner to their list, they told management that Faulkner titles could not be sold. See Klopfer to H.F. Juergen, Jan. 13, 1941, and Juergen to Klopfer, Jan. 24, 1941 (RH-FC: 10280-A, Box 3, Folder 42).

15. For a provocative analysis of Faulkner's art and his often turbulent emotional life (love affairs, marital unhappiness, and alcohol abuse), see David Minter, *William Faulkner: His Life and Work* (Baltimore, 1980). D. Klopfer to author, June 27, 1979.

16. See Blotner, 1,072-108; *Letters,* 139-55; and Minter, 184-91.
17. Cerf to Faulkner, June 30, 1942 (RH-FC: 10280, Box 3, Folder 39). Apparently the extra $1,000 Faulkner received in late June 1940 as part of the advance for the new book was charged against *The Hamlet,* because it was never discussed again. Eventually the original $2,000 advance was assigned to *A Fable* (1954).
18. Faulkner made four trips to Hollywood and back between July 1942 and September 1945. Here is the itinerary:

    Hollywood: July 1942 to December 1942.
    Oxford: December 1942 to January 1943.
    Hollywood: January 1943 to August 1943.
    Oxford: August 1943 to February 1944.
    Hollywood: February 1944 to December 1944.
    Oxford: December 1944 to June 1945.
    Hollywood: June 1945 to September 1945.
    Oxford: September 1945 to October 1948.

19. The idea for his fable (the new novel) derived from two Hollywood acquaintances, William Bacher (producer) and Henry Hathaway (director), who, in 1943, wanted Faulkner to develop a treatment and screenplay about Christ's reappearance and recrucifixion as the unknown soldier of W.W. I. Bacher advanced Faulkner $1,000 in August 1943 to work on it, with the understanding that Bacher, Hathaway, and Faulkner were to share in movie and dramatic rights, and Faulkner would hold literary rights to a novel and/or magazine sales. See Blotner, 1,149-50 and 1,178-80, and *Letters,* Faulkner to Ober, Nov. 17, 1943 (178-79); Faulkner to Cerf and Haas, Jan. 10, 1945 (188); and Faulkner to Commins, Feb. 4, 1954 (361-62).
20. See Haas to Faulkner, Jan. 16, 1945 (Harold Ober Collection, Univ. of Virginia, 8969, Box 1, 1944-45)—this letter states that a monthly advance was available. On revisions of the manuscript in the spring of 1945, see *Letters,* 190-92. For Faulkner's comments about an advance, see *Letters,* 180, and Blotner, 1,154.
21. Faulkner to Haas, Feb. 18, 1946 (*Letters,* 223).
22. Haas to Faulkner, Feb. 21, 1946 (RH-FC: 1280-A, Box 1, Folder 15), and Faulkner to Haas, Feb. 24, 1946 (*Letters* 225-26).
23. For the details of Faulkner's discontent with William Herndon, his Hollywood agent, and with Warner Brothers from 1941 to 1946, see Blotner, 1,073, 1,106-13, 1,117-94, 1,197, and 1,206-12; see *Letters,* 140-41, 153-63, 174, 176, 178, 180-81, 183, 190-95, 204, 209, 224-25, and 229-34; and for the emotional aspects, see Minter, 190-210. See also Haas to Faulkner, Feb. 26, 1946 (RH-FC: 10280-A, Box 1, Folder 15).

24. See Haas to Faulkner Mar. 21, 22, 29, Apr. 1, 2, and May 2, 9, and 14 of 1946 (RH-FC: 10280-A, Box 1, Folder 15); Faulkner to Haas, Mar. 30, May 5, and June 3, 1946 (*Letters,* 231–38; Ober to Faulkner, Mar. 28, 1946 (RH-FC: 10280-A, Box 1, Folder 15); and Faulkner to Ober, Apr. 18, 1946 (*Letters,* 232–33).
25. Haas to Faulkner, June 3, 1946 (RH-FC: 10280-A, Box 1, Folder 15).
26. See Blotner, 1,219–28, and *Letters,* 241–53. See also Haas to Faulkner, Nov. 14 and Dec. 13, 1946, and Mar. 7, 1947 (Blotner dates Faulkner to Haas, Mar. 24, 1947 [*Letters,* 247] incorrectly; this letter is actually Mar. 3, preceding Faulkner to Ober, Mar. 24, 1947 [*Letters,* 246]), Apr. 2, 1947 (RH-FC: 10280-A, Box 1, Folders 15 and 16).

    Faulkner drew $1,000 on April 1, 1946, and $500 a month until November 1, 1946, for a total of $4,000. Meanwhile, Ober sold two stories to the movies, netting Faulkner $6,000, and then Faulkner took on a freelance movie assignment at home in November and December. (This was unpublicized because it was a breach of his March 1946 agreement with Warner Brothers.) He received no further advances from Random House until April 1, 1947.

27. Faulkner to Haas, Aug. 24, late Aug. (nd), and Sept. 4, 1947 (*Letters,* 253–54), and Haas to Faulkner, Aug. 29 and Sept. 4, 1947 (RH-FC: 10280-A, Box 1, Folder 16).
28. Faulkner to Haas, Sept. 21, 1947 (*Letters,* 255).
29. *Letters,* 255–58. See also Haas to Faulkner, Sept. 30 and Oct. 14, 1947 (RH-FC: 10280-A, Box 1, Folder 16).

    By October 1, 1947, Random House had advanced Faulkner another $3,500 for a total of $7,500 since March 1946 and a grand total of $9,500 since 1940, which would rise to about $12,000 with the extra $2,400 Haas promised.

30. Faulkner to Ober, Oct. 30, Nov. 14 and 28, and Dec. 5, 1947 (*Letters,* 259–62).
31. See Cerf, "Report on Faulkner Book," Apr. 27, 1948 (RH-FC: 10280, Box 3, Folder 40).
32. Faulkner to Ober, Dec. 5, 1947 (*Letters,* 261–62).
33. On the unpopularity of nineteenth-century "classic" writers, see Henry Nash Smith, *Democracy and the Novel: Popular Resistance to Classic American Writers* (New York, 1978) and Richard Poirier's review "Classics and Commercials," *New York Review of Books,* Feb. 23, 1979, 40. (Poirier suggests that a more profitable perspective is a reversal of Smith's subtitle: "Resistance to Popularity"—and one I suspect is appropriate in Faulkner's case as well.) See also John Updike, "Reflection: Melville's Withdrawal," *New Yorker,* May 10, 1982, 120. For a general overview of American

publishing and mass audience, see Robert E. Spiller et al., *Literary History of the United States,* 3rd ed. rev. (New York, 1963), passim.

34. For a general analysis of the development of the modern book industry, see John Tebbel, *The Great Change, 1940–1980,* vol. 4 OF *A History of Book Publishing* (New York, 1981). Also see Merle Miller, "The Boom in Books," *Fortune,* Nov. 1945, 282. Overseas Editions was organized by the Council of Books in Wartime. Books were distributed by the Overseas Branch of the Office of War Information." The program called for distribution of 3.5 million books (50,000 each of 70 titles) and purchases of 300,000 extra books from American publishers for distribution in Western Europe (Tebbel, 55–56).

35. On wartime developments, see Tebbel, *Publisher's Weekly,* and Miller, "The Boom in Books," 146; "The Year in Books," *Time,* Dec. 20, 1943; Malcolm Cowley, "The Literary Business in 1943," *New Republic* 109 (Sept. 27, 1943): 417–19, and "Books by the Millions," *New Republic* 109 (Oct. 11, 1943): 482–85. See also the widely cited essay about the "standardization" of literature by James T. Farrell, "The Fate of Writing in America" (1945) in his *Literature and Morality* (New York, 1947), 35–78.

At the same time, there were concerns about the relationship between subsidiary rights, escalating costs, advances, profits, and literary quality. For example, see John K. Hutchins, "For Better or Worse, The Book Clubs," *NYTBR,* Mar. 31, 1946; Alfred R. McIntyre, "Crisis in Book Publishing," *Atlantic Monthly,* Oct. 1947, 107–10; Bennett Cerf, "Trade Winds," *SRL,* July 12, 1947, 4–5; Merle Miller, "The Book Club Controversy, *Harper's,* May and June 1948, 433–40 AND 518–24; and Philip Van Doren Stern, "Books and Best Sellers," *VQR* 18 (Winter 1942): 45.

36. For discussions of United States hegemonic intentions (economic, political, and military) and for early, "Grand Area" planning by the Council on Foreign Relations with respect to the British Empire in particular, see L.H. Shoup and William Minter, *Imperial Brain Trust* (New York, 1977), especially ch. 4, "Shaping A New World Order: The Council's Blueprint for Global Hegemony, 1939–1944," 117–87. See also W.R. Louis, *Imperialism at Bay: The United States and the Decolonization of the British Empire, 1941–1945* (New York, 1978), and Fred L. Block, *The Origin of International Economic Disorder: A Study of United States International Monetary Policy from World War II to the Present* (Berkeley, Calif., 1977), especially part 1.

For a careful historical discussion of U.S. goals during and after the war, see Gabriel Kolko, *The Politics of War: The World and United States Foreign Policy 1943–1945* (New York, 1968), and Joyce and Gabriel Kolko, *The Limits of Power: The World and United States Foreign Policy, 1945–*

1954 (New York, 1972). And for a discussion of the ideology of U.S. imperialism as it emerged and developed in the postwar era, see Noam Chomsky, *Towards a New Cold War: Essays on the Current Crisis and How We Got There* (New York, 1982); on history and propaganda, see also Jesse Lemisch, *On Active Service in War and Peace: Politics and Ideology in the American Historical Profession* (Toronto, 1975).

37. On the war and the paperback revolution, see L. Schick, *The Paperbound Book in America: The History of Paperbacks and Their European Background* (New York, 1958), especially part 2: "The Current Phase 1939–1957"; and Freeman Lewis, "Paperbound Books in America," in *Bowker Lectures on Book Publishing* (New York, 1959), 306–55. For a clear statement about the principal economic and demographic forces shaping the industry since 1945, see Dan Lacy, "Major Trends in American Book Publishing," in *Trends in American Publishing*, ed. K.L. Henderson (Chicago, 1968), 1–15, and see the essays in Chandler B. Grannis, ed., *What Happens in Book Publishing*, 1st ed. (New York, 1957). For an overview of bestsellers, see Alice P. Hackett, *Seventy Years of Best Sellers, 1895–1965* (New York, 1965), and James P. Hart, *The Popular Book: A History of American Literary Taste* (Berkeley, Calif., 1963).

38. For early analyses of the major changes in the book industry after the war, see Harold K. Guinzburg, ed., *Books and the Mass Market* (Urbana, Ill., 1953), and Hellmut Lehmann-Haupt, *The Book in America* (New York, 1951); see also Charles A. Madison, *Book Publishing in America* (New York, 1966). On the consolidation of the book industry and economic changes, see Malcolm Cowley, "The Big Change in Publishing," *Esquire* 545 (Dec. 1960): 309–15, and K.L. Henderson, ed., *Trends in American Publishing*. For more recent discussions of the shift from private companies to public corporations to subsidiaries of conglomerates, see Coser et al., and Benjamin Compaine, *The Book Industry in Transition: An Economic Study of Book Distribution and Marketing* (White Plains, N.Y., 1978). The "big money" phase has been reviewed in Thomas Whiteside, *The Blockbuster Complex* (Middletown, Conn., 1981)—also *The New York Times* has been, in recent years, following the developments in the book trade extremely carefully with dozens of articles on specific houses, mergers and acquisitions, the economics of book publishing, and cultural trends; see also Irwin Ross, "The New Golconda in Book Publishing," *Fortune* 96 (Dec. 1977): 110. For an example of the ideological and cultural impact of economic changes in the textbook industry, see Francis Fitzgerald's study of American history school texts, *America Revised* (Boston, 1980); see also American Textbook Publishers Institute, *Textbooks in Education* (New York, 1949).

39. *Publishers Weekly,* Jan. 26, 1946, 603–4. Cooperative efforts between government and industry were established, such as the Informational Media Guaranty Program (mainly for technical and scientific works) administered by the USIA under the Economic Cooperation Act of 1948 and the USIA Information Services Center Program.
40. "Distribution of American Books Abroad," in Grannis, *What Happens in Book Publishing,* 280–81. See also R.E. Barker, *Books For All: A Study of the International Book Trade* (Paris, 1956).
41. "American Books Abroad," *Library Trends* 5 (July 1956): 95. The entire number is devoted to the topic. The essays were collected as part of the National Book Committee's conference at Princeton in September 1955. Peter Jennison was one of the advisory editors.
42. For Cerf's memoirs, see *At Random.* For a summary of Random House developments, see Tebbel, *The Great Change,* 181–95, and passim. For an example of Cerf's celebrity status, see his profile in *Life,* Dec. 3, 1945, 64.
43. Edith Stern, "Random House," *SRL,* Dec. 6, 1941, 18, and John F. Baker, "Fifty Years of Publishing at Random," *Publisher's Weekly,* Aug. 4, 1975, 25. On editing and working at Random House, see Hiram Haydn's memoirs, *Word's and Faces* (New York, 1974), and Dorothy Commins, *What Is an Editor? Saxe Commins at Work* (New York, 1978). Klopfer Interview.
44. For Cerf's statement, see G. Gross, ed., *Publishers on Publishing* (New York, 1961), 473–88. For Cerf's commentary about publishing in the postwar era, see his memoirs and his regular column, "Trade Winds" in *SRL.*
45. See Tebbel, 76. For a representative example of a carriage trade publisher, see Geoffrey T. Hellman, "Alfred A. Knopf, Publisher," *New Yorker,* Nov. 20, 1948, 45, and also Alfred A. Knopf, "Book Publishing: The Changes I Have Seen," *Atlantic Monthly* 200 (Dec. 1957): 155–60. The classic pre-W.W. I economic analysis of the book industry reflecting its carriage trade orientation is O.H. Cheney, *Economic Survey of the Book Industry* (1931; New York, 1960); the 1960 reprint includes a good introduction which contrasts the basic changes over thirty years. William Miller, *The Book Industry* (New York, 1949), provides a postwar update of the Cheney report with analysis of the wartime "boom." On the paperback revolution, see Kurt Enoch, "The Paper-Bound Book: The Twentieth Century Publishing Phenomenon," *Library Quarterly,* July 1954, 211–25. Unfortunately, a comprehensive history of the paperback revolution has yet to be written; but in addition to Tebbel, there have been several recent attempts to deal with facets of paperback publishing—Thomas L. Bonn, *Under Cover: An Illustrated History of American Mass-Market Paperbacks* (New York, 1982); G. O'Brien, *Hardboiled America: The Lurid Years of Paperbacks* (New York, 1981); and a company history, Clarence Petersen,

The Bantam Story: Thirty Years of Paperback Publishing, 2nd rev. ed. (New York, 1975). And for a review of Armed Services Editions, see *A History of the Council on Books in Wartime, 1942-46* (New York, 1946) and John A. Jamieson, *Books for the Army (New York,* 1950).

46. *Letters,* 217-18.

47. His 1942 contract with Warner Brothers called for a $300 per week salary to start, and he was to rely on Hollywood paychecks until 1946. The details of his relationship with the studio in this period are presented in Blotner, 1,073, 1,106-13, 1,117-94, 1,197, 1,206-12, and in *Letters,* passim.

48. Cowley's three essays were: 1) "William Faulkner's Human Comedy," *NYTBR,* Oct. 29, 1944; 2) "William Faulkner Revisited," *Saturday Review* 28 Apr. 14, 1945); and 3) "William Faulkner's Legend of the South," *SR* 53 (Summer 1945).

   Robert N. Linscott, a Random House senior editor, had expressed an early interest in the possibility of creating a *Portable;* see ch. 1, 31. And for Cowley's request, in spring 1945, to Viking management to reconsider a *Portable,* see Cowley to Best, May 26, 1945 (postscript) and Best to Cowley, June 14, 1945 (Cowley Papers).

49. For the actual negotiations in 1945, see Cowley to Best, June 11, Best to Cowley, June 22, and Cowley to Best, June 30, 1945 (Cowley Papers). See also Best to Cerf, July 6, (includes Cowley's original outline for the proposed volume), Cerf to Best, July 10, Best to Cerf, July 13 and Cerf to Best, July 16, 1945 (RH-FC: 10280-A, Box 3, Folder 42).

   The final agreement was reached at a luncheon meeting between Best and Cerf on Monday, July 23, 1945. See Best to author, Dec. 3, 1977, and Cowley to author, Oct. 29, 1980. On August 9, 1945, Cowley wrote to Faulkner announcing the agreement, (*Faulkner-Cowley File,* 20-24).

50. Of course, after the Nobel Prize, the Faulkner *Portable* began to sell strongly, reaching a total of 210,000 copies by 1970. It continues to sell a steady 20,000 copies per year. See Cowley to Matthew Bruccoli, Oct. 13, 1970, in M.J. Bruccoli, ed., *Fitzgerald and Hemingway Annual, 1971* (Dayton, Ohio, 1971), 318.

   In the period from 1946 to 1950, Viking paid a total royalty of about $4,000, including the $2,500 guarantee. After deducting Cowley's $1,000 fee, $3,000 was shared equally by Faulkner and Random House.

51. *Faulkner-Cowley File,* 88 and 82-89. See also Blotner, 1,207-9, and 1,215-16, and *Letters,* 219-22, 228-29, and 235-37. In 1946, Blotner reported that Faulkner's "bank account had dwindled to $500" (1,205).

   The original trade editions of these novels had sold poorly: *The Sound and the Fury* (1929), 2,990 copies, and *As I Lay Dying* (1930), 540 copies;

see A. Erskine's summary of sales, Mar. 29, 1954 (RH-FC: 10280, Box 3, Folder 40).

For an interesting but incomplete commentary on Faulkner's relationship with his editor, Saxe Commins, see Dorothy Commins, *What Is an Editor? Saxe Commins at Work,* 194–232. Interview with author: Dorothy Commins, Nov. 12, 1980.

Finally, there was no clear rationale for selecting these two novels. Apparently in the 1930s, Cerf and Klopfer had wanted to reprint *The Sound and the Fury* and *As I Lay Dying,* but these novels had been set in type by Faulkner's then publisher [Jonathan] Cape and [Harrison] Smith—i.e., *Sanctuary* was published by Random House because plates existed. See Evelyn H. Glick to Cowley, Feb. 20, 1966 (Cowley Papers).

52. Interoffice Memo: Weybright to Philip Album, sales manager, Feb. 13, 1948. This memo dealt with complaints about obscene language in *The Wild Palms.* See also Weybright to Clifford Forster, American Civil Liberties Union, Mar. 11, 1948. In paperback, *The Wild Palms* was banned in a number of cities—this was never a problem with the original trade edition.

For actual New American Library sales and publishing figures, see Donald Demarest to Victor Weybright, Interoffice Memo: "W. Faulkner—Titles published by and under contract *NAL,*" May 14, 1951 (*NAL* Archives, Fales Library, New York University, "WF, General File").

53. Weybright to author, Dec. 19, 1977. Interview with author: K. Enoch, May 20, 1981. See also Weybright, *The Making of a Publisher: A Life in the* 20th Century Book Revolution (New York, 1966), passim.

54. Faulkner and Random House shared the guarantee. See Cerf to Weybright, Nov. 13, 1946; Weybright to Cerf, Nov. 21, 1946; Enoch to Cerf, Nov. 25, 1946; and Cerf to Weybright, Nov. 27, 1946 (*NAL* Archives, "Sanctuary"). Cerf also told Weybright of a request by New Directions to reprint *Light in August* in a special limited edition.

For Faulkner's permission to sell reprint rights to Penguin, see Haas to Faulkner, Dec. 2, 1946. Also in 1946, Haas arranged to release *Sanctuary* through the firm's hardbound reprinter, Grosset and Dunlap; see Haas to Faulkner, Dec. 13, 1946 (RH-FC: 10280-A, Box 1, Folder 15).

In the introduction to *Sanctuary* Faulkner claimed the novel was a "cheap idea" written quickly to make money. For a recent and thorough discussion of the novel, see Noel Polk's "Afterword," to *Sanctuary: The Original Text* (New York, 1981).

55. Weybright, 216–17. A review of the "Sanctuary" file in the *NAL* Archives sheds no further light on Poore's report on Faulkner sales. In the file, there is a statement from Random House noting that through October 1946 the

novel sold 31,175 copies in Modern Library and 25,491 in the trade edition for a total sale of 56,175 since 1932. In 1950, Poore reported 70,000, which indicated a yearly sale of slightly in excess of 3,500 copies, earning Faulkner little more than $300 (see above, 3). Poore's 70,000 is correct, but not quite as impressive when viewed as sales covering 18 years.

56. Weybright, 190–92 and 230–36. Arabel J. Porter to Weybright, Interoffice Memo, July 15, 1947 (*NAL* Archives, "The Wild Palms"). Enoch Interview.

   The Wild Palms became the first Signet novel when, in 1948, Enoch and Weybright separated from Allen Lane's Penguin Books of London—Signet became the *NAL* fiction imprint; and Mentor, the nonfiction.

57. Weybright to Haas, Aug. 20, 1947 (*NAL* Archives, "The Wild Palms").

58. Weybright to Cerf, Aug. 12, 1947; Haas to Weybright, Aug. 15, 1947; Weybright to Haas, Aug. 20, 1947; Haas to Weybright, Aug. 21, 1947; and Haas to Weybright, Aug. 29, 1947 (*NAL* Archives, "The Wild Palms"). See also Haas to Faulkner, Aug. 21, 1947, urging Faulkner to accept the reprint offer (RH-FC: 10280-A, Box 1, Folder 16).

59. Weybright to Haas, Feb. 5, 1948 (*NAL* Archives, "The Old Man").

60. *NYTBR,* Sunday, Feb. 8, 1948, 44. Of course, Clifton Fadiman was always hard on Faulkner—reviewing in the influential *New Yorker.* When asked to comment on the vast *NAL* sales in the late 1940s, Fadiman says he was impressed with the figures, but thought 95% of the readers, if interviewed, would admit to being "bored to death." C. Fadiman to author, June 20, 1979.

61. Weybright to Haas, Feb. 11, 1948 (*NAL* Archives, "The Old Man").

62. Blotner, 1,243–44.

63. Blotner, 1,254. And Erskine to author, Dec. 13, 1977, and June 12, 1979.

64. Cerf, "Report on Faulkner Book," Apr. 27, 1948 (RH-FC: 10280, Box 3, Folder 40). For another enthusiastic response, and a request for early publication of the novel, see Haas to Faulkner, May 3, 1948 (RH-FC: 10280-A, Box 2, Folder 17).

65. Blotner, 1,245–63, and *Letters,* 262–273. For details on Cerf's negotiations with *MGM,* see (RH-FC: 10280-A, Box 2, Folder 17).

66. Blotner, 1,262–63. For sales figures, see Haas to Faulkner, Sept. 30, 1948 (RH-FC: 10280-A, Box 2, Folder 17). For details on filming, see Blotner, 1,272-1,300.

67. Faulkner had liked the idea for the short story collection, and acknowledged receipt of the list of stories; but he was too busy finishing *Intruder in the Dust* to review it carefully. However, in preparation for the New York visit, he finally returned the list to Haas in late September with annotations. See Blotner, 1,261 and 1,270; see *Letters* 266, 273–75, and 277.

The original idea for a short story volume (organized in cycles) came from Cowley in 1945. See *Faulkner-Cowley File,* 34, and Faulkner to Cowley, Nov. 1, 1948 (*Letters* 277–79).

68. Commins to Faulkner, Dec. 8, 1948 (RH-FC: 10280-A, Box 2, Folder 17). See also Faulkner to Commins, Nov. 24, 1948, *Letters,* 280–81.

On November 15, Haas had reported to Faulkner that Commins was hard at work on preliminary organizing for a short story collection (RH-FC: 10280, Box 3, Folder 40). And on December 16, 1948, Linscott responded to an inquiry by Edmund Wilson about availability of early Faulkner titles, saying that Faulkner was out of print, but that plans were being made for gradually reissuing his work in the Modern Library (RH-FC: 10280-A, Box 1, Folder 17). Wilson wrote an important and influential review of *Intruder* for the *New Yorker.*

69. Commins to Faulkner, Jan. 21, 1949 (RH-FC: 10280-A, Box 2, Folder 18).

70. Erskine to author, June 12, 1979. See also Haas to Faulkner, Jan. 10, 1949 (RH-FC: 10280-A, Box 2, Folder 18). On reissuing *Light in August,* see E. Harper to Haas, Dec. 20, 1949 (RH-FC: 10280, Box 3, Folder 40), and Haas to Faulkner, Dec. 21, 1949 (RH-FC: 10280-A, Box 2, Folder 18).

71. *Knight's Gambit* sold 9,639 copies, according to the 1954 summary of Faulkner sales. If the sales figures for the three reprinted novels are reviewed, the limited demand was clear. As of 1942, sales for *The Wild Palms, The Hamlet,* and *Go Down, Moses,* were, respectively, 12,000, 7,000, and 4,000 copies (approximately); as of 1954, sales for the three titles were 13,749, 9,106, and 5,385.

72. Commins to Faulkner, Jan. 25, and Feb. 16, 1950 (RH-FC: 10280, Box 3, Folder 40). For delays on the W.W. I fable, see Blotner, 1,304–38; see also *Letters,* 297–308. (Haas and Faulkner also discussed, during the February 1950 visit, the possibility of publishing a 90,000-word excerpt from the manuscript.)

73. Blotner, 1,323, and *Letters,* 304. The stories were "Mules in the Yard," and "Shingles for the Lord."

74. Klopfer to Faulkner, July 7, 1950 (RH-FC: 10280, Box 3, Folder 40) and Blotner, 1,328–29.

75. Cerf to Faulkner, Oct. 16, 1950 (RH-FC: 10280, Box 3, Folder 40). For a congratulatory note on winning the Nobel Prize, see Haas to Faulkner, Nov. 10, 1950 (RH-FC: 10280-A, Box 2, Folder 19). See Blotner, 1,337–38 and 1,341–71. See also Bennett Cerf, *At Random,* 129–37.

No sales figures for the collected stories from the period August through November 1950 are available. The sales summary showed 25,255 copies sold, which was slightly more than the total for *Intruder in the Dust.* It is safe to assume that the sales for the first three months were in excess of 10,000 copies.

76. Weybright to Cerf, July 20, 1948 (*NAL* Archives, "Intruder in the Dust"), *NAL* guaranteed $1,000 for *The Old Man*.

77. Weybright, 199–225. *The Old Man* sold 245,000 copies, while *Intruder in the Dust* would sell 357,000 copies, just covering its guarantee. See D. Demarest to Weybright, May 11, 1951 (*NAL* Archives, "WF General Files"). On the negotiations for *Intruder in the Dust*, see *NAL* Archives, "Intruder in the Dust."

78. For the staff analysis, see Porter to Weybright, Oct. 19, 1949 (*NAL* Archives, "Pylon").

79. Porter to Weybright, Nov. 18, 1949 (*NAL* Archives, "The Wild Palms").

80. Weybright to Cerf, Jan. 16, 1950 (*NAL* Archives, "Knight's Gambit"). See also Haas to Faulkner, Jan. 23, 1950 (RH-FC: 10280-A, Box 2, Folder 19).

81. Demarest to Weybright and Enoch, Mar. 28., 1950 (*NAL* Archives, "Sartoris"). Demarest believed *Light in August* to be Faulkner's best book, but it was not available, having been already reprinted by New Directions and soon to be reissued in the Modern Library.

82. Weybright to Cerf, Sept. 19, 1950 (*NAL* Archives, "Pylon"). Of course, Weybright had been unable to decide for two years—so it was far from an urgent matter. Weybright lost his bet; *Pylon* sold 300,000 copies in the first year. (I assume he paid!)

83. Weybright to Cerf, May 21, 1951 (*NAL* Archives, "The Unvanquished"). Interestingly, just as in the case of *The Wild Palms,* Weybright was unable to find a copy of either *The Unvanquished* or *Sartoris* for the typesetter. He refused to pay $15.00 for a secondhand copy of *Sartoris* and borrowed one from Grosset and Dunlap instead. And when he asked Henry Maule at Random House to find two copies of *The Unvanquished,* Maule could not (*NAL* Archives, "The Unvanquished" and "Sartoris").

84. Enoch Interview. And Weybright explained:

> Faulkner's success in our editions did not surprise me. I expected it, just as I expected my early Mentor titles to succeed beyond the dreams of the sales department, who found them too highbrow to discuss with the wholesalers with whom they dealt in placing their titles in the racks at that time." [Weybright to author, Dec. 19, 1977]

85. *New York Times,* Nov. 16, 1950, 29. See also R. Haas to C. Poore, Nov. 16, 1950 (RH-FC: 10280-A, Box 2, Folder 19).

86. In 1942, for example, his royalty statement from Random House showed $300 earned for the year, representing sales of about 3,500 books. See R. Haas to Faulkner, Feb. 23, 1943 (RH-FC: 10280, Box 3, Folder 39).

CHAPTER THREE
The Origins of a New Literary Consensus

1. John T. Fain and Thomas D. Young, eds. *The Literary Correspondence of Donald Davidson and Allen Tate* (Athens, Ga., 1974), 363–64. See also Sidney Hook to Tate, Mar. 15, 1952 (Allen Tate Papers, Princeton University).

    Tate's speech on May 21 was adapted from his essay "The Man of Letters in the Modern World"; it was first given as a Phi Beta Kappa address at the University of Minnesota on May 1, 1952, and published in the *Hudson Review.*

2. For a recent overview of the postwar literary criticism and the origins and interconnections of its practitioners, see Grant Webster. *The Republic of Letters: A History of Postwar American Literary Opinion* (Baltimore, 1979); for the origins of the New Criticism, see especially the four chapters in part 2 "The New Critics as Tory Formalists," 63–209.

    For a discussion of modernism and southern literary culture, see Daniel J. Singal, *The War Within: From Victorian to Modernist Thought in the South, 1919–1945* (Chapel Hill, N.C., 1982); and for a social critique of the Southern Agrarians, see Alexander Karanikas, *Tillers of a Myth: Southern Agrarians as Social and Literary Critics* (Madison, Wisc., 1966).

3. Quoted in Singal, 219.

4. "The Profession of Letters in the South" (1935), quoted from Allen Tate, *Essays of Four Decades* (Chicago, 1968), 529.

5. See Ransom to Tate, Sept. 17 and late Sept. (nd), 1936 (Tate Papers). Faulkner, Hemingway, and Anderson were omitted from Ransom's list.

6. Tate to Davidson, Dec. 4, 1943, quoted from Fain and Young, *The Literary Correspondence of Donald Davidson and Allen Tate,* 328–29. For the rise of New Criticism, see Webster, 112 and passim.

7. Tate, "The Present Function of Criticism" (1940) in *Essays,* 198 and 202.

8. Tate, "The State of Letters," *SR* 52 (Autumn 1944): 609.

9. Ibid., 611.

10. Ibid., 613.

11. Alexander Bloom, *Prodigal Sons: The New York Intellectuals and Their World* (New York, 1986), 7. See all James B. Gilbert, *Writers and Partisans: A History of Literary Radicalism in America* (New York, 1968).

12. Bloom, 97.

13. William Phillips and Philip Rahv, "In Retrospect: Ten Years of *Partisan Review,*" in *The Partisan Reader: Ten Years of Partisan Review 1934–44*: An Anthology, ed. W. Phillips and P. Rahv (New York 1946), 679–88. For

a discussion of the role of the avant-garde and the cultural dissident, see William Barrett's review of *The Little Magazine: A History and a Bibliography,* entitled "Resistance," *PR* thirteen (Sept.–Oct. 1946): 479–88.

14. Philip Rahv, "Testament of a Homeless Radical," *PR* 12 (Summer 1945): 405.

15. See William Barrett, *The Truants: Adventures among the Intellectuals* (New York, 1982), 81–82 and 243–56. For the editors' response to letters about this editorial, see *PR* 13 (Nov.–Dec. 1946): 612–16. For a discussion of the evolution of the anti-Communist left to the liberal "vital center," see Bloom, passim, and Guilbaut, 195–205.

16. "Report to the Trustees' Committee on Humanities in American Institutions," Feb. 15, 1943 (Record Group [RG] 3, 911, Box 2, Folder 14, Rockefeller Foundation Archives [hereafter, RFA]). For a general overview of the Foundation activities, see the "Annual Reports" and Ray. B. Fosdick, *The Story of the Rockefeller Foundation,* (New York, 1952).

17. See "Humanities: Excerpt from 'Plans for the Future Work of the Rockefeller Foundation,' Nov. 1944 – used as basis for discussion at Trustees' meeting, April 4, 1945" (RG 3, 911, Box 2, Fld. 15, RFA). See also David H. Stevens, director of Humanities Division, Planning Memo, Sept. 2, 1944 (RG 3, 911, Box 1, Fld. 3, RFA).

18. See John Marshall, associate director of Humanities Division, Memo (on planned European trip), Sept. 1945 (RG 3, 911, Box 1, Fld. 3, RFA). At the April 1945 meeting, the trustees provided money to support the "Atlantic Awards in Literature" for younger British writers. Two grants totaling $71,000 were made to the University of Birmingham in 1945 and 1948, providing fellowships to 47 authors. For a summary of the program in support of British writers, see "The Encouragement of Creative Writing," Dec. 1950 (RG 3, 911, Box 1, Fld. 5, RFA).

   The Foundation was also a cosponsor with the Macmillan Company of Robert E. Spiller's symposium *Literary History of the United States* (New York, 1948), which was started in 1943. See "American Literary History" (RG 1.2, 200R, Box 273, Fld. 2610, RFA).

19. David H. Stevens, "The Humanities Program of the Rockefeller Foundation: 1942–1947," Apr. 15, 1948, 1–2, (RG 3, 911, Box 2, Fld. 14, RFA).

20. Ibid., 30. See also John Marshall, "Frontiers of the Mind," for his positive reaction to early drafts of the 1948 summary, Feb. 5, 1948 (RG 3, 911, Box 1, Fld. 4, RFA).

21. Stevens, 27.

22. Ibid., 28.

23. Ibid., 29, and John Marshall to David H. Stevens, Interoffice Memo, Oct. 6, 1943 (RG 3, 911, Box 1, Fld. 3, RFA).

24. See grant resolution prepared for Rockefeller Trustees, Jan. 10, 1944 [unless otherwise noted, material is found in RG 1.2.] (200R, Box 358, Fld. 3242, RFA). It was a one-time grant with no commitment for future funding.
25. John C. Ransom to David H. Stevens, Aug. 27, 1943 (200R, Box 358, Fld. 3242, RFA).
26. See Eliot to Tate, Nov. 11, 1942, Mar. 26, 1943, and April 16, 1945 (Tate Papers). And see Ransom to Tate, Nov. 22, 1943 (Tate Papers); see Tate to Stevens, Nov. 23, 1943, and Feb. 5, 1944 (Box 8, Blackmur Papers, Princeton University).

    Tate had also asked MacLeish to talk with Stevens about *Sewanee Review.* See MacLeish to Tate, Nov. 8, 1943, and Tate to MacLeish, Dec. 4 and 7, 1943 (Tate Papers). At the Library of Congress, in 1943, MacLeish negotiated a Rockefeller grant for a series of books on American civilization to be published by the Library.
27. For Blackmur's work in 1944 and his report, see "Literary Magazine Study, 1944" (200R, Box 243, Fld. 2906, RFA). The Foundation made a $12,000 grant to Princeton in 1943 to help begin revision of the university's program in the humanities. And in 1948, Blackmur was finally appointed to the English faculty, as part of a substantial Rockefeller grant to support seminars in literary criticism.
28. Richard P. Blackmur, "The Economy of the American Writer: Some Preliminary Notes," *SR* 53 (Spring 1945): 175–85.
29. Tate to Blackmur, Mar. 1944, Rahv to Blackmur, Apr. 20, 1944, and Schwartz to Blackmur, Nov. 28, 1943 (Box 8, Blackmur Papers).

    In 1943, according to James B. Gilbert, with Dwight MacDonald's departure, the magazine almost went bankrupt; Dwight and Nancy MacDonald had a family inheritance which they generously used to support *Partisan Review* until the political break in the summer of 1943 over the proper stance on the war (*Writers and Partisans,* 260–61). For MacDonald's resignation and the editorial response, see also *PR* 10 (July–Aug. 1943): 382–83. For a discussion of the *Review's* position on W.W. II and postwar anti-Stalinism, see also S.A. Longstaff, "*Partisan Review* and the Second World War," *Salmagundi,* no. 43 (Winter 1977): 108–29.

    For a sense of *Partisan Review's* cultural development during the war, see, for example, the 124-page, Summer 1944 issue, with contributions from Stafford, Koestler, Orwell, Blackmur, Gide, Greenberg, Richards, Rice, Barrett, Lowell, Chase, Schwartz, Mills, and Mizener.
30. See Blackmur to Marshall, May 4 and 14, 1945 ("Literary Magazine Study, 1945," 200R, Box 243, Fld. 2907, RFA).
31. See Ransom to Marshall, May 11, and Tate to Marshall June 7, 1945

(200R, Box 243, Fld. 2907, RFA). See Marshall's interview memo with Tate, May 15, and Marshall to Stevens, Interoffice Memo, May 16, 1945, entitled "Assistance to the Literary Magazines" (200R, Box 243, Fld. 2907, RFA). (Officers regularly wrote summaries of interviews in the form of memoranda for the Foundation records.)

32. Tate, "The State of Letters," *SR* 52 (Autumn 1944): 608–14. And for Tate's response to the Blackmur essay on the economic position of the American writer, see "The State of Letters," *SR* 53 (Summer 1945): 504–6.

33. William Phillips, "Middle-Aged Artists," *PR* 11 (Winter 1944): 119–20.

34. T.S. Eliot, "The Man of Letters and the Future of Europe," *SR* 53 (Summer 1945): 333–42. See also Tate to Eliot, Apr. 7, 1945 (Tate Papers).

35. Originally published in the *Virginia Quarterly Review* (Spring 1945), but quoted from Tate, *Essays of Four Decades,* 535–46.

36. Tate, *Essays of Four Decades,* 535–36.

37. Ibid., 545. This was also clearly reflected in Tate's work on the symposium dedicated to John Peale Bishop, *A Southern Vanguard.* With this collection he wanted to demonstrate the power of southern literature and to offer younger New Critics an influential forum. Unfortunately, except for Cowley's essay on Faulkner, the pieces by such second-generation critics as Robert W. Stallman, Herbert Marshall McLuhan, and Robert B. Heilman were a bit too derivative and pietistic. Both Tate and Gorham Munson, Prentice-Hall's editor for the volume, were disappointed that the collection was not as strong as they had hoped. See Munson to Tate, Aug. 7, 1946 (Tate Papers).

For the diffidence of the younger critics toward their mentors and toward southern culture, see McLuhan to Tate, June 11 and Sept. 13, 1945, written while McLuhan was preparing his essay for the volume. Interestingly, McLuhan in the second letter hailed Faulkner as a much more powerful postwar literary voice than Hemingway.

38. Tate, "Preface to Reactionary Essays on Poetry and Ideas" (1936), quoted from *Essays,* 611, and "Miss Emily and the Bibliographers" (1940), quoted from *Essays,* 154.

39. *American Harvest* (New York, 1942), 9–11.

40. *VQR* 18 (Spring 1942): 214–15.

41. Alfred Kazin, *On Native Grounds: An Interpretation of Modern American Prose Literature,* unabridged (1942; New York, 1970), 466–67.

42. Ibid., 467.

43. Ibid., 382 and 465.

44. Ibid., 457.

45. Ibid.

46. Delmore Schwartz, "The Fiction of William Faulkner," in *Selected Essays*

of Delmore Schwartz, ed. Donald A. Dike and David H. Zucker (Chicago, 1970), 277.

47. Ibid., 286.

CHAPTER FOUR
The Retreat from Radicalism and Literary Naturalism

1. "Introduction: Faulkner: Past and Future," in *Faulkner,* 10.
2. Malcolm Cowley, *And I Worked at the Writer's Trade: Chapters of Literary History, 1918–1978* (New York, 1978), 159.
3. Lawrence H. Schwartz, *Marxism and Culture: The CPUSA and Aesthetics in the 1930s* (Port Washington, NY, 1981), 51 and passim.
4. Malcolm Cowley, *Exile's Return: A Literary Odyssey of the 1920s* (New York, 1934), 294–303.
5. Edmund Wilson to Malcolm Cowley, Oct. 20, 1938, from *Edmund Wilson: Letters On Literature and Politics, 1912–1972,* ed. Elena Wilson (New York, 1977), 310. Cowley, *And I Worked,* 155.
6. Malcolm Cowley to Kenneth Burke, Dec. 17, 1940, quoted in David E. Shi, *Matthew Josephson, Bourgeois Bohemian* (New Haven, 1981), 207. (See also 14, below.)
7. Cowley, *And I Worked,* 158. For long quotes from his letter of resignation, see "In Memoriam," *New Republic* 103 (Aug. 12, 1940): 219–20, the League's response, and Cowley's rejoinder, *New Republic* 103 (Aug. 26, 1940): 279–80. For a revisionist analysis of left-wing cultural politics in the 1930s, see Schwartz, *Marxism and Culture.*

    Cowley's political affiliations during the 1930s are outlined in detail in letters to Robert Heilman (a second-generation New Critic and an Allen Tate disciple), English Department, University of Washington: Nov. 8, 1948 and Nov. 21, 1949 (Cowley Papers). Cowley had been invited to teach at the university and wanted Heilman to know of his political background.
8. *New Republic* 112 (Jan. 22, 1945): 121.
9. Ibid., 122.
10. *New Republic* 112 (Feb. 5, 1945): 180.
11. Ibid., 180.
12. Cowley, "Spender, Auden and After," *New Republic* 107 (Oct. 5, 1942): 419. See also Cowley, "Success Story: 1930–39," *New Republic* 107 (July 6, 1942): 25–26; Cowley, "Reading In Wartime," *New Republic* 107 (Sept. 14, 1942): 361; and Cowley to Stanley P. Young, Apr. 11, 1944 (Cowley Papers).

13. Cowley, *A Second Flowering: Works and Days of the Lost Generation* (New York, 1973), ix.
14. For a long discussion of his break with the radical movement and his future literary plans, see Cowley to Burke, Dec. 17, 1940 (Cowley Papers). For an assessment of Cowley's analysis of *his* generation, see Lewis P. Simpson, "Malcolm Cowley and the American Writer," *SR* 84 (Spring 1976): 221–47—a review of Cowley's *A Second Flowering*.
15. Cowley, *Faulkner-Cowley File*, 6.
16. Cowley to Stanley P. Young, Apr. 11, 1944, and Young to Cowley, Apr. 17, 1944 (Cowley Papers). The contract stipulated that Cowley had to devote his full-time efforts to research and writing; so after fifteen years with the *New Republic,* he resigned as of June 4, 1944. He was permitted to free-lance but had to pay back to the foundation 20% of those fees. See Cowley to Mary Mellon, June 3, 1944 (Cowley Papers). For a statement of his planned Faulkner study, see Cowley to Mary Mellon, Aug. 18, 1944 (Cowley Papers).
17. Cowley did make minor changes in this essay to reflect this criticism, but the influence of Tate and Gordon is more clearly seen in the essay that became the introduction to the *Portable.* See several letters not dated (probably 1944 or early 1945) from Gordon to Cowley. See also Tate to Cowley, Feb. 9, March 7, April 11, and May 7, 1945 (Cowley Papers). For earlier discussions about art, see Tate to Cowley, May 9, Dec. 12 and 17, 1934, and Apr. 26, 1936 (Cowley Papers).
18. For a succinct analysis of Cowley's view of the importance of myth and psychology, see Cowley to Burke, Dec. 9, 1948 (Cowley Papers).
19. "Not Men: A Natural History of American Naturalism," *KR* 9 (Summer 1947): 431.
20. Ibid., 429.
21. Ibid., 428 and 434–35.
22. *Exile's Return,* rev. ed. (New York, 1951), 289 and 295.
23. Malcolm Cowley, *The Literary Situation* (New York, 1954), 74.
24. Ibid., 87.
25. Ibid., 88.

CHAPTER FIVE
Forging a Postwar Aesthetic

1. John Marshall to David H. Stevens, "Grants to American Literary Magazines" (suggestions for action), Interoffice Memo, July 17, 1946; and John

Marshall to Blackmur, July 17, 1946 (including a copy of the memo to Stevens and other enclosures); and Blackmur to Marshall, Aug. 16, 1946 (Blackmur Papers, Box 7). For discussions about grants to literature, earlier in the year, see Delmore Schwartz to Blackmur, Feb. 10, Marshall to Schwartz, Mar. 4, and Schwartz to Blackmur, n.d. (probably mid-March), 1946 (Blackmur Papers, Box 8).

2. Stevens wrote a brief commentary in the margins of Blackmur's letter of Aug. 16 and discussed his doubts with Marshall on Aug. 21; Marshall responded in a handwritten note on Aug. 22 ("Literary Magazine Study, 1946," 200R, Box 243, Fld. 2908, RFA).

3. John Marshall, "Possible RF Assistance to the So-called Literary Magazines," Sept. 11, 1946 (Blackmur Papers, Box 7).

4. John Marshall, "A Suggested Procedure for the Award of Literary Fellowships in the United States," Sept. 11, 1946 (Blackmur Papers, Box 7).

5. See John Marshall, Interview Memo, Sept. 18, 1946; David Stevens, Interview Memo with Ransom, Aug. 13, 1946; and John Marshall to Blackmur, Oct. 15, 1946 (setting up final arrangements for the small panel to meet on Oct. 24 (Blackmur Papers Box 7).

6. All of the material concerning the activities of the Blackmur, Cowley, Trilling panel and responses from the larger group may be found in "Literary Magazine Study, 1946" (200R, Box 243, Fld. 2908, RFA).

Wilson's response is quoted from *Edmund Wilson: Letters On Literature and Politics, 1912–1972,* ed. Elena Wilson (New York, 1977), 443. For some time Wilson had felt that *Kenyon Review* was dull and sterile; perhaps his anger was the result of Ransom's refusal to publish his work. See Wilson to Tate, Sept. 28, 1943 (Tate Papers).

7. Lionel Trilling, "Introduction," *The Partisan Reader,* ix–xvi.

8. William Phillips and Philip Rahv, "In Retrospect: Ten Years of the *Partisan Review,*" in ibid., 679–88.

9. *PR* 11 (Spring 1944): 151.

10. See Marshall to Stevens, Interoffice Memo, Jan. 9, 1947, "Literary Magazine Study (1947–48," 200R, Box 243, Fld. 2909, RFA).

11. Marshall to Stevens, Jan. 9, 1947 (Ibid.).

12. Tate wrote to his successor at *Sewanee Review,* John Palmer, asking for a careful report to the Foundation. Tate wanted aid for the three journals, but he also wanted to see the Foundation set a new precedent for supporting such journals that would lead to even more generous action in the future. See Tate to Palmer, Jan. 28, 1947 (Tate Papers).

In Ransom's application there was also the request to extend the 1944 grant-in-aid, which was to expire this year. Ransom was pleased that the Foundation would subsidize rates to contributors, but he wanted more.

Ransom repeated his belief that journals dedicated to the highest standards required institutional support. He hinted that without additional support *Kenyon Review* might not survive. Marshall responded immediately. He made it clear that the Foundation would never take on the role as the primary benefactor of such journals, and that Ransom would have to get Gordon Chalmers, Kenyon College president, to guarantee the continuation of the journal. See Ransom to Marshall, Jan. 27, and Marshall to Ransom, Jan. 29, 1947 ("Kenyon Review and Kenyon College," 200R, Box 358, Fld. 3243, RFA). See also Ransom to Tate, Jan. 3, 1947 (Tate Papers).

13. See formal grant resolution in support of *Kenyon Review* and Marshall's analysis of Apr. 2, 1947; see also Marshall to Ransom, Apr. 3, 1947, in "Kenyon Review and Kenyon College" (200R, Box 358, Flds. 3242 and 3243, RFA).

14. "Art and Dogma," *New Republic,* Nov. 11, 1946, 634–36.

    Rahv and Phillips were extremely sensitive to this criticism, especially coming just when the entire matter of Foundation support was being decided; see their strident response to Schorer, *PR* 14 (Jan.–Feb. 1947): 106–8.

15. See Marshall to Stevens, Jan. 9, 1947 (with four pages of notes, n.d.), Trilling to Marshall, Mar. 25, 1947; Marshall to Trilling, Apr. 10, 1947; Stevens to Walter Stewart, Apr. 21, 1947; Stevens to Trilling, Apr. 29, 1947; and Marshall to Trilling, Jan. 19, 1948 ("Literary magazine Study, 1947–48, 200R, Box 243, Fld. 2909, RFA). The problem of *Partisan Review's* tax status was an issue, but probably not the primary difficulty with respect to the declination. See also 7, above.

16. See James B. Gilbert, *Writers and Partisans,* 274; Barrett, *The Truants,* 144–45; and "Angel with a Red Beard," *Time,* June 30, 1947, 64. Dowling began to withdraw support in 1950, and *Partisan Review* was forced to switch back to a bimonthly, and, by 1952, he ended his donations entirely.

17. See Palmer to Stevens, July 24, 1947, in "Sewanee Review, 1943–50" (200R, Box 416, Fld. 3587, RFA). Tate provided literary, financial, and political guidance to his successors as editor, including Palmer and then Monroe K. Spears. See also the Tate/Palmer and Tate/Spears correspondence in the Tate Papers.

18. See the resolution in support of the grant, Jan. 16, 1948, in "Sewanee Review, 1943–50" (200R, Box 416, Fld. 3587, RFA).

19. See John Marshall, Interview Memo, Jan. 15, 1947, "Princeton: Literary Criticism, 1947–49" (200R, Box 407, Fld. 3511, RFA). The new director of the Institute was, of course, Robert Oppenheimer, who was extremely interested in contemporary literature.

20. See "The Kenyon School of Criticism: A Plan for an Education Project in

the Humanities" ("Kenyon Review and Kenyon College," 200R, Box 358, Fld. 3242 and 3243, RFA).

21. Literary criticism in these terms was essentially an all-male institution. The rampant sexism was simply part of the elitism that infused literary criticism in the 1940s and 1950s. The plan for the school was more liberal; it would permit women students.

22. See Ransom to Marshall, Aug. 13, 1947. The development of Bentley's career was particularly rewarding because when he arrived from England he was, according to Ransom, primarily interested in journalism and "left-ish" politics. Ransom said that Bentley had been convinced to turn his full energy away from politics to literature, making valuable contributions to *Kenyon Review*. For a summary of grants, see Gordon Chalmers to Stevens, Dec. 22, 1948, which includes Ransom's observations about Bentley and others "Kenyon Review and Kenyon College" (200R, Box 358, Fld. 3243, RFA).

23. D'Arms to Stevens, Interoffice Memo, July 31, 1947, and Marshall to Stevens Aug. 22, 1947, (Fld. 3243).

24. Resolution in support of Kenyon School of English Studies, Oct. 17, 1947 (200R, Box 359, Fld. 3248, RFA).

Ransom sent Tate complete copies of all materials with respect to the creation of the Kenyon School. See Tate Papers, "Kenyon College and Kenyon Review" (school's prospectus in mimeographed form dated Nov. 15, 1947), and also the Tate/Ransom correspondence.

25. *SR* 55 (Autumn 1947): 610–26. For details of the Wellek and Warren grant, see RG 1.1, 200, Box 285, Flds. 3404–06, RFA.

26. "A Burden For Critics," *HR* 1 (Summer 1948): 173, 177–80, and 184. For reactions by Tate and Ransom see their correspondence for this period (Tate Papers).

27. See an excerpt of an Interview Memo, Marshall and Blackmur at Princeton, July 1948, "Princeton: Literary Criticism, 1947–49" (200R, Box 407, Fld. 3511, RFA). Marshall thought the piece was extremely important, and circulated the essay to the other Humanities officers. See Marshall's interview memo with Blackmur, Oct. 8, 1948, concerning appointments for Kenneth Burke and T.S. Eliot at the IAS.

It should also be noted that in November 1947, the new director of the Institute, Robert Oppenheimer, appointed his lifelong friend, Francis Fergusson, to a two-year general membership. As Blackmur wrote to Marshall, he was always pleased when such "coincidences" worked out so well; see Blackmur to Marshall, Nov. 22, 1947.

28. See Blackmur's "A Project for Literary Studies at Princeton University and the Institute for Advanced Study," Nov. 15, 1948, in "Princeton University:

Literary Criticism, 1947–49." See also Marshall's Interview Memo with Blackmur, Oct. 8, 1948.

29. Stevens to Dodds, Dec. 3, 1948; D'Arms, Interview Memo with Dodds, Dec. 21, 1948; Dodds to D'Arms (formal request to the Foundation). Feb. 3, 1949; D'Arms, Interview Memo, Feb. 4, 1949; Marshall, Interview with Fergusson, Feb. 10, 1949; see "Princeton University: Literary Criticism, 1947–49."

30. See grant resolution for support of an experiment in literary criticism, Feb. 18, 1949, "Princeton University: Literary Criticism, 1947–49."

See also Fergusson to Marshall, May 23, 1949; D'Arms, Interview Memo with Fergusson, Sept. 12, 1949; and D'Arms to Fergusson, Dec. 1, 1949 ("Princeton University: Literary Criticism, 1947–49"). For the evaluation of the program see material in "Princeton University: Literary Criticism, 1950–51, and 1952–57" (200R, Box 407, Flds. 3512 and 3513, RFA). Much of this evaluation was written by Robert Fitzgerald; see his recently published discussion of the seminars, *Enlarging the Change* (Boston, 1984).

31. For declination of further aid to the Kenyon School of English, see Marshall to Chalmers, Mar. 13, 1950, and Ransom to Marshall, Apr. 5, 1950, "Kenyon Review and Kenyon College" (200R, Box 359, Fld. 3249, RFA). After the Kenyon decision, Marshall met with Fergusson and Blackmur at Princeton to discuss the direction of the Princeton seminars. Marshall reported that both men agreed with the foundation action to cancel continued money for Kenyon. See Marshall, Interview Memo, Mar. 23, 1950, "Princeton University: Literary Criticism, 1950–51." For an earlier evaluation of the School see interview memos of Marshall and D'Arms, who met with Ransom, Trilling, Matthiessen, Chalmers, and Charles Coffin (dean of the Kenyon School) on Nov. 30, 1949.

When it was clear that the Foundation would not continue to support the School and that a move to Indiana was necessary, Coffin asked Tate, in the spring of 1950 to approach the Bollingen Foundation. Tate tried, but was refused. See Coffin to Tate, Apr. 20, 1950, and Tate to Coffin, May 1, 1950, and "Indiana University" (Tate Papers).

Ransom transplanted the School to Indiana and continued to have a very balanced faculty of New Critics and New York intellectuals: Ransom, Trilling, Rahv, Austin Warren, and Tate were the Senior Fellows, supported by Arvin, Bentley, Blackmur, Brooks, Burke, Chase, Ellmann, Empson, Fergusson, Fiedler, R. Fitzgerald, Frye, Howe, Jarrell, Kazin, Lewis, Lowell, Mizener, Read, Schorer, Schwartz, Shapiro, Spender, N. Stallknecht, Unger, Warren, Wellek, H. Whitehall, Winters, and Zabel.

See also Ransom to Tate, Sept. 6, 1950 (Tate Papers), discussing the

Kenyon School, and the important *Kenyon Review* project for 1950-51, "My Credo: A Symposium of Critics." Ransom also reported a new, exclusive arrangement with Random House; the company would give *Kenyon Review* $1,000 per year to inform Random House of young writers and new manuscripts (see below, ch. 7, 8). Ransom thought that the credos might make an interesting book.

32. See "Princeton University: Literary Criticism, 1952-57," particularly: D'Arms, Interview Memo with Walter S. Stewart, Aug. 19, 1951; Dodds to Marshall, Jan. 9, 1952; Fahs to Dodds, Feb. 7, and Dodds to Fahs, Feb. 21, 1952; and D'Arms to Fahs, Interoffice Memo, Mar. 10, 1952 (200R, Box 407, Fld. 3512, RFA).

    See also the Resolution in support of the Princeton grant, Apr. 2, 1952 (Fld. 3512).

33. For a summary of the program to the journals, and the shift to fellowships, see "Decentralized Awards Of Literary Fellowships," (memorandum for discussion at Sept. 1955 meeting of RF Executive Committee)—copy in "Partisan Review, 1954-61" (200R, Box 401, Fld. 3465, RFA); and "Literature and the Little Magazines," Nov. 1955—copy in "Sewanee Review, 1954-58" (200R, Box 416, Fld. 3588, RFA). For correspondence between officers and editors, see also "Kenyon Review, 1952-58" (Flds. 3245-47) and "Sewanee Review, 1951-58" (Flds. 3588 and 3589).

    Grant Resolution in support of *Kenyon Review,* June 20, 1952, "Kenyon Review" (200R, Box 358, Fld. 3242). See also Ransom to Chalmers, Jan. 22, 1952, and D'Arms to Chalmers, May 26, 1952 (Fld. 3242).

34. See correspondence between Spears and Fahs in the autumn of 1952, and the grant resolution, Jan. 16, 1953, "Sewanee Review, 1951-53" (200R, Box 416, Fld. 3588, RFA).

    The Foundation also made a fellowship grant for three years to the State University of Iowa for $40,000. When Tate, who had helped Spears prepare the *Sewanee Review* proposal, learned of the Iowa grant, he wrote to Marshall asking for money to support a program at his school, University of Minnesota. He said it was a small but strong program in writing, and argued that too many untalented young people were being encouraged to become writers. See Tate to Marshall Nov. 8, 1952, and Fahs (for Marshall) to Tate, Nov. 14, 1952 (saying no money available for graduate programs such as Minnesota's) (Fld. 3588). Iowa was supported because its writers' workshop program under Paul Engle had been in existence for a dozen years and had a history as an active center for creative writing.

35. See Marshal, Interview Memo, Nov. 16, 1950. At the beginning of 1951, Rahv again petitioned for money, and Marshall explained that, while *Partisan Review* was now technically eligible for support as a tax exempt corpo-

ration, nothing could be done until the grants to *Kenyon Review* and *Sewanee Review* were evaluated. See Marshall to Rahv, Jan. 8, 1951, "Partisan Review" (200R, Box 401, Fld. 3464, RFA).

36. See excerpts from the diaries of Fahs, Oct. 9, 1952, and Marshall, Nov. 5, 1952 (MacLeish, according to Marshall, was very much opposed to Foundation support for *Partisan Review* because he still saw it as too narrow and parochial). Marshall's analysis of *Partisan Review* was dated Jan. 10, 1953 (Fld. 3464).

37. See Marshall's analysis of Jan. 10, and Marshall to Fahs, Jan. 21, 1953 (Fld. 3464).

38. This material is located in the "Program and Policy" files of the Foundation's archives under "National Security" headings. See in particular "Officer procedures for avoiding grants to subversive individuals," Jan. 20, 1953; "Suggestions concerning policy for dealing with subversives or potential subversives in RF recommendations," Jan. 27, 1953; and Dean Rusk to Dr. Robert Waterson, Mar. 1, 1954 (RG 3, 900, Box 25, Fld. 200, RFA).

39. Rahv and Phillips, "The Problem of Democratic Culture and the Granting of Fellowships" ("Partisan Review," 200R, Box 401, Fld. 3464, RFA).

40. "Foreword" to *The New Partisan Reader* (New York, 1953), vi–vii. Rahv and Phillips were greatly influenced in preparing the grant proposal by Trilling's *Liberal Imagination,* especially his analysis of the separation between high culture and liberal politics, and by Jacques Barzun's provocative essay about institutional support for artists and writers, "Artist Against Society: Some Articles of War, *PR* 19 (Jan.–Feb. 1952): 60–77, and reprinted in the anthology (486–501).

41. See "Partisan Review," and see also Rusk to Phillips, Dec. 9, 1953 (200R, Box 401, Fld. 3464).

   In the fall of 1953, the officers also considered establishing a fellowship program through the National Institute of Arts and Letters, but the organization was listed in the "Guide to Subversive Organizations and Publications" of the House Committee of Un-American Activities. Also certain of the Institute's officer's had been cited. The officers did not proceed with this proposal. See "Decentralized Awards of Literary Fellowships," Sept. 1955.

42. See Marshall to Fahs, June 21, 1955, Interoffice Memo, "RF aid to contemporary literature in the United States" (RG 3, 911, Box 1, Fld. 7, RFA). See also summaries of fellowships, lists of awards, and bibliographies of fellows in "Decentralized Awards of Literary Fellowships." For a list of awards through 1958, see summary in "Hudson Review" (200R, Box 348, Fld. 3174. RFA). And for an overview of the entire program, see Fahs,

"Fiction in RF Humanities Program (Draft Memorandum for Staff Discussion)," Mar. 9, 1959 (RG 3, 911, Box 1, Fld. 8, RFA).

By 1957, the politics of Rahv and Phillips was so sanitized and their work on behalf of American Cold War culture so clear, the Foundation asked them to participate in a new humanities program, "Intercultural Understanding." The Foundation was planning to send literary men around the world to meet with writers, critics, and intellectuals in Europe, Eastern Europe, and the Far East. The travel grants to Rahv and Phillips were also tied to meetings sponsored by the Congress for Cultural Freedom. See "Partisan Review, Visits 1956–60" (200R, Box 401, Fld. 3466, RFA).

The entire fellowship program ended in 1958, when the officers decided that the publishing environment for fiction had improved. Also there had been some mild criticism of the fellowship program because the writers selected were too similar—with little support for the "wilder" literary figures of the 1950s. For discussion of the Foundation decision not to continue the fellowship program, see Ransom to Marshall, Apr. 17, 1958, in "Kenyon College and Kenyon Review" (200R, Box 359, Fld. 3247, RFA). (This 16-page letter provides an excellent overview of the entire relationship between the Foundation and the literary reviews.) For the Foundation position, see Marshall to Monroe K. Spears, Mar. 18 1958, and Spears's correspondence to Tate about the declination (Tate Papers).

And finally, in November 1958, when Rahv notified the Foundation that *Partisan Review* had shifted publishers to the American Committee for Cultural Freedom (to protect its tax exempt status), Marshall informed the editor that the Foundation could not move the third year of fellowships to a new publisher. He also told Rahv that there was no sense to reapply under ACCF, because the program would not be renewed to any of the journals. See Rahv to Marshall, Nov. 6, 1958, and Marshall to Rahv, Nov. 25, 1958, "Partisan Review" (200R, Box 401, Fld. 3465, RFA). And for a summary of support to writers, see Fahs, "Fiction in the RF Humanities Program (Draft Memorandum for Staff Discussion)," Mar. 9, 1959 (RG 3, 911, Box 1, Fld. 8, RFA).

43. Charles B. Fahs, "Defining a Humanities Program" (2nd tentative draft), Feb. 15, 1950, 2 and 7 (RG3, 911, Box 1, Fld. 5, RFA).

44. Ibid., 12–13. Fahs draft was presented formally, and virtually unchanged, as "The Program in the Humanities," Feb. 1951 (RG3, 911, Box 2, Fld. 15, RFA).

45. *Prodigal Sons,* 297. "The State of American Writing, 1948: A Symposium," *PR* 15 (Aug. 1948): 871 and 876.

46. *PR* 19 (May–June 1952): 426.

47. *PR* 19 (Mar.–Apr. 1952): 284.
48. Alfred Kazin, "Faulkner's Vision of Human Integrity," *Harvard Advocate* 135 (Nov. 1951): 33. This was a special Faulkner issue to commemorate the Nobel Prize.

CHAPTER SIX
The Triumph of the New Literary Consensus

 1. "The State of Letters: William Faulkner, 1897–1962," *SR* 71 (Jan.–Mar. 1963): 160–64. See also "A Southern Mode of Imagination," in *Essays of Four Decades*, 577–92, and "The Novel in the American South," *New Statesman* 57 (June 13, 1959): 831–32. The "fact" of Faulkner's genius is part of all of the standard biographies and secondary sources.
 2. Tate to Donald Davidson, Dec. 12, 1929, Fain and Young 243–45.
      It is worth noting that in the early 1930s, Tate worked closely with Stark Young to push Ellen Glasgow's reputation. See Tate to Glasgow and Young, 1932–34 (Tate Papers). In fact, Young told Tate that he helped Glasgow write some of the prefaces to the recently released collection of her work, Young to Tate, n.d., 1934 (Tate Papers).
 3. *VQR* 23 (Summer 1947): 423–38. In the same issue, see also Vincent Hopper, "Faulkner's Paradise Lost," 405–20. This was a derivative and uninteresting essay but, in the 1940s, the first on Faulkner in *VQR*.
 4. Peyre, 428.
 5. Ibid., 432.
 6. Ibid., 423.
 7. *NYTBR*, June 22, 1947, 29.
 8. *The Age of the American Novel: The Film Aesthetic of Fiction between the Two Wars*, trans. Eleanor Hochman (New York, 1972), 101. First published in 1948, Magny's analysis was an attempt to explain the modern novel in relation to cinema. For background, see Malraux's first postwar interview on new directions in the arts, where he predicted the emergence of postwar "moralist" fiction: "An Interview With Malraux," *Horizon* 12 (Oct. 1945): 236–42.
      For another early report on the status of American writing in Europe, see Robert Pick, "Old-World Views on New-World Writing," *SRL*, Aug. 20, 1949, 7 ff. And for an overview, see Thelma M. Smith and Ward L. Miner, *Transatlantic Migrations* (Durham, N.C., 1955).
 9. Magny, *Age of the American Novel*, 230.
10. Ibid., 186–87 and 54–56.

11. Ibid., 187. Trilling's idea was fully developed in "Reality in America," the lead essay in his influential *The Liberal Imagination*. Part 1 was originally published in *PR* (Feb. 1940) and part 2 in the *Nation* (Apr. 20, 1946).

12. James D. Wilkinson, *Intellectual Resistance In Europe* (Cambridge, Mass., 1981), 268–69 and 277.

13. Ibid., 1. In the postwar era of real, active, and effective anti-Communist crusading, such accommodation to cultural traditionalism merely accelerated the dominance of American art in the latter half of the 1940s. For example, see Stephen Spender, "We Can Win the Battle for the Mind of Europe," *New York Times Magazine*, Apr. 25, 1948, 15 ff.

14. For discussions of "liberal" intellectuals during the Cold War, see Bloom, *Prodigal Sons,* and Richard H. Pells, *The Liberal Mind in a Conservative Age: American Intellectuals in the 1940s and 1950s* (New York, 1985).

15. Faulkner to Harold Ober, Feb. 1, 1948. *Letters,* 262.

16. Faulkner to Robert Haas, Apr. 20, 1948, *Letters,* 266. Faulkner's idea for this novel was one he had been thinking about for eight years, a "blood and thunder" mystery story, the kind of book that the novelist always thought could find an audience: "original in that the solver is a negro, himself in jail for the murder and is about to be lynched, solves murder in self-defense" (Faulkner to Haas, Apr. 28, and June 7, 1940, *Letters,* 121–22 and 128). But it was also tied to an idea for another book (*The Reivers*), a Huck Finn story, as he called it, about a boy who grows up, almost overnight, to learn "courage and honor and generosity and pride and pity" (Faulkner to Haas, May 3, 1940, *Letters,* 124).

17. For the publishing history of *Intruder,* see ch. 2. For analyses of *Intruder* and its place in Faulkner's career, see Eric J. Sundquist, *Faulkner: The House Divided* (Baltimore, 1983), Walter Taylor, *Faulkner's Search for a South* (1983), and David Minter, *William Faulkner* (Baltimore, 1980).

And Bosley Crowther, in the *New York Times* called the film version of the novel one of the year's "pre-eminent" pictures and "one of the great cinema dramas of our time."

> For here, at last is a picture that slashes right down to the core of the complex of racial resentments and social discussion in the South—which cosmically mocks the hollow pretense of 'white supremacy'—and does it in terms of visual action and realistic drama at its best. [Nov. 23, 1949]

18. Harvey Breit, "Faulkner after Eight Years," *NYTBR*, Sept. 26, 1948, 4.

19. Introduction to Maxwell Geismar, "Ex-Aristocrat's Emotional Experience," *SRL*, Sept. 25, 1948, 8. Geismar's review is far more supportive

than his earlier commentaries on the novelist, but he was still highly critical of Faulkner's southern nationalism. See also Charles Glicksberg, who continued to read Faulkner as a reactionary naturalist: "The World of William Faulkner"; a review of *Intruder* in *Arizona Quarterly* 5 (Spring 1949): 46–58 and 85–88; and "William Faulkner and the Negro Problem," *Phylon* 10 (Spring 1949): 153–60.

20. Edmund Wilson, "William Faulkner's Reply to the Civil Rights Program," *New Yorker,* Oct. 23, 1948, 120 ff.

21. Malcolm Cowley, "William Faulkner's Nation," *New Republic* 119 (Oct. 18, 1948): 21–22, and Elizabeth Hardwick, "Faulkner and the South Today," *PR* 15 (Oct. 1948): 1130–35. Hardwick acknowledged Faulkner's literary genius but claimed that he misunderstood the contemporary South.

22. Andrew Lytle, "Regeneration for the Man," *SR* 57 (Winter 1949): 120–27. For another pietistic review, see Eudora Welty, "In Yoknapatawpha," *HR* 1 (Winter 1949): 596–98—the inaugural issue of the journal.

23. Paolo Milano, "Faulkner in Crisis," *Nation* 167 (Oct. 30, 1948): 496–97. Also Milano was a frequent participant in R.P. Blackmur's colloquia at Princeton.

24. Robert Hillyer, "Treason's Strange Fruit: The Case of Ezra Pound and the Bollingen Award," *SRL,* June 11, 1949, 11. And Editorial, *SRL,* June 11, 1949, 21.

25. Robert Hillyer, "Poetry's New Priesthood," *SRL,* June 18, 1949, 38.

26. Margaret Marshall, " 'The Saturday Review of Literature' Unfair to Literature," *Nation,* Dec. 17, 1949, 598. The letter of protest published with Marshall's commentary (599).

    For a summary of the plans to issue the letter and publish a response to Hillyer and the *SRL* see Tate to Fellows, Sept. 23, 1949 (Tate Papers). These plans were organized during the weekend meeting in mid-September with Leonie Adams, Louise Bogan, Karl Shapiro, Tate, and Willard Thorp. Included were outlines for the pamphlet and Shapiro's first draft of the protest letter.

27. See Barrett to John Berryman, Oct. 25; John Dos Passos to Tate, Oct. 26; Tate to Julien Boyd, librarian of Princeton University, Oct. 31; Van Wyck Brooks to Tate, Nov. 1, and Tate to Brooks, Nov. 12; Tate to MacLeish, Feb. 17, and Edmund Wilson to Tate, Apr. 27, 1950 (Tate Papers). See also Ernest Hemingway to Harvey Breit, July 9, 1950, in *Ernest Hemingway: Selected Letters,* 701–3.

    In the autumn of 1949, Tate and Huntington Cairns, secretary-treasurer of the National Gallery of Art, legal advisor to the Bollingen Foundation, and a member of its board of trustees, were negotiating on two matters. First, they were arranging to continue the poetry prize at Yale University, and, second, they were discussing the renewal of a grant to *Poetry,* which was necessary to prevent the demise of the journal.

28. Tate tried to get several publishers to sign the letter of protest, and in the exchange of correspondence with several he learned that Smith and Cousins had used the controversy to build circulation. This was also corroborated by Malcolm Cowley. See William Sloane, William Sloane Associates, Inc., to A. Tate, Oct. 20 and 26, 1949, Tate to Sloane, Oct. 22, see Tate to Lambert Davis, director of the University of North Carolina Press, Oct. 28, 1949; and Tate to Robert N. Linscott, senior editor, Random House, Oct. 28, 1949 (Tate Papers).

   Interestingly, Bennett Cerf, Faulkner's publisher, participated in the early rounds of the debate over Pound. See Robert A. Corrigan, *"What's My Line:* Bennett Cerf, Ezra Pound and the *American* Poet," *American Quarterly* 24 (Mar. 1972): 101–13.

29. Robert A. Corrigan, "Ezra Pound and the Bollingen Prize Controversy," in *The Forties: Fiction, Poetry, Drama,* ed. Warren French (Deland, Florida, 1969), 294.

30. Frank A. Ninkovitch, "The New Criticism and Cold War America," *Southern Quarterly* 20 (Fall 1981): 1–24.

31. See L. Adams to A. Tate, Jan. 1949 (probably January 28), and Tate to Adams, Jan. 31, 1949. Throughout the year, correspondence with the principals and his close literary colleagues indicated that Tate was leading a national campaign. For example, John Palmer, his successor as editor of *Sewanee Review,* asked how he could help and submitted a draft letter to Tate to check over and approve (Palmer to Tate, Sept. 29, 1949); and Phillip B. Rice, managing editor of *Kenyon Review,* wrote to approve of Tate's work in leading the offensive against Hillyer (Rice to Tate, Oct. 25, 1949). See also Cleanth Brooks to Tate May, and Aug. 5 1949; Eliot to Tate Oct. 7, 1949; and Mark Schorer to Tate, Oct. 14, 1949 (Tate Papers).

32. It is safe to say that Tate modeled his professional literary life on Eliot's. However, he saw Eliot as more than a mentor. When he wrote to congratulate Eliot on the Nobel Prize in November 1948, Tate said that Eliot was truly a moral example of the way an honorable man and artistic genius ought to conduct his life. For this Tate was thankful, but he also saw Eliot as mentor and literary father (Tate to Eliot, Nov. 5, 1948, [Tate Papers]). As Tate's own reputation and influence expanded, he would, of course, receive similar declarations of filial affection from his American disciples.

   As background to the process of awarding poetry prizes, there are documents in the Tate Papers regarding the award of the Harriet Monroe Poetry Prize in 1944 through the University of Chicago. The award was to be given to an American poet, with preference to modernists. Morton D.

Zabel, Allen Tate, and Louise Bogan served as the committee, with Zabel as chairman. Zabel offered two lists. First he presented older poets: Marianne Moore, Wallace Stevens, or Leonie Adams; then he suggested possible younger poets: Robert Penn Warren, John Bishop, Horace Gregory, Delmore Schwartz, Karl Shapiro, Randall Jarrell, and possibly James Agee. The committee decided on Marianne Moore, but Tate raised the issue of T.S. Eliot. Tate thought that Eliot deserved the award for *Four Quarters,* but Zabel and Bogan both felt that Eliot did not qualify because the terms of the award specified an "American" poet. Also Zabel thought that this award was, in a certain sense, beneath Eliot; he should be given the Nobel Prize. Finally, it should be noted that Pound, already indicted, was *not* even considered. See Zabel to Tate, early April, May 2, and 4, 1944; and Tate to Zabel, Apr. 19 and May 24 (Tate Papers).

33. Ernest Hemingway to Archibald MacLeish (Apr. 4 May 5, and Aug. 10, 1943), to Allen Tate Aug. 31, 1943), and to Malcolm Cowley Nov. 14, 1945) from *Ernest Hemingway: Selected Letters, 1917–1961,* 544–45, 548–51, and 605. On protecting Pound, see also letters from Tate to Eliot, 1943 to 1946, Tate to John Bishop (before his death in 1944), John Crowe Ransom, and Richard P. Blackmur (Tate Papers and Richard P. Blackmur Papers, Princeton University). On the question of Pound's sanity, see Julian Cornell to Tate and Tate to Cornell, Dec. 7 and 12, 1945 (Tate Papers).

    Delmore Schwartz in a letter to Blackmur said that he had raised the issue at *Partisan Review.* The view at the magazine was that he was not being tried as a poet and his actions could not be defended on the basis of his greatness as a writer. However, if he were attacked as poet they would defend him strongly (Delmore Schwartz to R.P. Blackmur, Nov. 1945 [Blackmur Papers, Box 8]).

34. E. Fuller Torrey, *The Roots of Treason: Ezra Pound and the Secret of St. Elizabeth's* (New York, 1983), xix, 4, 10, 174–75, 181–82, and 234–36; the MacLeish comment appears in his *Riders on the Earth* (New York, 1978), 120.

35. See Ninkovitch; Archibald MacLeish, *Poetry and Opinion,* 33–34, and *The Irresponsibles* (New York, 1940): and *The Case against the Saturday Review of Literature* (Chicago, 1949), published by *Poetry* under the direction of Hayden Carruth, then editor of the journal.

36. For details, see Corrigan, Ninkovitch, and *The Case against.*

37. K. Shapiro to A. Tate, Jan. 27, 1949 (Tate Papers).

38. For a discussion of the threatened congressional investigation and the decision to remove the award from the Library, see "Preface," "Statement of the Committee of the Fellows of the Library of Congress in American Letters," and Aline B. Loucheim, "The State and Art" (reprint from

the *New York Times,* Sept. 4, 1949) in *The Case against,* v-vi, 1–19, and 39–42. See also Ninkovitch.

39. Tate to Shapiro, Jan. 31, 1949 (Tate Papers).

40. Shapiro to Tate, Feb. 2, 1949, and Shapiro's statement quoted in *PR* 16 (May 1949): 518–19; Tate to Shapiro, Feb. 5, 1949 (Tate Papers). The official announcement was released by the Library on Feb. 20; for a reprint, see *The Case against,* 29–30. See also L. Adams's report (Feb. 4) to the Fellows of the meeting with Lowell, Shapiro, Adams, and Evans on Feb. 1 (Tate Papers). And see Tate to Shapiro, Apr. 22, and Shapiro to Tate, Apr. 26, 1949 (Tate Papers).

41. Shapiro to Tate, May 3, 1949 (Tate Papers).

42. Shapiro to Tate May 9 and 15, 1949 (Tate Papers). Shapiro's statement appeared in *PR* 16 (July 1949): 764.

43. *PR* 16 (June 1949): 666–68.

44. For example, see Luther Evans to editors of *SRL,* June 7, 1949. It was published July 2, 1949; quoted in *The Case against,* 23–28. For supporting letters that were not published in *SRL* by Mark Van Doren, William Meredith, William Van O'Connor, Cleanth Brooks, and Yvor Winters, see *The Case against,* 62–71. Katherine Anne Porter to Editors, *SRL,* July 3, 1949 (Tate Papers). This eloquent five-page letter was to be published in *The Case against,* but Porter withdrew permission when she learned it was to be shortened. See Carruth to Tate, Oct. 4, 1949; and Brooks to Tate, Aug. 5, 1949 (Tate Papers). See also *The Case against* 46–58.

45. *The Case Against,* 10 and 13.

46. Ibid., 34.

47. Ibid., 38.

48. William Barrett, "A Prize For Ezra Pound," *PR* 16 (Apr. 1949): 344–47; see also Dwight MacDonald to Tate, May 3, 1949 (Tate Papers).

Tate angrily protested Barrett's piece because it suggested that the jury acted out of anti-Semitic prejudice. This he interpreted as a personal attack on his honor and demanded an apology. Rahv disagreed with Tate's reading. Rahv saw no insinuation of anti-Semitism in the piece and even asked Lionel Trilling and Sidney Hook to reread it after Tate raised the question. Rahv claimed that Barrett did not intend to insinuate anti-Semitic prejudice, though the essay clearly was not polite. He also noted how complex all these issues were and reminded his friend that the award was a moral act as well as an aesthetic judgment, but Rahv took no personal stand in his response to Tate, simply inviting his friend to reply publicly in the May issue. See Tate to the Editors of *Partisan Review,* Mar. 30, 1949, and Rahv to Tate, Apr. 4, 1949 (Tate Papers). On Tate's threat to obtain personal "satisfaction" from Barrett, see Howe, *Margin of Hope,* 155. The memoirs usually present this threat of a duel as the comic highlight of the Pound affair and illustrative of the supposed distance still existing between reactionary New Critics and New York intellectuals.

Also Rahv had written to Tate about a recent letter from Eliot which, in effect, said that Barrett's essay was reasonable. Eliot thought it inadvisable, as a non-citizen, to defend the award in public, but told Rahv that the award to Pound could be defended because the anti-Semitic lines were nonessential to the poetry. See Rahv to Tate, Apr. 21, 1949 (Tate Papers).

See also Ninkovitch, *The Case against,* and letters from Adams to Tate, early May 1949, and Cleanth Brooks to Tate, May 1949 (Tate Papers).

49. *Commentary* 7 (May 1949): 418. In addition to statements by Shapiro and Tate, the May issue of *Partisan Review* contained responses by Auden, Davis, Greenberg, Howe, and Orwell.

50. *Commentary* 8 (Sept. 1949): 209.

51. Ibid., 210.

52. *Commentary* 8 (Oct. 1949): 365.

53. Ibid., 368.

54. *Memoirs of a Revolutionist: Essays in Political Criticism* (New York, 1957), 215–18.

55. *Poetry and Opinion: "The Pisan Cantos" of Ezra Pound: A dialog on the role of poetry* (New York, 1950), 47–48.

56. Horace Gregory, "Lit by the Critics Torch," *VQR* 25 (Summer 1949): 443–44.

57. *PR* 16 (June 1949): 666–68.

CHAPTER SEVEN
Faulkner's Postwar Reputation

1. At the *New Republic,* it was policy *not* to review books by staff members, but Cowley claimed that he was not the author of the *Portable.* In retrospect, Mayberry believed Warren's essay to be one of the most important pieces, in terms of literary influence, published during his tenure (Mayberry to author, Sept. 10, 1980). (And no doubt Gordon's review of the *Portable* appeared as the lead item of the influential *New York Times Book Review* with the help of Harvey Breit, then assistant editor of the *Review.*)

2. "The Snopes World," *KR* 3 (Spring 1941): 253; and his "Katherine Anne Porter (Irony with a Center)," *KR* 4 (Winter 1942): 29–42.

3. Warren, "William Faulkner," in Hoffman and Vickery, *William Faulkner,* 124.

4. Ibid., 113.

5. See Ransom to Tate, July 17, 1946 (Tate Papers), Warren to Cowley, July 18, 1946 (Cowley Papers). According to Caroline Gordon, in the 1930s when he met with the Agrarians, Faulkner was always drunk. Yet they admired his work, even though he was aloof and isolated. See Caroline Gordon to Cowley, two undated letters, probably in late 1944 or early 1945 (Cowley Papers). For a 1931 conference on southern writing in Charlottesville, see Blotner, 707–21.

   In the 1940s, Tate's only contact with Faulkner was a single exchange of letters when Tate asked the novelist to contribute a story to *Sewanee Review.* Faulkner said he had nothing available. See Faulkner to Tate, May 19, 1945 (Tate Papers).

6. Tate to Ransom, July 22, 1946 (Tate Papers).

7. Quoted from *Essays of Four Decades,* 124–140.

8. Ransom to Tate, Aug. 22, 1946 (Tate Papers). Tate was then a Holt editor. Also Ransom informed Tate the he had discussed with Trilling the possibility of an arrangement between the *Review* and one of the more prestigious New York publishers to include advertising, to steer younger novelists of promise to that house, and to arrange publication of special numbers in book form. Ransom speculated that Tate might be able to organize such a relationship with Holt. This arrangement was not consummated with Holt, but was forged later with Random House.

9. See Tate to Cowley, Aug. 15, 1946; Tate to Ransom, Aug. 30, 1946; Tate to Hytier, Sept. 12, 1946; Hytier to Tate, Oct. 18, 1946; Tate to Auden, Sept. 12, 1946; Auden to Tate, Sept. 15, 1946 (Tate Papers). See also Ransom to Tate, Sept. 19, 1946, in which he agreed to spend money to create a distinctive issue—even money for an original cover sketch (Tate Papers).

10. Beck to Tate, Oct. 21, Tate to Beck, Oct. 25, and Beck to Tate, Oct. 31, 1946 (Tate Papers). Kazin to Tate, Nov. 4, 1946, and Feb. 4, 1947 (Kazin recommended the French critic, Claude-Edmond Magny [Tate Papers]).

11. Ransom to Tate, Sept. 12, 1947 (Tate Papers).

12. The Chase and Bowling essays appeared in *KR* 10 (Autumn 1948): 539–51 and 552–66, respectively. For Bowling's piece as a precursor to the flood of technical criticism in the 1950s, see the five essays on *The Sound and the Fury* from Columbia University's *English Institute Essays: 1952* (New York, 1954).

13. Chase *Stone and Crucifixion,* 549 and 551.

14. *HR* 1 (Summer 1948): 222–31.

15. "Ernest Hemingway," *KR* 9 (winter 1947): 1–28.

16. For a brief discussion of the new successes of their literary friends see Morton D. Zabel to Tate, May 16, 1947 (Tate Papers).

On the rise in status, see also Eric Bentley, "The Meaning of Robert Penn Warren," *KR* 10 (Summer 1948): 407–24. Not only was Warren "the most considerable American writer to emerge since the twenties," but Bentley argued that Warren was no shallow provincialist. There was room in his fiction for the rest of the world too. He claimed that the power of modern literature in general (and for Warren in particular) was derived from the dialectical combination of naturalism and symbolism: "It is not that James or Lawrence or Proust or Faulkner 'combine' naturalism with symbolism. It is that a naturalist picture of things *becomes* symbolic if it is well enough done" (423).

17. Irving Howe, *William Faulkner: A Critical Study* (New York, 1952), 202.
18. On Faulkner and the significance of the southern literary tradition, see Howe to Tate, Oct. 9, 1948 (Tate Papers). See also Irving Howe, *Sherwood Anderson: A Biographical and Critical Study* (New York, 1951).

    It should also be noted that Howe was the recipient of a *Kenyon Review* fellowship and a participant in Blackmur's Princeton seminars. Interestingly, Howe had asked Trilling to help him secure a Rockefeller Foundation grant to support his work on a history of the Communist Party of the United States. The Foundation declined to support it.

19. "William Faulkner and the Quest for Freedom," *Tomorrow* 9 (Dec. 1949): 56; see also his "The South and Current Literature," *American Mercury* 67 (Oct. 1948): 494–503.
20. Howe, *William Faulkner*, 199 and 201.
21. Ibid., 3 and 8. See Howe's autobiography, *A Margin of Hope,* for a self-definition of his critical methodology. He believed that the label of social or political critic, which routinely has been applied to him, was not accurate.
22. Howe, *William Faulkner,* 20–24.
23. Ibid.
24. Ibid., 203. For their shared interest in the joys of literature, see Howe to Tate, Aug. 4, 1952 (Tate Papers).
25. "The Hero in the New World: William Faulkner's *The Bear,*" *KR* 13 (Autumn 1951): 660.
26. "Technique as Discovery," *HR* 1 (Spring 1948): 67–87. The details of the publishing history of this essay are discussed in Schorer to Tate, Jan. 18, 1948 (Tate Papers). Schorer held Tate in the same filial affection as Tate did Eliot; see Schorer to Tate, Feb. 16, 1950 (Tate papers).

    "Technique as Discovery" appeared in O'Connor's *Form of Modern Fiction* (1948) as the second essay, following O'Connor's introduction and preceding a reprint of Tate's "Technique of Fiction." It was not, however, included in Stallman's *Critiques and Essays in Criticism, 1920–1948* (1949).

27. "Technique," *HR* 1, 73–74.
28. Ibid., 78.
29. Ibid., 84.
30. Ibid., 87.
31. Ibid., 86–87.
32. See Schorer's prewar analysis "The Chronicle of Doubt" *VQR* 18 (Spring 1942), discussed in ch. 3.
33. *PR* 18 (Nov.–Dec. 1951): 690. On the need for a literary "genius," see John Aldridge's *After the Lost Generation: A Critical Study of the Writers of Two Wars* (New York, 1951), written, in part, while he was at Princeton under Blackmur's literary criticism program, and the massive *PR* symposium "Our Country and Our Culture," beginning in the May–June 1952 issue.
34. Trilling to Tate, Nov. 27. 1942 (Tate Papers). They did not carry on an extensive personal correspondence, but it was clear that they deeply respected one another and read each other's work carefully.

    Also, beginning in the early 1940s, there was a rather close affinity between Tate and other New York writers such as Rahv, McCarthy, Wilson, and Schwartz. Tate and Rahv grew particularly close after 1950. See for example, Rahv to Tate, Oct. 23, 1942, Nov. 9, 1945, Aug. 4, 1948, Feb. 19, Mar. 10, and 20, 1952, and Jan. 12 and 24, 1953; McCarthy to Tate, Oct. 4 and 16, 1942, and Apr. 6, 1945; Schwartz to Tate, May 2 and 23, 1941; and Dwight MacDonald to Tate, Feb. 13, 1942 (Tate Papers).

    Finally, see also "The State of American Writing, 1948: A Symposium," *PR* 15 (Aug. 1948): 855–95, with commentary by John Berryman, Leslie Fiedler, Clement Greenberg, John Crow Ransom, Wallace Stevens, Lionel Trilling, and H.L. Mencken.
35. Quoted in *The Liberal Imagination*, 280. This was a position in mild opposition to such critics as Wellek, Austin Warren, and Eliot who wanted to protect literature from the pressures of ideology. It was first delivered at a conference on American literature at the University of Rochester in February 1949, and published in the *American Quarterly* (Fall 1949).
36. Trilling, *Liberal Imagination*, 282. In Blackmur's long review of Trilling's essays, "The Politics of Human Power," *KR* 12 (Autumn 1950): 663–73, he claimed that Trilling was crossing boundaries, not leaving the arts in a separate category to represent a distinct kind of truth. Blackmur was sympathetic to Trilling's reading of contemporary literature, but not in accord with liberal democratic ideals. (It should be recalled that this issue contained the first part of the *Kenyon Review* symposium "My Credo.")
37. Trilling, *Liberal Imagination*, 287.
38. Ibid., 288.

39. Ibid., 291.
40. Trilling, "Life of the Novel," *KR* 8 (Autumn 1946): 665.
41. Trilling also claimed contemporary literature should encompass the Communist experience. To that end he wrote *The Middle of the Journey* (1947), a novel about the failure of Communism and its vulgarization of intellectual and cultural life—a common theme in the attack on Communism by anti-Stalinists.

    For a classic statement of how Communism corrupted culture and how far too many liberal intellectuals acquiesced in its deterioration, see Robert Warshow, "The Legacy of the Thirties: Middle-Class Mass Culture and the Intellectuals' Problems," *Commentary* 4 (Dec. 1947): 538 ff. The idea that the Communists had a pervasive hold over culture in the 1930s became a favorite myth for the new liberals in the early years of Cold War. It helped to create the illusion that the "fellow traveler" was a true danger in a democracy. The attack was led by essays in *Commentary* and the *New Leader*. For example, see Sidney Hook on academic freedom and Communists—e.g., "Academic Integrity and Academic Freedom: How to Deal with the Fellow-Travelling Professor," *Commentary* 8 (Oct. 1949): 329–39.

42. Quoted from *The Liberal Imagination,* 207, 213, and 215. ("Manners, Morals, and the Novel" was first read at a conference at Kenyon College and then published in *Kenyon Review* [Winter 1948].) See also "Art and Fortune," which was written, in part, as a corrective. (It was read first at the English Institute, Columbia University, and then was published in *Partisan Review* [Winter 1948].) Trilling believed that "Manners, Morals, and the Novel" had been misunderstood; it was not a call for a new "genteel" tradition in literature, he stated.

43. "Introduction," *The Liberal Imagination,* vii and xii–xiii.

44. "Beyond Liberalism," *Commentary* 10 (Aug. 1950): 188–92. One of the best critiques of Trilling's cultural politics, though written with the sympathetic biases of a member of the New York family, is found in Barrett's *The Truants,* 161–85.

    On the problem of achieving high quality in the arts in a society of mass culture, see Spender's "The Situation of the American Writer," *Horizon* 19 (Mar. 1949): 162–79. This was written after an eighteen-month visit to the United States. In 1952, when Spender planned to return to America to teach and lecture, he initially was denied a visa because of his early connections to the British Communist Party. Tate intervened, and, in part through the Congress of Cultural Freedom, Spender was eventually cleared for entrance. Later, Spender became enmeshed in the problems of CIA funding of *Encounter.* Some of these difficulties are revealed in letters to Tate from Spender, Irving Kristol, and Frank Kermode (Tate Papers).

45. Brooks, "My Credo," *KR* 13 (Winter 1951): 78 and 80.
46. Ibid., 80.
47. Dayton Kohler, "William Faulkner and the Social Conscience," *College English* 11 (Dec. 1949): 121, 122, and 127.
48. "William Faulkner: An American Dickens," *Commentary* 10 (Oct. 1950): 284.
49. "The Dark, Bright World of Faulkner," *NYTBR*, Aug. 20, 1950 1.
50. See Edward Weeks to Bennett Cerf, Apr. 4, 1951 (William Faulkner Archives, Univ. of Virginia, 10280, "William Faulkner: General Files, Box 3, Fld. 41).
51. Harvey Breit, "William Faulkner," *Atlantic* 188 (Oct. 1951): 54. See also his "Literary Portraits: A sense of Faulkner," *PR* 18 (Jan.–Feb. 1951): 88–94. Breit relied heavily on Cowley's language and analysis.
52. Ibid., 56.
53. *A Margin of Hope: An Intellectual Autobiography* (New York, 1982), 146–49.
54. Eliot, "Religion and Literature," *Essays Ancient and Modern* (New York, 1932), 92—quoted by Tate in his working papers on Pound and the "*Saturday Review of Literature* Controversy" (Tate Papers).

CHAPTER EIGHT
Conclusion

1. "Europe's Faith in American Fiction," *Atlantic Monthly* 188 (Dec. 1951): 52.
2. See especially Arthur Schlesinger, Jr., *The Vital Center: The Politics of Freedom* (1949; Boston, 1962), xxiii, and chs. 4 and 5, "The Challenge of Totalitarianism" and "The Case of Russia," 51–91; and Les K. Adler and Thomas G. Peterson, "Red Fascism: The Merger of Nazi Germany and Soviet Russia in the American Image of Totalitarianism, 1930s–1950s," *American Historical Review* 75 (Apr. 1970): 1046–64.
   For discussions of the shift to the right on the part of the anti-Communist, New York intellectuals in the *Partisan Review* circle and their advocacy of the avant-garde, see Gilbert, *Writers and Partisans,* Bloom, *Prodigal Sons,* and Terry A. Cooney, "Cosmopolitan Values and the Identification of Reaction: *Partisan Review* in the 1930s," *The Journal of American History* 68 (Dec. 1981): 590–98; and for a discussion of the anti-Stalinism of the 1930s and its ties to postwar anti-Communism, see John P. Diggins, *Up From Communism: Conservative Odysseys in American Intellectual History* (New York, 1975).

3. The postwar Red Scare created a pervasive, effective, and powerful "intellectual blacklist" which stifled social criticism. The sordid story of anti-Communism and the subsequent cultural and political repression has been well documented: On the CIA, the Congress for Cultural Freedom, and the American Committee for Cultural Freedom, see Christopher Lasch, "The Cultural Cold War: A Short History of the Congress for Cultural Freedom," in *Towards A New Past: Dissenting Essays in American History*, ed. Barton J. Bernstein (New York, 1968) 322–59. On intellectual repression, see David Caute, *The Great Fear: The Anti-Communist Purge under Truman and Eisenhower* (New York, 1978), especially part 6, "Purge of the Professions," 403–84, and appendix B, "The Tillett Survey: The Predicament of the Discharged Teachers," 551–56. On the corrosive nature of anti-Communism with respect to civil liberties, see Mary S. McAuliffe, *Crisis on the Left: Cold War Politics and American Liberalism, 1947–1954* (Amherst, Mass., 1978), and Robert Griffith and Athan Theoharis, eds. *The Specter: Original Essays on the Cold War and the Origins of McCarthyism* (New York, 1974).

4. This view is put forward quite candidly in their own recent memoirs: William Barrett's *Truants: Adventures among the Intellectuals* (New York, 1982); Irving Howe's *A Margin of Hope;* William Phillips's *A Partisan View: Five Decades of the Literary Life* (New York, 1983); and Norman Podhoretz's *Making It* (New York, 1967) and *Breaking Ranks* (New York, 1979).

5. Richard Ohmann, *English In America: A Radical View of the Profession* (New York, 1976) 88, and Ohmann to author, July 3, 1978.

6. For example, see C. Vann Woodward, "Why the Southern Renaissance?" *VQR* 51 (Spring 1975): 222–39; Michael O'Brien, *The Idea of the American South, 1920–1941* (Baltimore, 1979); Lewis P. Simpson, "Southern Fiction," in *Harvard Guide to Contemporary American Writing*, ed. Daniel Hoffman (Cambridge, Mass., 1979) 153–90; Richard H. King, *A Southern Renaissance: The Cultural Awakening of the American South, 1930–1955* (New York, 1980); and Daniel J. Singal, *The War Within: From Victorian to Modernist Thought in the South, 1919–1945* (Chapel Hill, N.C., 1982).

7. Nathan Glazer, "New York Intellectuals—Up from Revolution," *NYTBR*, Feb. 26, 1984, 35. An important aspect of Glazer's essay, which written in part as a commentary on the memoirs cited in 4 above, is to urge continued vigilance against Communism. The lesson of the early Cold War still has value, he claims, because there is an extant revisionism that suggests once again that being a Communist was not all that bad.

   Of course, this call to vigilance was present in the books themselves and in the book reviews which in turn were written by the friends of the authors.

For example, see Hilton Kramer's review of Barrett's *Truants*, which appeared as the lead essay, "Partisan Culture, Partisan Politics," in *NYTBR*, Feb. 7, 1982. And in direct response to Glazer's essay, see Sidney Hook and Arnold Beichman, letter, *NYTBR*, 25 March 1984, where they claim special honors for the *New Leader* and *Commentary* in the fight against Communism. For a recent strident and irrational attack on fellow-travelers, see also William L. O'Neill's, *A Better World: The Great Schism: Stalinism and the American Intellectuals* (New York, 1982).

8. Quoted from S.A. Longstaff, "Partisan Review and the Second World War," *Salmagundi*, Winter 1979, 128.
9. *Margin of Hope*, 149.
10. "Notes on the Decline of Naturalism," in *Image and Idea* (New York, 1949), 138.
11. Rahv, "The Cult of Experience in American Writing," *Image and Idea*, 21.
12. "The Understanding of Fiction," *KR* 12 (Spring 1950): 197.
13. Quoted from *Essays of Four Decades* (Chicago, 1968), 16.
14. Ibid., 589.
15. Howe, *William Faulkner*, 298.

Selected Bibliography:
Secondary Sources

The following is not a comprehensive listing of all sources either cited or read in the preparation of this book. The works catalogued below were key secondary sources and are offered as a general guide to extant research. For complete references to specific aspects of my analysis, the reader should consult the notes.

Adler, Les K., and Thomas G. Peterson, "Red Fascism: The Merger of Nazi Germany and Soviet Russia in the American Image of Totalitarianism, 1930s–1950s." *American Historical Review* 75 (Apr. 1970): 1046–64.

Aiken, Conrad. "William Faulkner: The Novel As Form." In *William Faulkner: Three Decades of Criticism,* ed. Frederick J. Hoffman and Olga Vickery, 135–42. New York, 1960.

Aldridge, John. *After the Lost Generation: A Critical Study of the Writers of Two Wars.* New York, 1951.

Arendt, Hannah. "Franz Kafka: A Revaluation (On the Occasion of the Twentieth Anniversary of his Death)." *PR* 11 (Fall 1944): 413–22.

Atlas, James. *Delmore Schwartz: The Life of an American Poet.* New York, 1977.

Ayme, Marcel. "What French Readers Find in William Faulkner's Fiction." *NYTBR,* December 17, 1950, 4.

Baker, Carlos, ed. *Ernest Hemingway: Selected Letters, 1917–1961.* New York, 1981.

Barker, R.E. *Books for All: A Study of the International Book Trade.* Paris, 1956.

Barrett, William, "American Fiction and American Values." *PR* 18 (Nov.-Dec. 1951): 681–90.

———. "Culture Conference at the Waldorf: The Artful Dove." *Commentary* 7 (May 1949): 487–93.

_____. "The 'Liberal' Fifth Column." In *The Truants: Adventures among the Intellectuals,* 243–56. New York, 1982.

_____. "A Prize for Ezra Pound." *PR* 16 (Apr. 1949): 344–47.

_____. "Resistance." *PR* 13 (Sept.–Oct. 1946): 479–88.

_____. *The Truants: Adventures among the Intellectuals.* New York, 1982.

Barzun, Jacques. "Artist against Society: Some Articles of War." *PR* 19 (Jan.–Feb. 1952): 60–77.

Bentley, Eric "The Meaning of Robert Penn Warren's Novels." *KR* 10 (Summer 1948): 407–24.

Berg, A. Scott. *Max Perkins: Editor of Genius.* New York, 1978.

Blackmur, Richard P. "A Burden for Critics." *HR* 1 (Summer 1948): 170–85.

_____. "The Politics of Human Power" *KR* 12 (Autumn 1950): 663–73.

Block, Fred L. *The Origin of International Economic Disorder: A Study of United States International Monetary Policy from World War II to the Present.* Berkeley, Calif., 1977.

Bloom, Alexander. *Prodigal Sons: The New York Intellectuals and Their World.* New York, 1986.

Blotner, Joseph. *Faulkner: A Biography.* New York, 1974.

_____. *Selected Letters of William Faulkner* New York, 1977.

Bosha, Francis J. "William Faulkner and the Eisenhower Administration." *Journal of Mississippi History* 42 (Feb. 1980): 49–54.

Bowen, Catherine D. "Harold Ober, Literary Agent." *Atlantic Monthly* (July 1960): 35–47.

Bowling, Lawrence E. "Faulkner: The Technique of *The Sound and the Fury.*" *KR* 10 (Autumn 1948): 552–66.

Breit, Harvey. "Faulkner after Eight Years." *NYTBR,* September 26, 1948, 4.

Brooks, Cleanth. "The Formalist Critic." *KR* 13 (Winter 1951): 72–81.

_____. "What Southern Literature Needs." *SRL,* Sept. 19, 1942, 8 and 29.

_____. *William Faulkner: Toward Yoknapatawpha and Beyond.* (New Haven, 1978).

_____. *William Faulkner: The Yoknapatawpha Country.* (New Haven, 1963).

Burnham, James. "The Unreconstructed Allen Tate." *PR* 16 (Feb. 1949): 198–202.

Cantwell, Robert. "The Faulkners: Recollections of a Gifted Family." In *William Faulkner: Three Decades of Criticism,* ed. Frederick J. Hoffman and Olga Vickery, 51–66. New York, 1960.

_____. "When the Dam Breaks." *Time,* January 23, 1939, 45–47.

Cash, W.J. *The Mind of the South.* New York, 1941.

Caute, David. *The Great Fear: The Anti-Communist Purge under Truman and Eisenhower.* New York, 1978.

Cerf, Bennett. *At Random: The Reminiscences of Bennett Cerf.* New York, 1977.

_____. "Trade Winds." *Saturday Review,* July 12, 1947, 12–13.

Chase, Richard. "Art, Nature and Politics." *KR* 12 (Autumn 1950): 580–94.

_____. "How To Read Faulkner." *Commentary* 14 (Aug. 1952): 188–91.

_____. "The Stone and the Crucifixion: Faulkner's *Light in August.*" *KR* 10 (Autumn 1948): 539–51.

Cheney, O.H. *Economic Survey of the Book Industry.* 1931, New York, 1960.

Chomsky, Noam. *Towards a New Cold War: Essays on the Current Crisis and How We Got There.* New York, 1982.

Columbia University. *English Institute Essays: 1952.* New York, 1954.

Commins, Dorothy. *What Is an Editor? Saxe Commins at Work.* Chicago, 1978.

Compaine, Benjamin. *The Book Industry in Transition: An Economic Study of Book Distribution and Marketing.* White Plains, N.Y., 1978.

Cooney, Terry A. "Cosmopolitan Values and the Identification of Reaction: *Partisan Review* in the 1930s." *Journal of American History* 68 (Dec. 1981): 590–98.

Corrigan, Robert A. "Ezra Pound and the Bollingen Prize Controversy." In *The Forties: Fiction, Poetry, Drama,* ed. Warren French. Deland, Fla. 1969.

_____. "*What's My Line:* Bennett Cerf, Ezra Pound and the American Poet." *American Quarterly* 24 (Mar. 1972): 101–13.

Coser, Lewis, et al. *Books: The Culture and Commerce of Publishing.* New York, 1982.

Council on Books in Wartime. *A History of the Council on Books in Wartime.* New York, 1946.

Cowley, Malcolm. *And I Worked at the Writer's Trade: Chapters of Literary History, 1918-1978.* New York, 1978.

_____. *Exile's Return: A Literary Odyssey of the 1920s.* New York, 1934.

_____. *The Faulkner-Cowley File: Letters and Memories, 1944-1962.* New York, 1966.

_____. "An Introduction to William Faulkner." *Critiques and Essays on Modern Fiction 1920-1951,* ed. John Aldridge, 427–46. New York, 1952.

_____. *The Literary Situation.* New York, 1954.

_____. "Not Men: A Natural History of American Naturalism." *KR* 9 (Summer 1947): 428–35.

_____, ed. *The Portable Faulkner.* 1946. Rev. ed. New York, 1967.

_____. Review of *Absalom, Absalom!, New Republic,* 89 (Nov. 4, 1936): 22.

_____. *A Second Flowering: Works and Days of the Lost Generation.* New York, 1973.

_____. "William Faulkner Revisited." *SRL* 28 (Apr. 14, 1945): 13–16.

_____. "William Faulkner's Human Comedy." *NYTBR,* Oct. 29, 1944, 4 +.

De Beauvoir, Simone, "An American Renaissance in France." *NYTBR,* June 22, 1947, 29 +.

De Voto, Bernard. "Witchcraft in Mississippi," *Minority Report*. Freeport, N.Y., 1971.

Diggins, John P. *Up from Communism: Conservative Odysseys in American Intellectual History.* New York, 1975.

Dike, Donald A., And David H. Zucker, eds. *Selected Essays of Delmore Schwartz.* Chicago, 1970.

Donald, David H. "What Set the Mind of the South Thinking." *NYTBR,* Oct. 31, 1982, 13+.

Eliot, T.S. "The Man of Letters and the Future of Europe." *SR* 53 (Summer 1945): 333–42.

_____. "Notes toward a Definition of Culture. *PR* 11 (Spring 1944): 145–57.

Emerson, O.B. "William Faulkner's Literary Reputation in America." Diss., Vanderbilt Univ., 1962.

Enoch, Kurt. "The Paper-Bound Book: The Twentieth Century Publishing Phenomenon." *Library Quarterly* 24 (July 1954): 211–25.

Etzold, Thomas H., and John L. Gaddis. *Containment: Documents On American Foreign Policy and Strategy. 1945–50.* New York, 1978.

Fadiman, Clifton. "Faulkner, Extra Special, Double-Distilled." *New Yorker,* Oct. 31, 1936, 78–80.

Fain, John T., and Thomas D. Young, eds. *The Literary Correspondence of Donald Davidson and Allen Tate.* Athens, Ga., 1974.

Farrell, James T. *Literature and Morality.* New York, 1947.

Faulkner, William. "The Stockholm Address." In *William Faulkner: Three Decades of Criticism,* ed. Frederick J. Hoffman, and Olga Vickery, 347–48. New York, 1960.

Fiedler, Leslie. "What Can We Do about Fagin? "The Jew-Villain in Western Tradition." *Commentary* 7 (May 1949): 411–18.

_____. "William Faulkner: An American Dickens." *Commentary* 10 (Oct. 1950): 384–87.

Fitzgerald, Francis. *America Revised.* Boston, 1980.

Fitzgerald, Robert. *Enlarging the Change: The Princeton Seminars in Literary Criticism, 1949–1951.* Boston, 1984.

Fosdick, Ray B. *The Story of the Rockefeller Foundation.* New York, 1952.

Geismar, Maxwell. *Writers in Crisis: The American Novel, 1925–1940.* 1942. New York, 1971.

Genovese, Eugene. *Roll Jordan Roll: The World the Slaves Made.* New York, 1976.

_____. *The World the Slaveholders Made: Two Essays in Interpretation.* New York, 1969.

Gilbert, James B. *Writers and Partisans: A History of Literary Radicalism in America.* New York, 1968.

Glazer, Nathan. "New York Intellectuals—Up from Revolution." *NYTBR,* Feb. 26, 1984, 35+.

Gordon, Caroline. "Mr. Faulkner's Southern Saga." *NYTBR,* May 5, 1946, 1.

_____. "Notes on Faulkner and Flaubert." *HR* 1 (Summer 1948): 222–31.

Graff, Gerald. "What Was New Criticism? Literary Interpretation and Scientific Objectivity." *Salmagundi,* Summer-Fall 1974, 72–93.

Grannis, Chandler B., ed. *What Happens in Book Publishing.* New York, 1957.

Greenberg, Clement. *Art and Culture.* Boston, 1961.

_____. "Portrait of the Artist as an American." *Horizon* 16 (Oct. 1947): 15–19.

_____. "The Present Prospects of American Painting and Sculpture." *Horizon* 16 (Oct. 1947): 20–30.

Griffith, Robert. "Dwight D. Eisenhower and the Corporate Commonwealth." *American Historical Review* 87 (Feb. 1982): 87–122.

Griffith, Robert, and Athan Theoharis, eds. *The Specter: Original Essays on the Cold War and the Origins of McCarthyism.* New York, 1974.

Gross, Gerald, ed. *Publishers on Publishing.* New York, 1961.

Guilbaut, Serge. *How New York Stole the Idea of Modern Art: Abstract Expressionism, Freedom, and the Cold War.* Trans. Arthur Goldhammer. Chicago, 1983.

_____. "The New Adventures of the Avant-Garde in America: Greenberg, Pollock, or from Trotskyism to the New Liberalism of the 'Vital Center.' " *October,* Winter 1980, 61–78.

Guinzburg, Harold K. *Books and the Mass Market.* Urbana, Ill., 1953.

Hackett, Alice P. *Seventy Years of Best Sellers, 1895–1965.* New York, 1965.

Hart, James P. *The Popular Book: A History of American Literary Taste.* Berkeley, Calif., 1963.

Hartwick, Harry. *The Foreground of American Fiction.* New York, 1934.

Haydn, Hiram. *Words and Faces.* New York, 1974.

Hellman, Geoffrey T. "Alfred A. Knopf, Publisher." *New Yorker,* Nov. 10, 1948, 44–56.

Henderson, Kathryn, L., ed. *Trends in American Publishing.* Champaign, Ill., 1968.

Hicks, Granville. *The Great Tradition: An Interpretation of American Literature since the Civil War.* New York, 1935.

_____. "The Past and Future of William Faulkner." *Bookman* 74 (Sept., 1931): 17.

Hillyer, Robert. "Poetry's New Priesthood." *SRL,* June 18, 1949, 38+.

_____. "Treason's Strange Fruit: The Case of Ezra Pound and the Bollingen Award." *SRL,* June 11, 1949, 9+.

Hoffman, Frederick J., et al., eds. *The Little Magazine: A History and a Bibliography.* Princeton, 1946.

Hoffman, Frederick J., and Olga Vickery, eds. *William Faulkner: Three Decades of Criticism*. New York, 1960.

Hook, Sydney. "Academic Integrity and Academic Freedom: How to Deal with the Fellow-Travelling Professor." *Commentary* 8 (Oct. 1949): 329–39.

Hopper, Vincent. "Faulkner's Paradise Lost." *VQL* 23 (Summer 1947): 405–20.

Howe, Irving. *Margin of Hope: An Intellectual Autobiography*. New York, 1982.

———. "The New York Intellectuals: A Chronicle and a Critique." *Commentary* 46 (Oct. 1968): 29–51.

———. *William Faulkner: A Critical Study*. New York, 1952.

Jamieson, John A. *Books for the Army: The Army Library Service in the Second World War*. New York, 1950.

Jennison, Peter. "American Books Abroad." *Library Trends* 5 (July 1956): 95.

"The Jewish Writer and the English Literary Tradition: A Symposium." *Commentary* 8 (Sept., Oct. 1949): 209+.

Karanikas, Alexander. *Tillers of a Myth: Southern Agrarians as Social and Literary Critics*. Madison, Wis., 1966.

Kazin, Alfred. "Faulkner's Vision of Human Integrity," *Harvard Advocate* 135 (Nov. 1951): 8+.

———. *On Native Grounds: An Interpretation of Modern American Prose Literature*. Unabridged. 1942, New York, 1970.

King, Richard H. *A Southern Renaissance: The Cultural Awakening of the American South, 1930–1955*. New York, 1980.

Kohler, Dayton. "William Faulkner and the Social Conscience." *College English* 11 (Dec. 1949): 119–27.

Kolko, Gabriel. *The Politics of War: The World and United States Foreign Policy 1943–1945*. New York, 1968.

Kolko, Gabriel, and Joyce Kolko. *The Limits of Power: The World and United States Foreign Policy, 1945–1954*. New York, 1972.

Kostelanetz, Richard. *The End of Intelligent Writing: Literary Politics in America*. New York, 1974.

Kristol, Irving. " 'Civil Liberties,' 1952—A Study in Confusion: Do We Protect Our Rights by Protecting Communists?" *Commentary* 13 (Mar. 1952): 228–36.

Lacy, Dan. "Major Trends in American Book Publishing." *Trends in American Publishing,* ed. K.L. Henderson, 1–15. Chicago, 1968.

Lasch, Christopher. "The Cultural Cold War: A Short History of the Congress for Cultural Freedom." *Towards a New Past: Dissenting Essays in American History,* ed. Barton J. Bernstein, 322–59. New York, 1968.

Lehmann-Haupt, Hellmut. *The Book in America*. New York, 1951.

Lemisch, Jesse. *On Active Service in War and Peace: Politics and Ideology in the American Historical Profession*. Toronto, 1975.

Lewis, Freeman. "Paperbound Books in America." In *Bowker Lectures on Book Publishing*, 306–55. New York, 1959.

Longstaff, S.A. "*Partisan Review* and the Second World War." *Salmagundi*, no. 43 (Winter 1977): 108–29.

Louis, W.R. *Imperialism At Bay: The United States and the Decolonization of the British Empire, 1941–1945*. New York, 1978.

Lytle, Andrew. "Regeneration for the Man." *SR* 57 (Winter 1949): 120–27.

McAuliffe, Mary S. *Crisis on the Left: Cold War Politics and American Liberalism, 1947–1954*. Amherst, Mass., 1978.

Macdonald, Dwight. *Memoirs of a Revolutionist: Essays in Political Criticism*. New York, 1957.

McIntyre, Alfred R. "Crisis in Book Publishing." *Atlantic* 180 (Oct. 1947): 107–10.

MacLeish, Archibald. *The Irresponsibles*. New York, 1940.

――――. *Poetry and Opinion: 'The Pisan Cantos' of Ezra Pound: A dialog on the role of poetry*. New York, 1950.

――――. *Riders on the Earth*. New York, 1978.

Madison, Charles A. *Book Publishing in America*. New York, 1966.

Magny, Claude-Edmonde. *The Age of the American Novel: The Film Aesthetic of Fiction Between the Two Wars*. Trans. Eleanor Hochman. New York, 1972.

Malraux, André. "An Interview with Malraux." *Horizon* 12 (Oct. 1945): 236–42.

――――. "On American Literature and Civilization." *Horizon* (Oct. 1945): 236–42;

Marshall, Margaret. " 'The Saturday Review of Literature' Unfair to Literature." *Nation*, Dec. 17, 1949, 598.

Milano, Paolo. "Faulkner in Crisis." *Nation* 167 (Oct. 30, 1948): 496–97.

Miller, Perry. "Europe's Faith in American Fiction." *Atlantic* 188 (Dec. 1951): 52–56.

Miller, William. *The Book Industry*. New York, 1949.

Minter, David. *William Faulkner: His Life and Work*. Baltimore, 1980.

Mizener, Arthur. "Truth Maybe, Not Fiction." *KR* 11 (Winter 1949): 685–88.

"My Credo (A Symposium of Critics)." *KR* 12 and 13 (Autumn 1950, Winter and Spring 1951.

Ninkovitch, Frank A. "The New Criticism and Cold War America." *Southern Quarterly* 20 (Fall 1981): 1–24.

O'Brien, Michael. "C. Vann Woodward and the Burden of Southern Liberalism. *American Historical Review* 78 (June 1973): 589–604.

_____. *The Idea of the American South, 1920-1941*. Baltimore, 1979.

O'Connor, William Van. "Arts and Letters: Lionel Trilling's Critical Realism." *SR* 58 (July–Sept., 1950): 482–94.

O'Donnell, George Marion. "Faulkner's Mythology." *William Faulkner: Three Decades of Criticism,* ed. Frederick J. Hoffman, and Olga Vickery, 82–93. New York, 1960.

Ohmann, Richard. *English In America: A Radical View of the Profession.* New York, 1976.

_____. "The Social Definition of Literature." In *What is Literature?* ed. Paul Hernadi, 89–101. Bloomington, Ind., 1978.

"Our Country and Our Culture (A Symposium)." *PR* 19 (May–June, July–Aug., Sept.–Oct. 1952): 282–597.

Pells, Richard H. *The Liberal Mind in a Conservative Age: American Intellectuals in the 1940s and 1950s.* New York, 1985.

_____. *Radical Visions and American Dreams: Culture and Social Thought in the Depression Years.* New York, 1973.

Peyre, Henri. "American Literature through French Eyes." *VQR* 23 (Summer 1947): 423–38.

Phillips, William. "Comment: The Politics of Desperation." *PR* 15 (Apr. 1948): 449–55.

_____. "Middle-Aged Artists." *PR* 11 (Winter 1944): 119–22.

_____. *A Partisan View: Five Decades of the Literary Life.* New York, 1983.

Phillips, William, and Philip Rahv, eds. *The New Partisan Reader: 1945-1953.* New York, 1953.

_____. *The Partisan Reader: Ten Years of Partisan Review 1934–44: An Anthology.* New York 1946.

Podhoretz, Norman. *Breaking Ranks: A Political Memoir.* New York, 1979.

_____. *Making It.* New York, 1967.

Poetry. The Case against the Saturday Review of Literature. Chicago, 1949.

Polk, Noel. *Sanctuary: The Original Text.* New York, 1981.

Porter, Arabel J., and Andrew J. Dvosin, eds. *Philip Rahv: Essays on Literature and Politics, 1932-1972.* Boston, 1978.

Price-Stephens, Gordon. "The British Reception of William Faulkner—1929–1962." *Mississippi Quarterly* 18 (Summer 1965): 119–200.

Rahv, Philip. "Art and the 'Sixth Sense.' " *PR* 19 (Mar.–Apr. 1952): 225–33.

_____. "Disillusionment and Partial Answers." *PR* 15 (May 1948): 519–29.

_____. *Image and Idea.* New York, 1949.

Ransom, John Crowe. "The Understanding of Fiction." *KR* 12 (Spring 1950): 189–208.

Sartre, Jean-Paul. "American Novelists in French Eyes." *Atlantic Monthly* 178 (Aug. 1946): 113–18.

_____. "Time in Faulkner: *The Sound and the Fury.*" In *William Faulkner: Three Decades of Criticism,* ed. Frederick J. Hoffman and Olga Vickery, 225–32. New York, 1960.

Schick, L. *The Paperbound Book in America: The History of Paperbacks and Their European Background.* New York, 1958.

Schlesinger, Arthur. *The Vital Center: The Politics of Freedom.* 1962. New York, 1949.

Schorer, Mark. "Art and Dogma." *New Republic* 65 (Nov. 11, 1946): 634–35.

_____. "The Chronicle of Doubt." *VQR* 18 (Spring 1942): 214–24.

_____. "Technique as Discovery." *HR* 1 (Spring 1948): 67–87.

Schwartz, Delmore. "The Duchess' Red Shoes." *PR* 20 (Jan.–Feb. 1953): 55–73.

Schwartz, Lawrence H. "Malcolm Cowley's Path to William Faulkner." *Journal of American Studies* 16 (Aug. 1982): 229–42.

_____. *Marxism and Culture: The CPUSA and Aesthetics in the 1930s.* Port Washington, N.Y. 1981.

_____. "Publishing William Faulkner: *The 1940s.*" *Southern Quarterly* 22 (Winter 1984): 70–92.

Shi, David E. *Matthew Josephson, Bourgeois Bohemian.* New Haven, 1981.

Shoup, L.H., and William Minter. *Imperial Brain Trust.* New York, 1977.

Simpson, Lewis P. "Southern Fiction," *Harvard Guide to Contemporary American Writing,* ed. Daniel Hoffman, 153–90. Cambridge, Mass., 1979.

Singal, Daniel J. *The War Within: Modernist Thought in the South, 1919–1945.* Chapel Hill, N.C., 1982.

Smith, Henry Nash. *Democracy and the Novel: Popular Resistance to Classic American Writers.* New York, 1978.

Smith, Thelma M., and Ward L. Miner, *Transatlantic Migration: The Contemporary American Novel in France.* Durham, N.C., 1955.

Sosna, Morton D. *In Search of the Silent South: Southern Liberals and the Race Issue.* New York, 1977.

Spender, Stephen. "Beyond Liberalism." *Commentary* 10 (Aug. 1950): 188–92.

_____. "The Situation of the American Writer." *Horizon* 19 (Mar. 1949): 162–79.

_____. "We Can Win the Battle for the Mind of Europe." *New York Times Magazine,* April 25, 1948, 15+.

Spiller, Robert E., et al. *Literary History of the United States.* 3rd ed., rev. New York, 1963.

"The State of American Writing, 1948: A Symposium." *PR* 15 (Aug. 1948): 855–96.

Steiner, George. "The Scandal of the Nobel Prize." *NYTBR,* Sept. 30, 1984, 1+.

Stewart, Randall. "Poetically the Most Accurate Man Alive," *Modern Age* 6 (1962): 82.

Sundquist, Eric J. *Faulkner: The House Divided.* Baltimore, 1983.

Tate, Allen. *Essays of Four Decades.* Chicago, 1968.

———. *Memoirs and Opinions.* Chicago, 1975.

———. "The State of Letters: William Faulkner, 1897-1962." *SR* 71 (Jan.-Mar. 1963): 160-64.

———, ed. *A Southern Vanguard.* New York, 1947.

Tate, Allen, and John Peale Bishop. *American Harvest.* New York, 1942.

Tebbel, John. *The Great Change, 1940-1980.* Vol. 4 of *A History of Book Publishing.* New York, 1981.

Torrey, E. Fuller. *The Roots of Treason: Ezra Pound and the Secret of St. Elizabeth's.* New York, 1983.

Trilling, Lionel. "Introduction." *The Partisan Reader,* ed. William Phillips and Philip Rahv, ix-xvi. New York, 1946.

———. *Liberal Imagination.* 1950. New York, 1976.

———. "The Life of the Novel." *KR* 8 (Autumn 1946): 658-67.

Warren, Austin, and René Wellek. "The Study of Literature in the Graduate School: Diagnosis and Prescription." *SR* 55 (Autumn 1947): 610-26.

Warren, Robert Penn. "Ernest Hemingway." *KR* 9 (Winter 1947): 1-28.

———. "Katherine Anne Porter (Irony with a Center)." *Kenyon KR* 4 (Winter 1942): 29-42.

———. "The Snopes World." *KR* 3 (Spring 1941): 253-57.

———. "William Faulkner." In *William Faulkner: Three Decades of Criticism,* ed. Frederick J. Hoffman and Olga Vickery, 109-240. New York, 1960.

Warren, Robert Penn, ed. *Faulkner: A Collection of Critical Essays.* Englewood Cliffs, N.J., 1966.

Warshow, Robert. "The Legacy of the Thirties." *Commentary* 4 (Dec. 1947): 538-42.

Webster, Grant. *The Republic of Letters: A History of Postwar American Literary Opinion.* Baltimore, 1979.

Wellek, René, and Austin Warren. *Theory of Literature.* New York, 1949.

Welty, Eudora. "In Yoknapatawpha." *HR* 1 (Winter, 1949): 596-98.

Weybright, Victor. *The Making of a Publisher: A Life in the 20th Century Book Revolution.* New York, 1966.

———. "Paperback Books." *The Reader's Encyclopedia of American Literature,* ed. Max J. Herzberg, 849-52. New York, 1962.

Whiteside, Thomas. *The Blockbuster Complex.* Middletown, Conn., 1981.

Wilkinson, James D. *Intellectual Resistance in Europe.* Cambridge, Mass., 1981.

Wilson, Edmund. "William Faulkner's Reply to the Civil Rights Program." *New Yorker,* Oct. 23, 1948, 120 ff.

Wilson, Elena, ed. *Edmund Wilson: Letters on Literature and Politics, 1912–1972.* New York, 1977.

Woodward, C. Vann. *The Burden of Southern History.* New York, 1960.

_____. "Why the Southern Renaissance?" *VQR* 51 (Spring 1975): 222–39.

Index

Frequently cited periodicals have been identified by the following abbreviations: *HR, Hudson Review; KR, Kenyon Review; NYTBR, New York Times Book Review; PR, Partisan Review; SR, Sewanee Review; SRL, Saturday Review of Literature; VQR, Virginia Quarterly Review.*